Salt  Light

---

Meditations on the Sermon on the Mount

*How Jesus' Best Known Sermon
Turns Religion on Its Head*

James Jennings

Table of Contents

To grandmother Laura and Aunt Tommy who taught me the value of obedience and generosity

To Mason and Sandy who invited me to meet the revolutionary Jesus

To Keith and Rich whose songs introduced me to faith's passionate potential

To Jeanette whose love and companionship mends and frees me to follow my identity in Christ

For those who long to be lights in an increasingly dark world

Preface

Faith transforms. Faith gives hope and purpose. For me, faith is my life's greatest source of joy. Still, other things compete for my attention, pushing my faith into the back seat. Out of a desire to revitalize my faith, I decided to begin a personal study of Jesus' Sermon on the Mount in the book of Matthew, chapters five, six, and seven.

As I posted my thoughts, on social media, about what I was reading, a few friends encouraged me to make my complete study available. While the primary purpose for this study was personal, it's my sincere hope that it will challenge, encourage, and prompt others to discover Christ's sermon anew. Doing this study has been a boon to the growth of my faith. I anticipate I will review it regularly and add to it as I learn new things.

I begin with two hypotheses:

First, the core of what it means to be a follower of Jesus is expressed in the Sermon on the Mount. In my opinion, no other section of scripture expresses what Jesus wants from us as clearly as this sermon does. It is the foundation for following Jesus. It eclipses any creeds, man-made doctrine, or Church tradition. I believe it stands alone and above all other scripture. No theological concept, examination of Church history, apostolic letter, or teaching from any Church father carries the weight of those three chapters. In short, if we want to think like Jesus and live like Jesus, the Sermon on the Mount should be written on our hearts. Everything else is milk, and it is meat. We should continually be contemplating its application in our lives.

Second, it's our responsibility to understand what Jesus is saying. To grasp that, we have to study, pray, and search our souls. There are complex concepts and seemingly impossible challenges here. There are only two sources that speak to this, with authority. Only the totality of scripture can shine a light on the meaning of any single verse. This means you may need to grapple with verses that appear to contradict the others. I will get into this in more detail later. The other source is God's Spirit. God does not hand us a Bible and abandon us. If we carefully listen for His voice, He will open our hearts and minds. He will prompt us to ask questions and challenge our presuppositions. He will transform us if we allow Him to.

Beyond the entirety of scripture and God's illumination of what we read, we can also listen to the views of others. God may reveal a truth to someone else that brings an answer into focus. They may know some historical or linguistic detail that might shed light on a verse. Many references are available that can assist in providing context or understanding the meaning of words. Still, no one else can be an authority on how to interpret Jesus' teachings. The protestant reformer, Martin Luther, said, "Every man his own priest." That doesn't mean that you have to be an expert. It means that you must wrestle with what Jesus is asking of you and not blindly follow the interpretation of others. You may find that some of what you have been taught doesn't match what you hear Jesus saying. You may be right, or you may not be. Approach it with humility and determination. Still, if the answer you are given by others seems flimsy, challenge it. Go to God, pray, study, and seek the answer for yourself.

Much of this is my take on what is recorded in Jesus' sermon. I have tried to read scholarly opinions, word studies, related scriptures, and historical perspectives. I have prayed and tried to approach it with honesty, yet this still represents my understanding of these verses and their relevance. My interpretation of these passages is well-considered and valid. Still, your interpretation is equally worthwhile if you consider these passages with an open heart, study, and a willingness to change.

Only Jesus is the authority. Anyone else who claims to fully understand is simply mistaken. My goal isn't to persuade you to see this as I do. I hope that you will challenge yourself to genuinely meditate on Jesus' words and let God transform you, regardless of where it takes you.

There is a contrast between religion and genuine faith

in our current challenged and often disturbed world. Faith has always fostered lasting peace, compassion, mercy, and hope. In contrast, religion has often engendered ignorance, arrogance, tribalism, and selfishness. Faith moves us two steps forward, while religion pulls us two steps backward. Jesus emulated faith and opposed religion. If it doesn't look like Jesus' Sermon on the Mount, it's not faith and is likely to do more harm than good. There's a reason that Jesus preferred to dine with tax collectors and prostitutes rather than the religious leaders of his day. He knew which were closer to the kingdom of heaven. He recognized a field ripe for harvest and one where no amount of tending would produce fruit. If he was here today, I suspect this would still be his inclination.

As I've said, this is my personal interpretation of the verses. It is also my personal sense of the state of the world, the health of the Church, and whether we reflect the values that Jesus teaches here. As I write about Jesus' words, I've tried to let the following values guide me:

Live Simply. Forgive Freely. Love Fully.
Embrace Truth. Honor Wisdom. Listen Openly.
Speak Gently. Explain Honestly.
Consider Criticism Respectfully.

At the start, let's be honest. We all fail. Flaws and willful selfishness are part of our DNA. If any of us stand next to Jesus, an honest eye will recognize that we all need transformation. This is true for me and for the entirety of the Church. Some of what I have written here is critical. As much as I criticize the Church, I am harsher in my criticism of myself. I have struggled to remove a log from my own eye during too many segments of my faith journey. Splinters remain and I don't speak from a place of superiority. Neither do I want to be dishonest in what I see representing Jesus in our world.

I love the Church. Within this thing, we call *the Church* are many different groups. It includes people from every spectrum of our journey of faith. Many genuinely love God, desire to live like Jesus, and care for their neighbor. Many live selfless lives of integrity. Some are like the Bereans:

> *"The people here were of more noble character than those in Thessalonica, since they received the word with eagerness and examined the Scriptures daily to see if these things were so."* -- Acts 17:11 (CSB)

When I offer criticism, I don't intend to paint with too broad a brush. I recognize that many are genuinely trying to follow Jesus. Some do so remarkably. They live as Jesus' hands and feet. I aspire to be more like them.

The Church that Jesus built is integral to his mission of establishing the kingdom of heaven. Frankly, without a healthy, growing Church, the kingdom Jesus visualized will never fully develop. Fortunately, Jesus promises that he will build his church and *"the gates of Hades will not overcome it"* -- Matthew 16:18. That promise doesn't mean that the Church won't go through periods where it loses its way. It doesn't mean that deception

5

and idolatry will never threaten our mission. I believe that we are in the midst of a time like that.

We are told:

> *"Iron sharpens iron, and one person sharpens another."* -- Proverbs 27:17 (CSB)

Regardless of how careful and loving we are, the process of sharpening iron will produce resistance. That resistance nearly always creates heat.

> *"for the Lord disciplines the one he loves and punishes every son he receives."* -- Hebrews 12:6 (CSB)

> *"The one who follows instruction is on the path to life,*
> *but the one who rejects correction goes astray."* -- Proverbs 10:17 (CSB)

This seems clear. We all need correction. Consider what Jesus said to the religious leaders of his day or how he addressed the seven Christian Churches, in the book of Revelation, chapters two and three. Consider how John the Baptist and the Old Testament prophets confronted the people of God during their day. There's no denying that, at times, the Church needs to examine itself and change course.

Both Jesus and the prophets could be brutal in their correction. Jesus, *Meek, and Mild* said the religious leaders were vipers who would be eaten by the devil. He warned the seven Christian churches that, without change, he would *"remove your lampstand," "fight against them," "strike her children dead," "come like a thief,"* and *"vomit you out of my mouth."* Even in those early days, the norm was a vital need to repent. How much more is it needed today? The old testament prophets spoke to God's people about their need to repent:

> *"Therefore, say to the house of Israel, 'This is what the Lord God says: Repent and turn away from your idols; turn your faces away from all your detestable things."* -- Ezekiel 14:6 (CSB)

I think we fool ourselves if we believe the need for Church repentance stopped back then and doesn't apply to us. It applies to the universal Church and to me.

> *"For the time has come for judgment to begin with God's household, and if it begins with us, what will the outcome be for those who disobey the gospel of God?"* -- I Peter 4:17 (CSB)

Still, I am not Jesus. While I've felt for decades that the gift of prophecy was something God had given me, I leave it to Him to confirm that. Nevertheless, our reaction to a prophetic message should be:

> *"We also have the prophetic word strongly confirmed, and you will do well to pay attention to it, as to a lamp shining in a dark place, until the day dawns and the morning star rises in your hearts."* -- II Peter 1:19 (CSB)

This should be weighed against the warning to beware of false prophets. The Apostle Peter warns:

> *"There were indeed false prophets among the people, just as there will be false teachers among*

7

you. They will bring in destructive heresies, even denying the Master who bought them, and will bring swift destruction on themselves." -- II Peter 2:1 (CSB)

Ultimately, I don't ask you to accept my criticism as prophetic. I believe I'm speaking what God has laid on my heart, but I'm human and could be wrong. I only ask that if you feel criticized, recognize that I am not attacking you personally. False prophets don't care about you or the health of the Church. I would far prefer that I am wrong and Christ's mission succeed than be proven right and see the gospel suffer.

While we all need to examine ourselves and adjust course, my primary concern is with the segments of our faith that are commonly identified as conservative and liberal. I will explain more later but there are aspects in either extreme that have veered from looking like Jesus. While there is needed growth within the moderate, mainstream Church, I am most worried by the extremes. In recent decades, conservative elements have made up the loudest voices and have been the most visible and concerning. Many independent, fundamentalist, pentecostal, and evangelical voices have tended to reflect a worldview that conflicts with much of scripture and with Jesus' character. Sadly, actions from many in those groups have done tremendous harm to the spread of the gospel. Their extreme views have also caused significant damage to the social fabric. I have been sharing my faith with unbelievers since I became a Christian, back in 1974. It is monumentally harder to talk about Jesus today.

That's not because of sin in the world, but the world's perception of the Church. That negative perception has much foundation in reality.

Likewise, in response to extremes on the right, there are many liberal faith groups that have tended to discard much of the good with the bad. In the short term, the actions of the liberal Church are not as harmful but could have a disastrous effect on the Church in future generations. I will say that as I have spoken with those who have run from the right to embrace the left I have found they are mostly open to honest dialogue and consideration. That seems hard to find with the conservative Church.

I share many personal insights here. I don't do this because learning about me is important. It's simply part of my journey to discover how Jesus' sermon applies to me. I have been very transparent in my writing. I can be pretty tough on myself. I have to be because I can be tough on others. I don't criticize myself or others because it's fun. I just believe that we need to be free, and only truth frees us.

Note that this study begins with three days of introduction and preparation. The study of Christ's sermon begins in earnest on Day Four. I believe these days of preparation provide a meaningful foundation for what is to follow. If you find something here that displeases you, I encourage you to continue. There will be days that are entirely agreeable and some which you may contend with. Prayerfully consider them and move on.

I am grateful for the help and assistance of others in completing this study. Jon and Mary Perry have read and provided needed editing. It was their encouragement to write a book that helped to push me forward. Our work with them in loving our Muslim neighbors has been a joy and I so appreciate them.

Doing this study has helped grow my faith. I hope that it helps you, too. Please share the things you learn with others. Feel free to share this book with others. I hope that you will join me, seated on that hillside, listening to the One whose words give life.

"Let anyone who has ears listen." -- Matthew 11:15 (CSB)

Day One: Introduction

"But I have this against you: You have abandoned the love you had at first." -- Revelation 2:4 (CSB)

I enjoy writing. Writing prose, songs, and poetry has always been a part of my life. I'll have an idea and I'll sit and begin a stream of thought. Sometimes I'll realize that I've lost track of the original idea that motivated me to write. Usually, the best response is to put it aside and try to return to my original inspiration.

Some time ago, I recognized that I had lost focus on some crucial aspects of my faith. Much like the Church of Ephesus, I had lost track of my first love. While that love wasn't dead, many other things, thoughts, concerns, and interests (and sins) were crowding it out. I found myself wanting to reignite my devotion to Jesus and renew my faith.

At moments like this, I find myself wishing that I had a time machine. With it, I could go back to the early days of the Jesus Movement, where our idealism and love for Christ was so breathtakingly simple, innocent, pure, and honest. I often think about those days. We walked everywhere with our Bibles, not to beat someone over the head with it, condemn them, or use it to justify our cultural identity. We longed to learn more about Jesus. We wanted to share what we learned with others. I think that recently, I discovered that time machine.

I can't locate many of those joyful, long-haired ex-hippies, who weren't concerned about money or power, and simply trusted God. Many of them no longer exist. Still, at least in my mind, I can return to the small, gray, spartan room in a military school in Front Royal, Virginia. That is where I first opened my copy of *Good News for Modern Man* and experienced the lightning strike of Jesus' words from the Sermon on the Mount.

In January 1974, I was an eighteen-year-old boy. I had come, like many of us, from a dysfunctional home. My father left when I was six and my mother was often missing. I rarely sensed adequate affection or support from adults or peers. I was severely insecure. I have vivid memories of hunger, and poverty, and little to no adult involvement in my life. My days were a toxic mix of bullying, depression, and isolation. I daily escaped into television and books. In the ninth grade, I was sent to military school. I weighed eighty-five pounds, and my self-esteem was non-existent. For the next four years, I focused on schoolwork, trying to fit in, and avoiding the bullying that was now twenty-four hours a day. By the time I was a senior, I was an angry agnostic. My informal Senior photo was of me, in a graveyard, with gray and white orbs floating around my head.

That was the before picture, which came face to face with the words of Jesus, as he spoke to a crowd, on a hill outside of Jerusalem. I had heard these words before but this was the first time I truly listened. For me, reading these themes, which Jesus likely repeated often, takes me back to the joy and freedom that I first experienced all those years ago.

I first read the Sermon on the Mount back in January 1974, and today, it still leaves me weak in the knees and hungry to hear more. Throughout this year, I have been living in those three chapters. Since 1974, I have called myself Christian and Evangelical. I've followed the crowds to small group studies and megachurches. I've listened to Christian Music and attended conferences and seminaries. I've led worship, shared my faith, and struggled to be more authentic. I suppose those things have their place, but when I place the total of their impact on my soul next to those chapters in the Book of Matthew, they seem unremarkable. I had some truly good experiences there and a handful of lasting relationships. I learned a few important lessons and met some people who challenged my view of the world. Still, nothing slays my fragile grasp on our delicate, insubstantial, and material world like those three chapters.

Those chapters make me uncomfortable embracing a conservative or liberal worldview. Simple, liberal and tenuous answers are no match for Jesus. They show me that it's impossible to

> "Be perfect, therefore, as your heavenly Father is perfect." -- Matthew 5:48 (CSB)

and regard sin lightly. Likewise, unmerciful and rigid

conservative judgments are alien to Jesus' compassion and demand that we love our neighbor as ourselves:

> *"The second is, Love your neighbor as yourself."* -- Mark 12:31 (CSB)

I'm left realizing that no man-derived ideology gives me hope or peace. Only Jesus' words do that.

So, I decided to study those three chapters as in-depth as possible. In Jesus' words, I find statements that are more loving than I can grasp and some so terrifying and seemingly brutal that they leave me feeling helpless.

I don't know where I fit, or even if I fit, in many parts of the American Church that I used to call home. Part of that is on me. Part is because it's becoming exceedingly rare to see Jesus' words being reflected in this thing we call *Church*. Too often, I sense an opposing message. If Jesus were here today, I'm not sure he'd feel at home there, either. (Note that I use *Church* when I am speaking of the universal church or a church movement. I use *church* when speaking of an individual assembly.)

Still, my home is with Jesus, and I choose, moving forward, to place more focus on the face of Jesus. Nothing else gives me peace or leads me to any meaningful joy. There is a place for political discourse and a call to repentance. Still, if I stay there all the time, at the expense of simply sitting at Jesus' feet, I become like Martha, slaving away in the kitchen. Meanwhile, Mary took just a little time to consume a meal that wouldn't be forgotten in a week. I can almost hear Jesus addressing me, as he did Martha:

14

"The Lord answered her, "Martha, Martha, you are worried and upset about many things, but one thing is necessary. Mary has made the right choice, and it will not be taken away from her." -- Luke 10:41-42 (CSB)

Can we spend some of this next six weeks, together, chewing on Jesus' sermon? That is something that would benefit us all.

In what is to follow, I will walk through the various verses and consider where I've lost my way, where I've been obedient, and what I believe I must do, moving forward. I will comment on where I believe segments of the Church need to examine themselves. Nothing here means I disagree with what I believe was my past prophetic calling to speak truth to power. Still, after forty years, I sense that God is releasing me from making that my primary focus. I will speak to that here but my primary interest in this book is to consider Jesus and how to return to him, in earnest. I want and need to get back to what I experienced in that tiny room, at military school, in 1974. There I first opened my *Good News for Modern Man* and read about Jesus. His words broke me and gave me new life. Jesus has, I believe, been a part of my journey since then, but it's time to return to the basics. I'm convinced that Jesus' most well-known sermon is the place to begin. I hope that what is written here encourages and challenges you to join with Jesus. If you've never met him, there is no one more important. If you used to love him but have forgotten, I hope this draws you back to your first love.

Today's Verses to consider:

"But seek first the kingdom of God and his righteousness, and all these things will be provided for you." -- Matthew 6:33 (CSB)

What are "*these things*" that Jesus promises those who seek God's kingdom above all else? Perhaps they are eternal treasures, God's direction, clarity of purpose, and a life absent worry for our daily needs.

"You expected much, but then it amounted to little. When you brought the harvest to your house, I ruined it. Why? " This is the declaration of the Lord of Armies. "Because my house still lies in ruins, while each of you is busy with his own house." -- Haggai 1:9 (CSB)

If we question why we struggle to merely survive, perhaps this verse provides insight.

Day Two: How to Read the Bible

"The Word became flesh and dwelt among us. We observed his glory, the glory as the one and only Son from the Father, full of grace and truth." -- John 1:14 (CSB)

One thing that is beautiful about the Bible is that it is meant to be approachable. Before the Reformation, very few individuals had copies. Today, one is on the shelf of nearly every American home. Sadly, they are often unread, ignored, or misunderstood. Very few of us are fluent in Hebrew, Aramaic, or Greek. Most of the world doesn't read those languages. This forces us to make a choice. Do we encourage everyone who wants to learn from and be inspired by scripture to first understand a handful of ancient and seemingly alien languages? Alternatively, should we have language experts do their best to accurately translate those texts into our language?

In making this choice, there was a trade-off. When we translate scripture, we raise the probability of being accused of corrupting the text and the minuscule possibility that we actually will. Other religions and skeptics often employ the former claim to justify rejecting the Jewish/Christian scriptures. This is a largely unfounded criticism. There have been scores of English translations of the Bible over the years since the originals were written. Still, they essentially agree in ninety-nine percent of what is recorded. None of the disagreements impacts any central doctrine. However, some have amplified minor issues into significant disputes, perhaps based on questionable translations and potential bias.

Yes, there have been some minor translation errors. More importantly, culture and idioms change. While one translation may have made sense in sixteenth-century England, it may mislead in twenty-first-century America. Even then, it was not fully understood. Translating ideas, values, and environment from first-century Palestine to any other time and culture will always present challenges and likely misunderstanding.

In a perfect environment, to fully grasp the meaning and purpose of any statement, including scripture, I would have to live in the time and at the place where the original statement was written. I would have to fluently speak the language, understand the idioms and dialect of the writer. I would have to be thoroughly acquainted with the culture, politics, history, environment, and circumstances being addressed in the text and the underlying motivation for what is written. I would have to know the people mentioned. I would have to understand the background and intent of the person writing the text. Even knowing all of that, no communication is perfect. Send an email or write a Facebook post and a significant percentage will likely misunderstand at least some of what you're trying to say. Sometimes, even a change in punctuation can transform the meaning of a statement. "I'm giving up overeating for a month." can morph into: "I'm giving up. Overeating for a month."

Think about the ingredients you need to bake a cake. What happens if you leave out some of its ingredients? Now, consider the things required to understand the intent of a passage. If you remove some or most of those ingredients, how would that affect your understanding of the passage? You live in a different culture. You know little to nothing of the environment or circumstances, the people being discussed, the idioms, or the challenges and difficulties they faced. Put a few thousand years between yourself and those events. The original texts of what we now define as scripture have long since vanished. The text has been masterfully, but imperfectly, pieced together by taking the thousands of fragments from different early centuries, comparing, organizing, and contrasting them to later complete copies of the texts. Additionally, you'll have to trust early Church leaders, many of whom had deep ties to the political state, to decide which of those texts are deemed to be *from God* and above being questioned. The result is the Bible. Inspired. Imperfect.

What we have today is remarkable. We can be confident

that our translations convey a message which is very close to the original. There are minor differences between translations. There have been times when translators allowed their own agenda to intentionally change the meaning of a handful of verses. Still, it is largely consistent and dependable.

The same can't be said of the reader- the one who interprets the words. Most of us are lacking the key ingredients to fully understand. Consider the things I mentioned above. The things which make up the context, the pretext, the subtext, are often entirely missing. We are missing significant pieces of the puzzle. When you combine that reality with ignorance and arrogance, the Bible (like any religious text) can move from being a thing of beauty and value to become a tool for harm.

Almost none of us are Bible scholars, yet far too many American Christians talk about the Bible like they think they are. Some insist on a literal reading of scripture but it takes little time to discover they mean only the verses they choose to take literally. To be clear, I am not a biblical scholar. I am a layperson with limited training. I had an unremarkable year and a half of seminary training. I have access to sources that would have been unavailable to any pastor, a century ago. They are a significant help. Additionally, I have a keen desire to question and understand what is written. Many others can speak with more authority to the language or history of the text. I know my limitations. I can only speak to what seems accurate, but I am open to hearing from those who have a more thorough foundation. With that said, even the most remarkable students of the Bible will never fully grasp the author's original intent. The only thing more dangerous than an ignorant man is an ignorant man who believes that he is an expert.

When we read the scriptures, I think the primary, and first quality, that we should possess, before we are handed a Bible is humility. Jesus didn't have the complete canon of scripture. Of course, he didn't need it because he was, and is, the living Word of God. King David had even less of the sacred texts. So, why should we listen to these, who didn't have the entirety of the Bible to work with, when the know-it-all down the road has the entire text? Because they spoke with humility, honesty, and authority.

God has sent us His Spirit to dwell within us. It wasn't because He needed a place to stay or because our hearts offered such great accommodations. He places the Spirit within us to shine light before our feet and direct us. So, when we read scripture, we shouldn't expect our pastor, teacher, parent, or anyone else to interpret it for us. If they are skilled and have done the work to objectively get some of the necessary ingredients, they can help us understand the context. They can challenge us, but they can't, and should never, be trusted to interpret it for us authoritatively. Even the best of them speak from their own personal worldviews. It is God's job to authoritatively interpret what we read, not theirs. If we allow Him to, if we seek Him diligently, He will guide our hearts and minds.

"So, then, you are no longer foreigners and strangers, but fellow citizens with the saints, and members of God's household, built on the foundation of the apostles and prophets, with Christ Jesus himself as the cornerstone. In him the whole building, being put together, grows into a holy temple in the Lord. In him you are also being built together for God's dwelling in the Spirit." -- Ephesians 2:19-22 (CSB)

The Bible is meant to be approachable. It is intended to help us begin to understand. It's also intended to leave us with a sense of awe and a heart full of questions. God doesn't intend for us to use it as if we have all the answers. It isn't meant to replace God. It is paper and words, which can point us to the Living Word. Some of those words are addressed directly to us. Some simply tell a story of how God worked in the lives of people millennia ago. Some illustrate concepts in a way that primitive people could understand a central point. Only God's Spirit can guide us. If you want to understand God, then don't build a relationship with a book. I believe Jesus' words are accurately recorded in the gospels. If you read his words with an open heart, I think you will fall in love with him.

While all scripture is inspired by God, He never held a pen in hand and rarely dictated specific words. The thrust of scripture was not to create a set of rules and punishments. It was not intended to develop divisive theological creeds. Its purpose is to tell the story of God's love for man and His plan to reconcile us to Him. All of that culminates in the life of Jesus. The scriptures exist for the sole purpose of bringing us to our Creator, restoring our connection with Him, and challenging us to love our neighbor as selflessly as God loves them. Minus that, the Bible is simply a fascinating collection of history, allegory, poems, parables, and principles. It is worth studying in school, but it is merely another book if we miss its singular purpose. God is not a book publisher. He is in the business of transforming lives. If we want to be changed, I believe the best way is to know Jesus and follow his example. The Sermon on the Mount is the cornerstone of that foundation.

Today's verse to consider:

"The people here were of more noble character than those in Thessalonica, since they received the word with eagerness and examined the Scriptures daily to see if these things were so." -- Acts 17:11 (CSB)

Day Three: Reading Ourselves

"Looking at him, Jesus loved him and said to him, "You lack one thing: Go, sell all you have and give to the poor, and you will have treasure in heaven. Then come, follow me." But he was dismayed by this demand, and he went away grieving, because he had many possessions." -- Mark 10:21-22 (CSB)

As we encounter Jesus, we all come with our own personal baggage. Often, the baggage is something we must immediately leave behind if we want to follow Jesus. Some bags he allows a lifetime for us to release. Other bags contain things that we can delude ourselves into believing are perfectly consistent with following Jesus. However, the truth is that regardless of how good the world or members of our church see us, God sees us differently.

"But the Lord said to Samuel, "Do not look at his appearance or his stature because I have rejected him. Humans do not see what the Lord sees, for

humans see what is visible, but the Lord sees the heart." -- I Samuel 16:7 (CSB)

Those who share our culture and background may view some things to be perfectly fine because our culture has embraced them. They may condemn things simply because that's what is condemned in our culture. When we choose to follow Jesus, then he should decide what bags we must leave behind. When I speak of "culture" I'm not referring solely to secular culture. By culture I'm referring to our view of the world. This will be a combination of what we have learned from secular culture and also the culture of our religion, churches, and all spheres of influence.

Recently, I've been attending an online church (not really a formal church, but more of a gathering of mostly young believers). It's been encouraging because most of us are part of a diaspora. We are followers of Jesus, who are looking for a home with others who authentically love God, with all our hearts, and love our neighbors as ourselves. Unfortunately, we no longer felt at peace in the churches we came from due to the often suffocating degree of homogeneity and partisan culture there.

Many of us are refugees. We have been forced to leave behind both the good and the bad of the churches we knew. Reluctantly, we chose to strike out on our own. Just as the Israelites felt they had to escape Egypt to survive, many of us have felt the same need to escape. We may have sensed our faiths were being threatened there. We have experienced harsh criticism, sensed condemnation, condescension, dismissal, betrayal, disrespect, and accusations. We have lost friends, family, and even our identity. We have lost our sense of home.

Since 1980, I've believed that much of the Church was traveling a dangerous road, where politics and culture gradually replaced Jesus at the altar. I think of a scene from the first *Indiana Jones* movie. In the scene, Indie is trying to steal a valuable antiquity. He calculates the weight of the item and gradually replaces it with sand. This is a good picture of what I have seen happening in segments of the American Church. Unfortunately, more than forty years of pleading, reasoning, arguing, and prayer have made little difference. Strained relationships and loneliness have been the most abundant fruit. I recently felt that God was telling me that I had done what He wanted, and it was time to lay down my burden and move on. Perhaps, you're hearing that too.

Primarily, I am concerned about the millions of others, especially among the young. They no longer find they can be a part of their original stream of the faith because it challenges and offends their moral sense of the world. They have good reason to reject much of what passes for following Jesus these days. Perhaps they are incorrect in some of their criticism.

Two groups may be reading this. I suggest that both groups need to approach our differences with caution. To the first group, you may be comfortable with the state of the current Church in America. You may defend its connection with conservative politics and cultural identity. In that case, I encourage you to spend some time reading and meditating on Jesus' most well-known sermon. If considered deeply and honestly, it should leave none of us *comfortable*. You may be where God wants you to be. Only God can reveal that. Still, consider Jesus' words to the Church of Ephesus:

> *"Yet I hold this against you: You have forsaken the love you had at first. Consider how far you have fallen! Repent and do the things you did at first. If you do not repent, I will come to you and remove your lampstand from its place."* -- Revelation 2:4,5 (NIV)

Jesus has said this to me on more than one occasion. I just encourage you to consider whether he is saying this to you.

To the second group, you may have left the Church and are *deconstructing* your faith. Many of us have memories of first hearing Jesus' words and want something unbound by American culture. Any culture. We can agree on that. Still, be careful. If you have fled the conservative church of your youth, you may be tempted to overcorrect. Not everything you were taught was without merit. Yes, there are things there that need to change. I believe you are right to be disappointed and offended about some things. I hope you will consider two points. First, put aside any anger that you feel toward those you believe represent a faith that seems alien and harmful. Understand that most have arrived at that place without sinister motives. Just as God has shown you grace, extend grace to them. Second, recognize that those churches have taught and continue to teach much that is true. Don't scrap everything that you have been taught simply because you believe that some aspects are wrong. Consider what you have been taught and look at Jesus. Let Jesus be the one to determine what is and what isn't worth keeping. As you are *cleaning house*, go to Jesus before you toss something out.

People from every culture, time, and ideology have tried to appropriate Jesus or claimed that God was on their side. The reality is that Jesus is beyond any man-made ideology, culture, party, or worldview. He came to join us, but we have to go to him to fulfill that union. We have to leave behind the baggage of our politics, practices, worldly religion, and even our cultural identity and seek him. Jeremiah tells us of God's promise:

> *"You will seek Me and find Me when you seek Me with all your heart."* -- Jeremiah 29:13 (NIV)

Suppose a portion, or the preponderance of our identities, are tied to our political view of the world, our national identity, our racial, social, or even familial ties. In that case, that is a part of us that we may have made unavailable to give to God. We can't seek Him with *all our heart* if any part of our heart is committed elsewhere. It is a barrier to seeking Him with our whole hearts. Like the rich young ruler, I think many have walked away from Jesus' call on their lives. Unlike him, though, they don't grieve because they are misled into believing that they can both have Jesus and keep their treasure. They falsely believe that they can follow the kingdom of heaven and the kingdom of man. Perhaps, they have created a counterfeit Jesus in their image, who supports their own worldview. What is needed is to do the hard work of giving their attachments and culture to the biblical Jesus with permission to mold them in his image. This is true of conservatives and liberals alike.

Jesus isn't available as either a Liberal's mascot or a Conservative's soldier. He isn't a White European or a Black African. He came, as a Brown-Skinned Palestinian Jew, but more broadly, as all of us. He calls us out of those ways of thinking. Because we are called to love both God and neighbor, there may be times when we defend values that the world defines as Conservative or Progressive. Still, no genuine follower of Jesus can fully identify as either.

Jesus' values should always overrule values we receive from friends, family, political, or cultural influences. Those things are temporal. Only Jesus provides eternal values that we should pursue. A follower of Jesus must derive their identity by walking in his footsteps. No one else can *fill his sandals*. The world, and its groups, always have an agenda, and their goals will never fully align with Jesus'.

For lovers of Jesus, following our culture (liberal or conservative) and simultaneously following Jesus isn't an option. Many believe that it is, and I won't argue with them. I will leave it to someone else to make that clear. I am concerned, though, about those who have left their culture's churches behind but have no direction on how to follow Jesus. Many are put off by the Republicanism of their churches, only to exchange it for a Democratic church. Some are so offended by what they see as dishonest and unkind behavior that they reject Jesus, as well.

"Do not conform to the pattern of this world, but be transformed by the renewing of your mind. Then you will be able to test and approve what God's will is—his good, pleasing and perfect will." -- Romans 12:2 (NIV)

Today's Question:

Is Paul's challenge here to find a way of making Jesus fit into our home culture? Do we allow our culture to create a Jesus in our own image? Isn't Paul's challenge to look to the real Jesus to transform our lives, recreate our connection with God and the world we live in?

Day Four: Introduction to the Sermon

"When he saw the crowds, he went up on the mountain, and after he sat down, his disciples came to him." -- Matthew 5:1 (CSB)

What we refer to as *the Sermon on the Mount* appears in three of the four synoptic gospels (the books of Matthew, Mark, Luke, and John). It appears, seemingly in full, in the book of Matthew, chapters five, six, and seven. We find portions of it in the book of Luke, in chapters six, eight, eleven, twelve, thirteen, fourteen, and sixteen. That recording is referred to as *the Sermon on the Plain*. Portions are also seen in the book of Mark, in chapters one, three, four, nine, and eleven. I've always thought of this as a single event. Perhaps it was a sunny afternoon on a hill outside Jerusalem. Much of his sermon is communicated in snippets, in Luke and Mark. For this reason, it seems likely that what we see in Matthew were themes that Jesus returned to often during his ministry.

Matthew chapter five begins with a section we know as

the *Beatitudes* (the Blessings). It's most likely that Jesus was so passionate about these ideas that he returned to them often when he spoke to the crowds. His disciples likely heard these themes so often that they stuck in their minds, and it is why they chose to record them in the gospels.

While his disciples must have heard these themes often, these words were also intended for the crowds. In this verse, we see that Jesus chose to teach these Blessings to the disciples, as well as when the crowd was there. They weren't intended simply for the handful who traveled with him daily, but perhaps those who had never heard him before and who represented a wide range of people. In today's *Post-Christian* world, these teachings are more important than ever. The crowds likely included the wealthy, the poor, religious leaders, the unchurched, political zealots, and Roman soldiers and politicians. Since he said these truths so often and to so many, I think it's likely that Jesus saw these themes as foundational to the kingdom of God, which he was inviting us to. They give us a baseline for our faith and for those who want to know Jesus and his message.

Jesus' Sermon, as recorded in Matthew, begins with a list of blessings. These are for those who he sees as citizens of *the kingdom of heaven* or *the kingdom of God*. What is most apparent in his list is that it is the very opposite of the values of the kingdom of man. In today's world, our cultural beatitudes might read more like this:

"Blessed is the man who is wealthy, for he has greater value and has earned it.

Blessed are the powerful, for might makes right. They make the law, and they are above the law.

Blessed are the arrogant, for they never question or doubt their superiority.

Blessed are those who party and praise, for they are not negative and will be unmoved by suffering.

Blessed are those who know everything about God, for they believe He is easy to understand.

Blessed are those who don't struggle with sin, for they know that being perfect is impossible, and they are better than those people over there.

Blessed are those who are strong and are quick to fight, for they will make peace, for their friends.

Blessed are the beautiful, the celebrity, the loudmouth, and the trendy, for they will tell us what to think and what we should value.

Blessed are you when everyone agrees with you and defends your right to impose your beliefs and views on others."

Jesus provides a list of values that is the opposite of this. In some cases, he includes a list of *woes* (warnings) to those on the opposite list. Looking at these warnings helps to explain his blessings.

"But woe to you who are rich,

for you have received your comfort.
Woe to you who are now full,
for you will be hungry.
Woe to you who are now laughing,
for you will mourn and weep.
Woe to you
when all people speak well of you,
for this is the way their ancestors
used to treat the false prophets." -- Luke 6:24-26
(CSB)

I don't believe that Jesus' list of blessings is an entrance exam into heaven. Still, they are qualities that his followers and true citizens of the kingdom of heaven will respect, and seek, even if they do not possess them. I also don't believe his *woes* are a list of what will prevent entrance to heaven. Still, they do list qualities that we should never become comfortable with.

As we go through them, it's critical to ask ourselves if these characteristics reflect us and those we look to for spiritual or lifestyle guidance. I don't believe that there is a definitive understanding of what each of these blessings means. When I was in college, we were often given poems and assigned the task of interpreting their meaning. Since none of us wrote those poems, we had to guess what the author meant based on clues in the verses. Reading different commentaries on these verses makes it clear that the same is true with the Beatitudes. Fortunately, these verses do provide some clues. Some are relatively clear, and some are a bit less so. Even if we don't get a definitive answer, they raise important questions that every faithful follower of Jesus should struggle with. These were a foundational teaching by the one we consider our savior. Everything else that we identify with must make peace with these characteristics if we want to be worthy of the kingdom that Christ has prepared for us.

Today's Prayer:

Lord God,

Reveal to me my true nature. Give me a desire for qualities that You long to bless and unease with those things that may lead to woeful misgivings.

"Search me, God, and know my heart; test me and know my anxious thoughts. See if there is any offensive way in me, and lead me in the way everlasting." – Psalm 139:23,24 (NIV)

Day Five: The Poor in Spirit

"Blessed are the poor in spirit,
for the kingdom of heaven is theirs." -- Matthew 5:3
(CSB)

W hy should we value Jesus' words? I think that's a good starting point. Of the scores of billions of people who have inhabited our tiny planet and the countless words they have uttered, why should these words of Jesus stand out as so important? Consider the following passage:

"The Son is the image of the invisible God, the
firstborn over all creation. For in him all things
were created: things in heaven and on earth, visible
and invisible, whether thrones or powers or rulers
or authorities; all things have been created through
him and for him.

He is before all things, and in him all things hold
together. And he is the head of the body, the church;
he is the beginning and the firstborn from among
the dead, so that in everything he might have the
supremacy." – Colossians 1:15-18 (NIV)

In this passage, Paul tells us of Jesus' rightful authority and privilege. It is Jesus' kingdom. He is the firstborn over all creation. He is before all things. He is the head of the Church. All of God's fullness is in Jesus.

So, if Jesus has such authority and rightful privilege, why is it that he went to the cross? Why did Jesus stumble along the way? Simon of Cyrene was forced to step in and carry it for a time. Jesus was the "*image of the invisible God.*" So, how could the weight of that piece of wood overpower the creator of the universe? Undoubtedly, it would have caused me to stumble, but why Jesus? Why would Jesus, present at creation, become so weak that he needed help to carry the cross? I think it was because he willingly chose to identify with the crushed and broken of this world. While earthly kings would demand to sit, robed and honored, like Herod, or Pontius Pilate, Jesus wanted to join us in our suffering. He was born among animal droppings. He lived a life of poverty. He never had a wife. He never had children. He never held an earthly position of honor or power. He wasn't known to be a tall and imposing man or particularly handsome. In fact, in a passage from Isaiah, chapter fifty-three, we Christians believe that it speaks of Jesus when it says:

> *"He was despised and rejected by mankind, a man of suffering, and familiar with pain.*
> *He was despised, and we held him in low esteem.*
> *He took up our pain and bore our suffering.*
> *He was pierced for our transgressions, he was*

crushed for our iniquities.

He was oppressed and afflicted, yet he did not open his mouth.

He was led like a lamb to the slaughter.

By oppression and judgment He was taken away.

He was cut off from the land of the living.

He was assigned a grave with the wicked.

He had done no violence, nor was any deceit in His mouth. Yet it was the LORD's will to crush Him and to cause Him to suffer.

After the anguish of His soul, He will see the light of life and be satisfied." – portions of Isaiah, chapter fifty-three (NIV)

If this is truly a prophetic foretelling of Jesus, I think it shines a light on the meaning of the first of Jesus' blessings, in the Sermon on the Mount.

"Blessed are the poor in spirit,
for the kingdom of heaven is theirs." -- Matthew 5:3 (CSB)

"Blessed are you who are poor, for yours is the kingdom of God" – Luke 6:20 (NIV)

As the gospel writers record their memories of these events, there is a difference in the blessing. Did the two writers make a mistake? I don't think so. I believe that Jesus said both statements, but at different times. Why is there a difference, and what do they both have in common? Both are saying that God loves and understands those who are crushed under the weight of this world. He loves those who recognize their abject spiritual need for God's direction and comfort. He also loves and understands those who have physical, medical, emotional, and financial needs.

Jesus says that people like this are not only blessed but that He joins with them. He understands what it is like to feel the severe and gnawing pain of malnutrition. He understands what it means to be stripped naked, to be beaten, to be mocked, and to be cursed. Just like David, of the Psalms, Jesus understands the feeling of what it is like to feel abandoned by God.

Speaking of Jesus, Paul reminds us:

> *"For we do not have a high priest who is unable to empathize with our weaknesses, but we have one who has been tempted in every way, just as we are, yet he did not sin."* –Hebrews 4:15 (NIV)

When we suffer, we are blessed. This isn't just because we have a future hope of deliverance from suffering, as Job did. We are also blessed because we are not alone or forgotten by our Creator in our suffering. God doesn't want us to suffer, but He wants to draw near us when we experience it. The kingdom of God, the kingdom of heaven is ours because it is His Son's kingdom and he has also suffered. Christ joins with us, identifies with us in our suffering, and gives us a promised resurrection, but is also a companion during our trials. We call Jesus *the suffering servant*, not only because he experienced suffering but because he came to serve the suffering.

Today's prayer:

Heavenly Father,

Today, help me empathize and identify with those who make up the *Have-Nots*. Soften my heart to their circumstance. Guide me in how You want me to give them assistance, encourage them, promote just policies that provide them with a path forward. Thank You that Your son laid down his rights and became flesh to identify with us. Help me to follow in his steps.

Day Six: Those Who Mourn

"Blessed are those who mourn,
for they will be comforted." -- Matthew 5:4 (CSB)

Why mourn? At first glance, my thought is that you mourn when you recognize that you have lost something- a loved one, a relationship, a home. Following on the heels of the *poor in spirit* or simply the *poor* being blessed, I'm thinking that this is the second of the first two steps of receiving God's blessing. In the first step, we are blessed when we recognize our poverty- *poor in spirit*. We realize that something valuable is missing. We accept the reality of our utter dependence on God. In this step, we go beyond recognizing our dependence to actually FEELING and grieving the loss.

I often think of the world's first refugees- Adam and his family. They had dwelt, in peace, in a place where they felt the absolute love and acceptance of their father and Creator. They had experienced an existence that didn't know pain, hardship, sickness, or death. They had never felt shame, remorse, loss, anger, doubt, jealousy, anxiety, or hate. They had lived an existence that was God's original intent for all of us. This is the answer when people ask, "Why does God allow evil and pain."

His plan was for none of that. He didn't bring evil or suffering into the world. We did. We still do.

So, Adam and company find themselves on the other side of the gate, with the door to the Garden closed, locked, and guarded. Locked inside is that existence that he traded for *the knowledge of good and evil*. Previously, they only knew good, but they, and we, chose to also know evil. God certainly knew both Good and Evil but can understand it without being corrupted by it. Men are far more easily corruptible.

No longer was Adam able to walk, in the Garden, with his Creator. No longer was he able to live, in perfect harmony, with God's creation. Now, his *dominion* over creation was not an extension of his father's stewardship of the world but a daily struggle to survive. Adam would never again experience the possibility of enjoying a serene, family life in God's peaceful garden. He would see one son murder another. He'd live to experience hardship, pain, and loss that would have been alien had he not rebelled against his loving Creator and father.

It's likely that Adam rose every day, mourning his worst decision. Every time he ached, hungered, or wept, it's likely he thought of the day he chose to heed a voice that wasn't God's. Every time he was cold, angry, or lonely, I suspect he genuinely grieved. I think, perhaps, this is the sort of mourning that Jesus is referring to. Perhaps, it is the kind of mourning that he promises us will be comforted in God's timing.

It is easier for us to lose sight of Adam's loss because we never had it. None of us has ever existed in a place like the Garden. Regardless of how charmed or fortunate we are, none of us has ever experienced the sort of peace that Adam experienced before he was ejected from there. If we're honest, we all know that something is desperately wrong with our existence. We all know that there is something terribly off-kilter with the horrendous and obscene starvation of children in Yemen or desperate refugees from too many nations to count. This is made even worse because it is entirely the fault of political heartlessness or selfishness. We all know that something is broken in our world, where basic civility, decency, and humanity become increasingly challenging to find.

I believe that Jesus is reminding us to mourn over the loss of our original and intended inheritance. He is reminding us to be aware of what was lost in the Garden. He is reminding us that we should mourn over that loss and not make the same mistakes, day in and day out. Each day, we make choices. Sometimes, we choose the noble, the good, the decent, the loving. Some days, I find myself preferring the easy, the expedient, the temporal, the inferior. Jesus calls me to mourn that first catastrophic choice and to learn from it. No serpent will come into my home and offer fruit to me, but he does lie to me and tell me that compromise with God is OK. If I genuinely mourn Adam's horrific choice in the Garden, I will also mourn my own awful choices and try to make better ones.

The gate to the Garden isn't open to me today. I believe that Jesus came, as the Second Adam, to provide a way back, though. When I hear him offer me this blessing, I mourn what has been lost, but I also rejoice, believing that there is a blessing prepared for those who mourn.

In the Book of Revelation, Jesus puts meat on the bones of this promised, future blessing when he says:

> "Then I heard a loud voice from the throne: Look, God's dwelling is with humanity, and he will live with them. They will be his peoples, and God himself will be with them and will be their God. He will wipe away every tear from their eyes. Death will be no more; grief, crying, and pain will be no more, because the previous things have passed away.
>
> Then the one seated on the throne said, "Look, I am making everything new." He also said, "Write, because these words are faithful and true." -- Revelation 21:3-5 (CSB)

Today's challenge-

Consider what my selfishness and disobedience have cost me and the harm that it has done to others. Lead me to acknowledge my faults, ask for forgiveness, and do my best to repair what I have broken. Prompt me to embrace my grief over what is lost, but rejoice in what is yet promised. Find comfort in the promise that God Himself is now my *Comforter* and will ever be.

Day Seven: The Humble

"Blessed are the humble,
for they will inherit the earth." -- Matthew 5:5 (CSB)

Jesus isn't alone in making this seemingly counter-intuitive statement. David says something nearly identical.

"But the meek will inherit the land and enjoy peace and prosperity." -- Psalms 37:11 (NIV)

What does it mean to be meek? As I observe the world around me, these verses seem to contradict everything that I see. Is Jesus naive, or is he saying something that contradicts our understanding of the day-to-day reality of the world? How can a meek person possibly inherit anything but poverty and powerlessness?

The word meek can also be translated gentle. Jesus lived in utter confidence in God's direction in his life. His form of meekness is disciplined strength. It's the foundation of all lasting power and purpose. As with the previous blessings, being poor in spirit and mourning, to be meek is to recognize who we are when set next to our Creator. This realization will always lead us to humility. When you meet someone arrogant, you can be confident that they don't have an understanding of who their Creator is. I wouldn't want to drink a glass of lemonade, prepared by a five-year-old, without their parent's guidance, regardless of how confident they are. To be meek is to appreciate the fact that, in our own strength, we are limited and flawed. That said, Jesus also recognizes that, in God, we are:

> "more than conquerors, through him who loved us"
> -- Romans 8:37 (NIV)

It acknowledges that whatever strength we have will never be adequate on its own, but that God's resources are limitless. Our capabilities will eventually fail to meet the need of the day. Only those whose trust is, ultimately, in God will endure. However strong we are, we will, in time, tire, and then we must lean on God for strength. This is described in the passage below:

> "Do you not know?
> Have you not heard?
> The Lord is the everlasting God,
> the Creator of the whole earth.
> He never becomes faint or weary;
> there is no limit to his understanding.
> He gives strength to the faint
> and strengthens the powerless.
> Youths may become faint and weary,
> and young men stumble and fall,
> but those who trust in the Lord
> will renew their strength;
> they will soar on wings like eagles;

they will run and not become weary,
they will walk and not faint." -- Isaiah 40:28-31
(CSB)

I think that Jesus provides some examples of what he means by being *meek*. He tells us later in his sermon:

"You have heard that it was said, An eye for an eye and a tooth for a tooth. But I tell you, don't resist an evildoer. On the contrary, if anyone slaps you on your right cheek, turn the other to him also. As for the one who wants to sue you and take away your shirt, let him have your coat as well. And if anyone forces you to go one mile, go with him two. Give to the one who asks you, and don't turn away from the one who wants to borrow from you." -- Matthew 5:38-42 (CSB)

What Jesus is telling us is that in the economy of God's kingdom, unlike the kingdom of man, we are to surrender our rights to God. Paul goes into further detail on this:

"Do nothing out of selfish ambition or vain conceit. Rather, in humility value others above yourselves, not looking to your own interests but each of you to the interests of the others." -- Philippians 2:3-4 (NIV)

Here, neither Jesus nor Paul are saying that we are powerless or are to be doormats. They are reminding us that God is the source of our power and that God will protect us. He is telling us to get our priorities in order. They call us to re-imagine a world where *looking out for number one* is turned on its head. In God's economy, we put God and others ahead of ourselves. That doesn't mean that we ignore our needs, but we don't confuse our needs with our wants. In His economy, we go to God to provide us *our daily bread* -- Matthew 6:11, but we never place our wishes before the needs of others.

Let's be candid. Jesus is promoting a form of humility, meekness, and selflessness that rarely results in either wealth or power in today's world. Studies have shown that sociopaths and people with narcissistic qualities are overrepresented among CEOs and political leaders. This is true today more than ever. More often than not, people who are selfless and gentle rarely find themselves in positions of power. Those who hold positions of power and genuinely care for others often find themselves, in this life, at a disadvantage.

When Jesus says that the meek will be blessed by inheriting the earth, he wasn't promising wealth or power today. In fact, I think that he was calling us to lives of simplicity. While the *prosperity gospel* cult may present the lie that material wealth is the fruit of faith, nothing in scripture supports that. Instead, Jesus was promising an inheritance. We don't receive an inheritance until there's a death. Make no mistake, this world's order is temporary and will pass away. This blessing is primarily a promised, future blessing. If America is anything, it is cocky. It is overly confident. It can be arrogant. To follow Jesus is to go against the stream of American culture. God does promise to provide for our needs and won't necessarily call all of us to a life of poverty. Still, He clearly calls us to:

> *"Therefore, as God's chosen people, holy and dearly loved, clothe yourselves with compassion, kindness, humility, gentleness and patience."* -- Colossians 3:12 (NIV)

Living lives like this promise us both a future inheritance, peace in this life, and a better world for all of us. We can live in the economy of this world's kingdom or live by the values of God's kingdom. We can't be followers of Jesus and live looking out for number one. God's rich inheritance is for those who meekly place others' needs before our own wants.

Today's prayer:

Father God,

You are the source of all humility. Help me see myself, as You see me- entirely adequate to live a life trusting in You, experiencing Your presence, and loving my neighbor.

Day Eight: Hunger and Thirst

"Blessed are those who hunger and thirst for righteousness, for they will be filled." -- Matthew 5:6 (CSB)

*"Blessed are you who are hungry now,
because you will be filled.
Blessed are you who weep now,
because you will laugh."* -- Luke 6:21 (CSB)

As with the first of Jesus' blessings, we see that Luke records a somewhat different version of this blessing. Again, I do not believe that this is in error. I suspect that Jesus repeated these blessings often, and he expressed both. The Gospel of Matthew had a greater focus on a Jewish audience, so Matthew recalls the clearly spiritual aspect of hunger. Perhaps, it is because Luke was a physician that he remembers that Jesus also saw and cared about the physical hunger and needs of those he loved. Luke also recalls another aspect of this blessing:

"Blessed are you who weep now, for you will laugh." -- Luke 6:21b (CSB)

David expressed this when he said:

"You turned my wailing into dancing; you removed my sackcloth and clothed me with joy" -- Psalms 30:11 (NIV)

Jesus wasn't some cold-hearted preacher who only cared about people's souls. He cared about their stomachs as well as their souls. He loved the whole person. God didn't create us as spiritual orbs of light. He made us flesh. Jesus became flesh and walked with us. When the people in the crowd became hungry, he didn't tell them to sit down, shut up, and consider their eternal destiny. No, he fed them. We see the story of Jesus feeding the multitude in all four of the synoptic gospels. While many of the stories and parables of Jesus are told in only one or two of the gospels, the writers felt that this story was significant enough that it is recounted in each of the gospels. I like how Matthew and Mark say:

"When Jesus landed and saw a large crowd, he had compassion on them and healed their sick." -- *Matthew 14:14 (NIV)*

Mark 6:34 adds *"because they were like sheep without a shepherd."*

This story displays Jesus' compassionate heart, but also his qualifications as a worker of miracles. In fact, Matthew also recounts that, in addition to feeding them, he also healed them. Sick people will often weep. I believe that many saw their "*wailing turn into dancing*" that very day. Jesus not only fed their spirits

51

but also made them physically whole.

Matthew's version places more emphasis on the spiritual hunger that Jesus was looking for. Another story illustrates this hunger. When Jesus met the Samaritan woman at the well in Sychar, he asks her for water. This was shocking because Jews had a very condescending view of Samaritans and shunned them. Jesus shrewdly points out that he has something eternal to offer her, unlike the water from the well. He tells her:

> *"Jesus answered, 'Everyone who drinks this water will be thirsty again, but whoever drinks the water I give them will never thirst. Indeed, the water I give them will become in them a spring of water welling up to eternal life.'"* -- John 4:13,14 (NIV)

His response just confuses her. She replies:

> *"The woman said, 'Sir, give me this water so that I won't get thirsty and have to keep coming here to draw water.'"* -- John 4:15 (NIV)

She is only thinking about her physical need for water and how she hates the daily struggle of getting water. She incorrectly believes he is offering some magical, physical water. This is not the *thirst for righteousness* that Jesus wants to bless.

It isn't until he reveals his supernatural knowledge of her that she develops that form of thirst. Jesus tells this Samaritan woman about details of her life that he couldn't know naturally. When she recognizes that he is a prophet, she brings up the religious differences between Jews and Samaritans, thinking this disqualifies her. He could have confirmed that her theology was not orthodox and needed to change before her spiritual thirst could be satiated. He could have insisted that she "worshiped a different God" because she had a different theological understanding of God's nature. Instead, he says:

> *"yet a time is coming and has now come when the true worshipers will worship the Father in the Spirit and in truth, for they are the kind of worshipers the Father seeks."* -- John 4:23 (NIV)

Jesus' words changed her, and she went and told everyone about him. This woman began thirsting for a jug of water. Ultimately, she thirsted for Jesus and his righteousness.

It is all too easy for us to believe that God either only cares for the physical or just the spiritual. Excluding either is not biblical and demeans God's intentions. Some see God as only concerned about our eternal souls. They believe that God, and the Church, by extension, are only in the business of filling heaven. I question whether they even get that right. Others have abandoned Jesus' call for us to:

> *"Go, therefore, and make disciples of all nations, baptizing them in the name of the Father and of the Son and of the Holy Spirit, teaching them to observe everything I have commanded you. And remember, I am with you always, to the end of the age."* --
> Matthew 28:19-20 (CSB)

They have Jesus' compassionate heart for the physical but miss that we are both physical and spiritual beings. If we don't care about a person's physical need, we lie when we say we care about their spiritual need. Likewise, if we ignore someone's spiritual need we can't truly care for the whole person. At the well in Sychar, the woman is introduced to Jesus with only her physical needs in mind. Jesus skillfully reminds her that she is thirsty for more than a pitcher of water.

Those who have no physical hunger, or thirst, are often blind to the fundamental needs of others and can become callous. When you never have to worry about where your next meal comes from, you quickly take it for granted. Jesus felt compassion for those who lived lives of want. In fact, he identified and joined with them in a life of poverty. To the homeless, he could honestly say that he lived the life of a homeless man:

> *"Jesus replied, "Foxes have dens and birds have nests, but the Son of Man has no place to lay his head." --* Matthew 8:20 (NIV)

To those who were hungry, he could identify with the feeling of genuine and extreme hunger:

> *"After fasting forty days and forty nights, he was hungry." --* Matthew 4:2 (NIV)

While it's nearly impossible to not recognize our physical hunger or thirst, it is surprisingly easy to starve spiritually and not even be aware of it. It's possible to so fill up on junk food that you die of malnutrition. Many of us, both inside and outside the Church, are blind to their own spiritual malnutrition. I've certainly had my times of trying to fill up my soul with other things, things that still leave me thirsty. For a time, they can distract from what actually feeds my soul. Jesus tells me that I am truly blessed when I set aside this world's *fast food* and recognize my need for something lasting.

The righteousness that Jesus wants us to hunger for is not some external, religious behavior. He wants to transform our hearts. He wants us to hunger to be like him. He wants us to:

> *"Be perfect, therefore, as your heavenly Father is perfect."* -- Matthew 5:48 (CSB)

That is not something that a single meal will satisfy. It takes a lifetime of healthy *eating*. Sometimes, it will mean practicing something that I seriously lack-consistent discipline and self-control. Paul reminds us:

> *"No discipline seems pleasant at the time, but painful. Later on, however, it produces a harvest of righteousness and peace for those who have been trained by it."* -- Hebrews 12:11 (NIV)

God cares about our whole person- both our physical well-being and our spiritual health. Both our physical and our spiritual diets are essential.

Today's challenge:

Make a list of the things that you do each day to take care of your physical health. Compare that to the list of the daily activities which feed your soul. Consider what you need to change to be healthy, both physically and spiritually. Ask God to give you the thirst and the discipline to grow in health. Consider if there is something you can do to help someone else in their journey.

God,

help us to hunger and thirst for things which You will bless. Prompt me to care about my neighbor's needs- both physical and spiritual.

Day Nine: The Merciful

"Blessed are the merciful,
for they will be shown mercy." -- Matthew 5:7 (CSB)

What does it mean to be merciful or full of mercy? Mercy and compassion go hand in hand. While they are very much alike, I believe there is a slight difference that Jesus might be talking about here. Both are qualities of kindness, but mercy is also tied to one's rights and a sense of debt. Two stories in scripture illustrate the differences between compassion and mercy.

In the *Parable of the Good Samaritan* -- Luke 10:25-37, Jesus tells us one of his most well-known stories. While the incident he illustrates may have been fictional, it would have struck home with those who heard it. A man travels through a dangerous area when he is robbed, beaten, and left for dead. This poor, unfortunate soul is presented with three opportunities for rescue. The first two come in the form of highly respected and religious folk. They certainly know that God wants us to be compassionate, but their response is to ignore the broken man. His problem was, at best, simply an inconvenience to them. The third is a Samaritan man, who steps in to do far more than simple compassion would dictate. He transports the man to get help and pays for his care. What is remarkable about this story is that Samaritans were a group who were the targets of great prejudice and mistreatment by Jewish culture. I can imagine one of the Pharisees saying of the Samaritans, "They don't send us their best." Samaritans were the immigrants, Muslims, and disrespected minority of their day. Still, Jesus chose one of them to illustrate undeserved and unexpected kindness and compassion. That said, the broken man had not harmed the Samaritan. He was not in debt to the Samaritan. The Samaritan didn't have to let go of a grudge against the broken man or have to forgive anything before he could help. He simply had a soft heart and the ability to empathize with the broken man's pain and responded with godly compassion.

I think a more accurate illustration of God's mercy is presented in the Old Testament story of Joseph. In the Book of Genesis, we are told the saga of Joseph, the youngest of the twelve sons of Jacob (Israel). Jacob doted on Joseph, leading to his brothers' jealousy and betrayal. In chapters thirty-seven through fifty, Joseph's brothers sell him into slavery, and he is taken to Egypt. There, he experiences incredible injustice, slander, imprisonment, and mistreatment. Fortunately, his natural talent, and God's favor, eventually place him in a position of political influence. Because of this, many years later, when Joseph's brothers are suffering because of famine, they find themselves, illegal immigrants, standing before a powerful man, the brother they betrayed. If it had been any other group unknown to Joseph, an act of generosity would have represented simple compassion. However, this group had done treachery to Joseph. He had to respond with more than his simply compassionate heart. There was an almost unforgivable offense, yet Joseph forgives, feeds, welcomes, and loves them. He expresses his motivation this way:

> *"But Joseph said to them, "Don't be afraid. Am I in the place of God? You intended to harm me, but God intended it for good to accomplish what is now being done, the saving of many lives."* -- Genesis 50:19,20 (NIV)

Joseph, here, asks, "*Am I in the place of God?*" While he isn't, he does give us a potent image of God's character. He illustrates both God's strength and the heart of God's mercy. He was willing to see God's hand in allowing an injustice that must have broken his heart. He was able to forgive their betrayal. He willingly erased an overwhelming debt owed to him by his brothers.

While genuine compassion seems difficult to find these days, almost anyone can be compassionate. Compassion is the baseline of what God expects from every soul. Empathy, caring, and kindness should be the natural state of mankind. As we see much of it today, humanity has become so corrupted that simple compassion seems alien and heroic. Our nation's acceptance of clinical narcissism and political sociopaths indicates just how far our world, and the Church, have wandered from God's plan for us. I don't believe that Jesus, in this blessing, is saying, "If you see a hungry man, don't mock him, and maybe give him a buck, you will be blessed." God expects a baseline of compassion from *"even the tax collectors"* -- Matthew 5:46. No, I think he is pointing to the importance of forgiveness of debt. Jesus illustrates this in his *Lord's prayer*:

> *"Forgive us our debts, as we also have forgiven our debtors."* -- Matthew 6:12 (NIV)

Joseph's act of forgiveness transcended simple compassion because it utterly obliterated a tremendous debt that he could have justly held over the heads of his treacherous brothers. Even before he verbally offered them mercy, he must have understood God's sovereign control over his trying experiences. He knew that resentment and bitterness do more damage to us than it does to the ones who would understandably deserve the focus of our anger. Joseph was merciful to his brothers when he was in the pit and waiting to be sold into slavery. Joseph was merciful to Potiphar's wife when her lies unfairly sent him to prison. How was he merciful to them? He didn't dwell on his own mistreatment. Knowing that God was allowing injustice against him, for a greater reason, freed him from being trapped by self-pity or a desire for revenge. His being merciful, full of mercy toward those who betrayed him, tore down the barriers that might have prevented God from:

> "*he showed him kindness and granted him favor in the eyes of the prison warden.*" -- Genesis 39:21 (NIV)

Simply showing compassion for a stranger or friend is not the mercy that Jesus is telling us God will bless. It is showing grace and forgiveness to those who do not seemingly deserve it. In the here and now, we experience this mercy because it brings us peace:

> "*I have told you these things, so that in me you may have peace. In this world you will have trouble. But take heart! I have overcome the world.*" -- John 16:33 (NIV)

Additionally, this form of mercy- the forgiveness of debt, the erasure of a grudge, and loving our enemy, is the formula God will use in His judgment of us. In the parable of *The Unforgiving Debtor*, Jesus introduces us to a poor man who owes a significant amount of money. When the debtor is brought before the king he owes the money to, the lender feels compassion and pity and mercifully forgives the man, what he is owed. In a rare example, Jesus here tells a story of a rich man showing mercy to a poor man. Later, this poor man confronts an even poorer man and demands to be paid. The debtor has the more destitute man thrown into prison when he can't pay what he owes. When the merciful king hears of this, he demands that the original debt be paid and throws the debtor into prison -- Matthew 18:21-35. Jesus says that God will judge us similarly:

"This is how my heavenly Father will treat each of you unless you forgive your brother or sister from your heart." -- Matthew 18:35 (NIV)

He repeats this karmic promise:

"For if you forgive others their offenses, your heavenly Father will forgive you as well. But if you don't forgive others, your Father will not forgive your offenses." -- Matthew 6:14-15 (CSB)

The same is repeated throughout scripture:

"To the faithful you show yourself faithful, to the blameless you show yourself blameless." -- II Samuel 22:26 (NIV)

Today's challenge:

While we can't fully understand how God will judge us, we know that mercy will undoubtedly play a role- both our mercy and God's. Ask God: "How can I be more kind-hearted and compassionate? How can I be genuinely gentle and caring and be willing to forgive debts, even the seemingly overwhelming ones?"

Note too that Joseph's forgiveness doesn't erase the harm that his brothers did. Joseph was unique in that he was able to miraculously rise above their treachery. Had his enslavement resulted in lasting harm his brothers could not have justly said, "Get over it. That was years ago." Godly justice would have required them to acknowledge what they had done was evil and take concrete steps to make Joseph whole. God may miraculously step in to heal the damage done by our selfishness but justice demands both repentance and restitution. Even when we are not directly responsible for an injustice, followers of Jesus will identify with its victims, just as Jesus came to identify with us.

Day Ten: The Pure in Heart

"Blessed are the pure in heart,
for they will see God." -- Matthew 5:8 (CSB)

While so many of Jesus' words have comforted me, this blessing frightens me. Looking back on my days, I wouldn't categorize large portions of it as exemplifying purity. It's ironic because before I chose to follow Jesus, I briefly studied Eastern Mysticism and was very attracted to the spiritual concept of asceticism. The TV show *Kung Fu* had a profound impact on my young mind. Being free from worldly anchors, embracing simplicity, peace, and pursuing a life of the mind and spirit seemed far more attractive than what I saw in most American culture. The problem was and still is that I am an altogether undisciplined person. My moderately ADHD mind, combined with the lasting effects of a dysfunctional childhood, has made it all too easy to be impure- both in my thinking and my actions. I say this with both shame and a genuine desire to shed my old *dragon skin* and be fully reborn.

So, when I hear Jesus talk about purity, and later, his call for me to

"Be perfect, therefore, as your heavenly Father is perfect." -- Matthew 5:48 (CSB)

I feel inadequate, unworthy, and orphaned. How can I be a genuine child of God? I ask as the apostle Peter did:

"Who then can be saved?" -- Matthew 19:25 (NIV)

Fortunately, Jesus' answer to Peter is what I lean on:

"With man this is impossible, but with God all things are possible." -- Matthew 19:26 (NIV)

Still, I think that the Church often gets the concept of purity wrong. We confuse purity with being puritanical. To be puritanical is to be strict, straight-laced, and unsmiling. The last thing that God wants from us is to walk around with some imaginary stick up our rear. The Psalmist paints a very different picture of purity:

"You make known to me the path of life; you will fill me with joy in your presence, with eternal pleasures at your right hand." -- Psalm 16:11 (NIV)

The puritanical mind sees all pleasure as ungodly. Still, we are reminded that we are to be joyful, even when our circumstances are horrible:

"Though the fig tree does not bud and there are no grapes on the vines, though the olive crop fails and the fields produce no food, though there are no sheep in the pen and no cattle in the stalls, yet I will rejoice in the LORD, I will be joyful in God my Savior." -- Habakkuk 3:17,18 (NIV)

Every puritanical preacher who condemns dancing ignores the scriptures that call us to dance and the Spirit of God who wants us to experience real and lasting joy in the here and now.

I think of a commercial that was common when I was a boy. *Ivory Soap* used to advertise that it was "99 and 44/100ths percent pure". They said it was "so pure, it floats." I'm not sure how purity and floating are related. I suspect purity was referring to its Chemical composition- "the absence of impurity or contaminants in a substance." In Algebraic Geometry, purity means *a lack of unmixedness*.

These expressions of purity have to do with maintaining the essential ingredients as much as possible and recognizing how outside elements dilute the substance.

In much of the religious world, the concept of purity is solely focused on the outward. According to many of the religious and pious, God is pleased when we behave outwardly, in specific ways. They teach that avoiding certain words, some foods, and various forms of media will keep us pure. We are told to avoid socializing with *those people*. So when Jesus willingly chose to eat in the home of a tax collector, along with prostitutes, you can still almost hear the audible gasp from the self-righteous. Yet, God has always been far more concerned with the inner motivation than with the outward manifestation.

> *"The LORD does not look at the things people look at. People look at the outward appearance, but the*

LORD looks at the heart." -- I Samuel 16:7b (NIV)

The religious of this world often miss the point. Yes, God calls us to lead disciplined and holy lives. He calls us to simplicity and selflessness. He doesn't condone hedonism or debauchery, but primarily, it's not about living lives that prohibit certain things. The purity of heart that Jesus wants to bless is a life that is primarily focused on loving God, and neighbor. He wants us to see everything else in light of that love. Suppose you avoid everything the religious label as wrong, but God isn't at the center of your life. In that case, you are, in chemical terms, mixing different substances. A straight-laced man who lives by the motto "I don't drink, cuss, smoke, or chew, and I don't go with girls who do" can be farther from purity of heart than someone who does those things.

One of my favorite preachers, Tim Keller, says of idolatry that it is "Turning a good thing into an ultimate thing." The human heart can only hold one god at a time. That's why the first of the Ten Commandments is:

" I am the Lord your God, who brought you out of the land of Egypt, out of the place of slavery.
Do not have other gods besides me." -- Exodus 20:2-3 (CSB)

Purity of heart means taking that command seriously. It doesn't mean that you can't love other things or have other passions, but it does mean that we have to remember who our Creator is. This isn't because of God's fragile ego or that He will become jealous if we

67

don't pay Him enough attention. It's because WE need Him. We NEED Him. We need HIM. Other things will distract us. They may give us a jolt for a day or two, but only a real connection with our Creator is the source of true lasting peace.

I have certainly had my days where I took something good (and occasionally something terrible) and turned it into an ultimate thing. When I placed those things ahead of my Creator, I handed them the wheel and control. It wasn't always immediate, but invariably, they always drove me away from God and off the road. I quickly found peace disappearing in my rearview mirror. I am nowhere near "99 and 44/100ths" percent pure, but I long to be more like Jesus each day. The more I seek a life that prioritizes loving God, and my neighbor, the more I get a sense of His presence in my life and a confidence that I see Him in the world around me. Purity is not about avoiding things that I want. It's about desiring God so much that He changes my heart to pursue what He wants for me. Purity of heart is the abundance of God's light in our lives. It's impossible to grab darkness and remove it from a room, but the shadows disappear when we turn on the light.

Today's thought:

I'm done focusing on my own flaws, weaknesses, and impurity. God knows me better than I know myself, and yet, He loves me:

> *"for He knows how we are formed, he remembers that we are dust."* -- Psalm 103:14 (NIV)

Going forward, I choose to focus, instead, on God's sufficiency, through whom "*all things are possible.*" He gives me the desire to pray, as the Psalmist did:

"Create in me a pure heart, O God, and renew a steadfast spirit within me." -- Psalm 51:10 (NIV)

If you are struggling with temptation, regret, guilt, or shame, take comfort, knowing that it is no surprise to God. He gives us this promise:

"because of your partnership in the gospel from the first day until now. I am sure of this, that he who started a good work in you will carry it on to completion until the day of Christ Jesus." -- Philippians 1:5-6 (CSB)

Day Eleven: The Peacemakers

"Blessed are the peacemakers,
for they will be called sons of God." -- Matthew 5:9
(CSB)

While the movie was attacked by the religious community, Monty Python's *The Life of Brian* never mocked Jesus. It did richly mock religion. One of its most humorous moments was the only time the character of Jesus is actually in the film. A man, who is hard of hearing, makes his way to the crowd attending Jesus' Sermon on the Mount. This man hilariously misunderstands this particular blessing:

"Blessed are the cheesemakers! What's so blessed about the cheesemakers?" - Monty Python- *The Life of Brian*

He should have sought out Jesus to be healed. While the idea that Jesus would bless cheesemakers is humorous, the idea of blessing peacemakers seems more ludicrous. Statues typically honor those remembered as heroes of war, victims of war, and politicians who monetize and promote war. There are parks, streets, and towns named after people known, almost exclusively, because of their prowess in waging war. With all this nation's memorials, why are there few memorials to those who have gone against the flow and waged peace? It is because, as much as we want to call ourselves a *Christian* nation, we seem to value peace less than violence. We couch our love of violence with terms like *heroism* and *valor*. While those qualities are sometimes there, acting with violence can be done without courage, honor, or dignity. The same is not true of promoting peace. It often takes far more courage, self-control, and humanity to seek peace, but peace is not man's natural state.

In this blessing, Jesus is praising a rare quality and the type of soul that truly pleases their Creator. Is Jesus saying that we should all cower, run, and hide from conflict in God's kingdom? No. The world is often unjust, and we all experience anger. Even Jesus had moments of rage. On one occasion, he could have been accused of going overboard in expressing his outrage:

> *"Jesus entered the temple courts and drove out all who were buying and selling there. He overturned the tables of the money changers and the benches of those selling doves. "It is written," he said to them, "'My house will be called a house of prayer,' but you are making it 'a den of robbers.' "* -- Matthew 21:12,13 (NIV)

In other gospels, this incident is given more detail. In Mark, it explains that Jesus:

"and he would not allow anyone to carry merchandise through the temple courts." -- Mark 11:16 (NIV)

In John, it is even more explicit in the expressed fury that Jesus demonstrated in this incident:

"So he made a whip out of cords, and drove all from the temple courts, both sheep and cattle; he scattered the coins of the money changers and overturned their tables." -- John 2:15 (NIV)

So, what about this got under the skin of the *Prince of Peace*? Was he upset that the dealers in the courtyard were somehow harming the Temple's pomp, decorum, and ceremony? Was he irritated that the dealers were trying to make a living? Was he upset that people were required to pay a Temple tax? I don't believe so. Let me tell you why I believe he was *royally ticked*.

In Jesus' day, all observant Jews had to go to the Temple to make sacrifices. These sacrifices were seen as essential to cover their sins before they could enter the Temple and worship. Only certain sacrifices were deemed acceptable. Many were farmers who raised animals they could bring to sacrifice. However, not all had access to animals that could be offered, and not all had enough money. Travelers would trek to the Temple and purchase animals to sacrifice when they arrived. The leaders of the Temple had allowed sellers access to the Temple's courtyard to sell these animals.

Additionally, the travelers would have come with Roman coins to do business. These coins had the image of Caesar on them. The Pharisees wouldn't accept Roman currency with Caesar's image. Travelers were required to exchange Roman currency for Temple currency when worshipers came. There was often a significant markup on this. The result of all this was that poor people were being robbed. What little they had to purchase animals to cover their sins was being lost to the greed of the money changers. It's also possible money was going into the pockets of the Temple's religious leaders.

Consider the atmosphere of a bustling marketplace just outside the Temple. There was the sound of animals, along with the smell of their waste. Sellers were arguing and bartering. This would have been a distraction from any true worshipers who were there to connect with their Creator. On top of this, Jesus came to do away with any possible need to sacrifice to cover sins. He came to be the complete and final sacrifice so that we never again have to slaughter an innocent animal to stand clean before our Creator.

Combining greed with fraudulent religion is a perfect recipe for making Jesus angry.

Here is the tension that is the hallmark of our faith. The same man who says that peacemakers will be called "*sons of God*" fashioned a whip, turned over tables, and forcefully drove out the money changers. Later, he tells us:

> "*But I tell you, don't resist an evildoer. On the contrary, if anyone slaps you on your right cheek,*

turn the other to him also." -- Matthew 5:39 (CSB)

Which is it? Was Jesus being inconsistent? Was he being a hypocrite? No. Jesus wants us to both seek peace and seek justice. I think it's reasonable to ask how consistently today's Church is earnestly seeking either.

When the Temple Guard came to arrest him in the garden, he doesn't fashion a whip and fight -- Matthew 26:47-56; John 18:1-12. When it is his own cheek, he turns it and even heals the soldier's ear that Peter cuts off with his sword. He says to Peter:

> *"Put your sword back in its place," Jesus said to him. "For all who draw the sword will die by the sword."* -- Matthew 26:52 (NIV)

Jesus is talking, once again, about our hearts and our motivation. We are to seek peace. He was not naive. He understood our often violent and unjust nature better than any of us. He knew that the world is not filled only with puppies and flowers. His first concern, though, is our intent. Paul speaks of this:

> *"If it is possible, as far as it depends on you, live at peace with everyone."* -- Romans 12:18 (NIV)

What about when it is beyond us? What about the times when outside forces seek to *strike us on our cheek*? On more than one occasion, Jesus was faced with a religious mob who intended to harm him. In those cases, he neither *turned the other cheek* nor picked up a whip. He put space between himself and those who wished him harm.

74

"All the people in the synagogue were furious when they heard this. They got up, drove him out of the town, and took him to the brow of the hill on which the town was built, in order to throw him off the cliff. But he walked right through the crowd and went on his way." -- Luke 4:28-30 (NIV)

His first response to danger was not to acquire a better weapon. He didn't *Stand His Ground*. His response was to avoid unnecessary conflict. Jesus advises his disciples that if they are not welcomed, what their response should be:

"If anyone will not welcome you or listen to your words, leave that home or town and shake the dust off your feet." -- Matthew 10:14 (NIV)

Scripture, and Jesus, place a premium on living lives that promote, protect, and produce peace- not just for ourselves, but for our neighbors. When he calls us to be peacemakers, he doesn't mean that we should cloister ourselves away from a troubled world. Christ doesn't suggest we only concern ourselves with our own peace. He implies that we (all believers) have a role to play in promoting justice and peace. Without justice, there can be no authentic peace.

In the economy of God's Kingdom, the mere absence of violence is not peace. The absence of injustice is peace. Simply ignoring injustice, in the name of avoiding offense, or irritating others, is not the peace that Jesus is encouraging. The peace he calls us to is summed in his prayer:

"Your kingdom come.
Your will be done
on earth as it is in heaven." -- Matthew 6:10-9 (CSB)

When Jesus calls us to be makers of peace, we should consider the peace which God intends for us in eternity. Because God is the preeminent maker of peace, He wants us to model peace, through justice, in the here and now. Peacemakers are rare because they live in the heart of God's plan for the kingdom of heaven. They disdain violence, control their temper, and place the needs of others over their own. They recognize the role that justice plays in God's plan for His kingdom.

If you want to be a true child of God, you won't be adopted because you agree with some theological doctrine or join some religious group. If you want to sincerely know God as Father, then be a peacemaker. Promoting peace takes far more courage than any act of war. God is preparing a more fitting memorial, honoring makers of peace, which will outlast any earthly memorial to any soldier.

Today's prayer:

"Lord, make me an instrument of your peace:
where there is hatred, let me sow love;
where there is injury, pardon;
where there is doubt, faith;
where there is despair, hope;
where there is darkness, light;
where there is sadness, joy.

O divine Master,
grant that I may not so much seek
to be consoled as to console,
to be understood as to understand,
to be loved as to love.
For it is in giving that we receive,
it is in pardoning that we are pardoned,
and it is in dying that we are born to eternal life." --
Attributed to St. Francis of Assisi, though likely
anonymous.

Day Twelve: The Persecuted Part I

"Blessed are those who are persecuted because of righteousness, for the kingdom of heaven is theirs."
-- Matthew 5:10 (CSB)

"Blessed are you when people hate you, when they exclude you and insult you and reject your name as evil, because of the Son of Man." -- Luke 6:22 (NIV)

Jesus' blessings all seem to have a common theme- for a specific, challenging action or condition, there will be a positive response from God. Perhaps, if someone is disrespected or lacking in this world, God will more than compensate for it in His timing. If you're hungry, you will be fed. If you're sad, you will be comforted. If you show mercy, you will receive mercy. If you hunger for righteousness, you will be filled. If you try to make peace, you will see God.

Sometimes the condition or action is ours to control. Sometimes, it is out of our hands. In this blessing, we see a situation that results from our choices and is also beyond our control. The harsh here and now that Jesus says will eventually result in blessing is being persecuted. He's not talking about any persecution but persecution for the sake of righteousness.

Additionally, I think he's addressing a degree of mistreatment. Persecution is more than simply being disliked by someone. He's talking about being significantly mistreated or experiencing hostility solely because of a desire to foster righteousness.

Being mistreated is the common condition of humanity and has always been. Sometimes, that mistreatment is minimal. Good-natured ribbing, not being able to get a date, and not being popular doesn't even rise to the level of mistreatment. Mistreatment may mean being lied about, openly mocked, or criticized, but I doubt that is what Jesus means by persecution. Persecution moves beyond an occasional, unwarranted insult or unfair hurdle to being regular harassment, often violent. Real persecution is an attack on a person's identity and their most fundamental freedoms. It creates a condition where the person is forced to move from living to simple survival.

Real persecution does happen and is far too common. In Jesus' day, the Samaritans were mistreated and perhaps persecuted. Today, people are victimized because of their race, nationality, religion, and sexual orientation. Uyghur Muslims have been forced into Chinese concentration camps. Palestinians are being driven from their homes. Iraqi Christians have been forced out, primarily as a result of the US invasion. There has been a systematic destruction of American indigenous tribes. Whether it's any of these things or the cultural domination of minorities in Western nations, it's beyond dispute that mistreatment and persecution are a part of the human experience. What is shocking, though, is that when it's someone else's tribe being persecuted, those in power often deny that it's persecution. When even a minimal slight is experienced by those in power, they quickly claim they are being persecuted.

All of these examples of persecution are outrageous. They are an injustice, entirely condemned by God's nature. They are a threat to humanity. Still, they aren't what Jesus was referring to here. A person can be the victim of real persecution and not inherit the kingdom of heaven. God hates all injustice and feels empathy for all victims of persecution. But, Jesus gives a unique promise to those who have life and liberty threatened merely because they seek righteousness.

We should clarify that there is a significant difference between the outward appearance of religious acts and the sort of righteousness that Jesus is addressing. I don't believe that Jesus is saying here that God will bless those criticized for acting like pious jerks. He is not saying that if someone is called a bigot because they promote laws that harm their neighbor, and use the cover of scripture, that God will reward them. God is far more likely to reward the non-religious, who are being attacked by sanctimonious Pharisees than He is to reward the Pharisees. He is blessing the promotion of righteousness, not phony religion. Let me give you an example of my own journey through Phariseeland.

80

In 1976, I was a young, zealous, Jesus freak. I saw everything in simplistic, black and white terms. Subtlety and grace were not qualities that I'd yet learned to appreciate. I spent the Summer in New Hampshire. I was there with *Campus Crusade for Christ*. As part of our mission, I regularly went onto the beach and boardwalk. There, I talked to people about Jesus and their eternal destiny. I must have thought that I knew the entirety of God's plan or the person's heart. We led a young lady to pray to *receive Jesus*. Now, coming from the protestant South, I was unfamiliar with New England's Catholicism. This young lady invited me to her family's Catholic church for Sunday Mass. It happened to be *Annunciation Sunday*, where the service was focused on Mary. I was already aware that Catholicism taught that you could pray to people other than Jesus to intercede to God on our behalf. This service said that Mary would do that. My fundamentalist brain couldn't accept that. While I still believe, on this issue, that their theology is skewed, my response was even more wrong. After the service, I confronted the priest and told him that he would be judged for sending his congregation to hell. The response was predictable. He told me to leave and not come back.

I don't remember, but I probably felt that I was being persecuted for righteousness' sake. In fact, I had just been rude, unpleasant, ungracious, unkind, and unwise. If anything, that day demonstrated how far I was from God's kingdom. Over the decades, I've seen many others do exactly what I did, with the same result. Few

American Christians comprehend persecution because we are, for the most part, the powerful majority. We have an outsized influence in the political and economic segments of our nation. In my opinion, white, American Christianity has far more experience doling out persecution than it has in receiving it. I've been called a religious fanatic and a Jesus freak. I've had atheists assume that I'm scientifically illiterate and entirely absent of any ability to think critically. That criticism was primarily a reaction to genuinely ignorant and awful things that others have said or done in the name of my faith. I've found, in most cases, that a kind and patient response will, at least, open a door for dialogue.

I've never experienced genuine persecution. The closest I've come to it is from the same source that first persecuted Jesus, and the disciples. That source is other religious people. In any nation where religion has power and influence in government, persecution that comes will likely be at the hands of the religious. It will also, likely, be against an individual, or group, intently seeking righteousness.

This brings us to the distinction between faith and religion. I won't go into detail here, but Jesus calls us to a life of genuine faith. He does not promote a life of religion. Faith doesn't feel threatened when it is confronted with a different view of the world. Faith has no desire to control others, to arrogantly impose our view. Faith recognizes our own limitations and is humble. Organized religion is often the opposite.

"You will seek me and find me when you seek me

with all your heart." -- Jeremiah 29:13 (NIV)

"For such people are false apostles, deceitful workers, masquerading as apostles of Christ. And no wonder, for Satan himself masquerades as an angel of light." -- *II Corinthians 11:13,14 (NIV)*

The prophet Jeremiah reminds us that we find God by seeking Him. Simply claiming to know Him isn't enough. Neither is believing what our friends tell us about Him. We only find Him by diligently and personally seeking to find Him.

"For now we see only a reflection as in a mirror; then we shall see face to face. Now I know in part; then I shall know fully, even as I am fully known." -- I Corinthians 13:12 (NIV)

Paul reminds us that we have limited knowledge. To say that we understand God is the height of arrogance and dishonesty. To know and understand God is a progressive journey. That journey must involve asking questions, struggling with assumptions, adjusting our views, and challenging flimsy answers that merely protect orthodoxy and the status quo. Sometimes, the status quo and the orthodox are correct, but a person of faith should not lean on either in their search for God.

Naturally, a life of faith will result in occasional conflict with those who have convinced themselves that they know the unknowable. That conflict should be approached with respect, empathy, and openness but won't always result in an easy resolution or Kum Ba Yah moment. Sometimes, it will result in fractured relationships and distance. Even this is not persecution, though it grieves God's heart.

You and I may never know real persecution. We live in a nation of laws, where most in power identify as Christian. Only God knows how many actually are. Before joining with them, we must discern how closely their actions, principles, and values match Jesus'. Whether their values match our culture's values is irrelevant. Perhaps the best way to prevent our future persecution is to protect the religious freedoms of those who aren't in our tribe or share our particular flavor of belief. The second way that we protect our children from persecution is to remember our true mission and guard our behavior:

> *"And he has committed to us the message of reconciliation. We are therefore Christ's ambassadors, as though God were making his appeal through us. We implore you on Christ's behalf: Be reconciled to God."* -- II Corinthians 5:19,20 (NIV)

What would happen to an ambassador who was openly selfish, ignorant, bigoted, violent, unkind, and hurtful, or who defended such policies? It's unlikely they would hold that position for long. Jesus calls us to be his ambassadors in this world. Far too many of us promote and defend hateful, ignorant, selfish, and harmful policies and views. The world isn't blind to any of this. Many truly good people reject our religion because they see it as evil. That isn't always their fault. Increasingly it is ours. They reject our religion because they don't see our faith. The Church has defended potentially vile and harmful policies, politicians, and social mores for some time. This could be the most significant factor increasing the possibility that we may all experience persecution one day.

Today's thought:

> *"in fact, everyone who wants to live a godly life in Christ Jesus will be persecuted."* -- II Timothy 3:12 (NIV)

Most of us will rarely, if ever, experience genuine persecution. Some of this is because of laws that provide us religious freedom. However, we should consider whether we are not being persecuted because we fail to look like Jesus. It's unlikely we'll receive persecution because we go to church or have a *Christian* bumper sticker on our car. These things have become a part of our culture. If Jesus calls us to go beyond *Christianizing* our culture, to radically following him, and we obey, perhaps that is when we might experience actual persecution.

If you want God to bless you, remember that you represent Jesus. If you ever experience persecution because you are genuinely trying to be like Jesus, authentically striving to know God, and love your neighbor, then know that God is with you and offers you Himself as comfort. If you are criticized and mistreated because you are not acting like Jesus but as a Pharisee, God still loves you, but don't expect to be blessed for that.

Day Thirteen: The Persecuted Part II

"You are blessed when they insult you and persecute you and falsely say every kind of evil against you because of me. Be glad and rejoice, because your reward is great in heaven. For that is how they persecuted the prophets who were before you." -- Matthew 5:11-12 (CSB)

This blessing largely seems to repeat what was in the previous one. Here, Jesus continues to emphasize that what we do *"For his sake"* may result in persecution. What does he mean in that phrase- *"For my sake?"* Is he saying, "If you do something for me, I'll owe you?" Is this his way of asking us to do something that benefits him? On the surface, that seems almost selfish. He uses a similar phrase here:

"For whoever wants to save their life, will lose it, but whoever loses their life for me will find it." -- Matthew 16:25 (NIV)

I don't think he's asking us to build him a cathedral or give him something shiny. Suppose you go back to

Jesus' summation of the law and prophets. In that case, I think he is talking about genuinely and selflessly loving God and neighbor. Perhaps, he gives a hint here:

> *"Truly I tell you, whatever you did for one of the least of these brothers and sisters of mine, you did for me."* -- Matthew 25:40 (NIV)

When we take care of, protect, and honor our neighbor, we show love for God, and Jesus sees that as service for his sake. It's unlikely that giving a buck to a homeless man will result in even criticism, much less persecution. What happens if you move beyond a bandage response to addressing the real needs in the world around us? Suppose we press for actual systemic change to the world's system. I believe it is a system that promotes poverty, sickness, and violence. In that case, persecution may follow. The forces of the status quo that may reject proposals to *"love your neighbor, as yourselves"* are often some in the religious community.

Sadly, while faith comes from God, frees men, and promotes justice, religion often enslaves men and defends injustice. Jesus may be referring to this here when he references the persecution of *"the prophets that were before you."* Prophets, for the most part, don't confront sin in the secular world. They confront evil among those who are supposed to be different. While kings were often the tool used to harm Old Testament prophets, sin was often promoted, endorsed, or ignored by religious leaders. This was complicated by ancient Israel's attempt to have a form of theocratic government, which was often synonymous with the

Church.

Today's thought:

In trying to live out Jesus' call on your life, do you have a tender heart that grieves over the pain and injustice visited on the world by selfish, ignorant, and violent people? Do you seek to promote significant changes to prevent that and restore your neighbor? Do the priorities and policies you support oppose or promote Jesus' prayer that God's will be done on Earth, as in heaven? If so, you will likely find conflict. God has promised that a reward is prepared for those persecuted because they love God and neighbor. I don't believe that reward is only in the future. God is with you now. He is your comforter and protector.

Day Fourteen: Beatitudes Summary

This brings me to the end of the portion of the Sermon on the Mount that we call the Beatitudes. Before I move forward, I'd like to review what I've learned in the first twelve verses of Matthew, chapter five. There may have been a single event that correlates with this sermon. However, it seems likely that these were themes and statements that Jesus returned to regularly as he was speaking to the crowds. These weren't messages directed only to his disciples, the religious elite, or the Romans. He was addressing the public crowds, who would have represented all walks of life. These universal messages were the baseline of what he meant by the kingdom of heaven. They weren't spoken in theological or high-minded terms. They were simple, direct, and the foundation of his entire ministry. In the Beatitudes, Jesus paints a picture of life in the kingdom of heaven.

Jesus spoke regularly about *the kingdom of heaven* and *the kingdom of God*. I believe that he used these terms interchangeably. In his exchange with the rich young ruler, he uses both phrases to mean the same thing:

"Then Jesus said to his disciples, truly I tell you, it is hard for someone who is rich to enter the kingdom of heaven. Again I tell you, it is easier for a camel to go through the eye of a needle than for someone who is rich to enter the kingdom of God." -- Matthew 19:23,24 (NIV)

As an aside, the word translated here as camel may be incorrectly translated. The Greek word for camel is *kamelon*. The Aramaic word for rope is *kamilon*. Whether it meant camel or thick thread, Jesus is pointing to how much wealth interferes with our spiritual walk. What was this kingdom that he kept referring to? Was it just some future, eternal existence that the *saved* will experience? I don't think so. While Jesus clearly taught some future redemptive healing in eternity, I believe that when Jesus spoke of the kingdom, he meant it to be for the here and now. Early in Jesus' ministry, he visited a synagogue from his home community in Nazareth. He stood and read a section from Isaiah:

"The Spirit of the Lord is on me,
because he has anointed me
to preach good news to the poor.
He has sent me
to proclaim release to the captives
and recovery of sight to the blind,
to set free the oppressed,
to proclaim the year of the Lord's favor.

He then rolled up the scroll, gave it back to the attendant, and sat down. And the eyes of everyone in the synagogue were fixed on him. He began by saying to them,"Today as you listen, this Scripture has been fulfilled." -- Luke 4:18-21 (CSB) - Jesus reading Isaiah 61:1,2

Jesus was not merely promising a future and heavenly kingdom. What was truly radical about Jesus' teaching was that he was calling for:

"Your kingdom come. Your will be done on earth as it is in heaven." -- Matthew 6:10-9 (CSB)

This promise was given to the poor, to those in chains, and to the blind. These blessings were for the *Have-nots*. I believe that Jesus wanted his followers to promote God's kingdom in the here and now. I don't mean that he expected his followers to set up a theocratic political system. It wasn't his goal to force religion on anyone. I believe that he encourages us to embody the values of God's kingdom while living in the earthly realm.

In the first twelve verses, Jesus lists conditions that will result in God's blessing. What strikes me is how different these conditions are from what many contemporary religious leaders typically promote. In the Beatitudes, Jesus says that in his kingdom, including the here and now, you will be blessed if you:

 - are poor in spirit (or materially poor)
 - mourn (or weep)

- are meek
- hunger and thirst for righteousness (or are physically hungry)
- are merciful
- are pure in heart
- are peacemakers
- are persecuted for righteousness' sake
- are reviled and persecuted falsely on Jesus' account.

Nowhere here does Jesus say that you will be blessed because you believe in some specific doctrine. Nowhere does he even mention religion or theology. Jesus doesn't even tie blessing to acts that we do for God or the Church. That isn't to say that he is discouraging sound doctrine or faith, but he clearly lists blessings that supersede those things. This tells us so much about what God values. God doesn't care about your religion. I know some will disagree, but it is true. He isn't moved by what creeds you can recite. He isn't interested in your theological insights or interpretations. God is looking beneath those things. He is interested in our hearts and how our hearts impact our treatment of others and our love for our Creator. These prerequisites for God's blessing are tied to conditions we experience and our response to those circumstances. They often demonstrate a recognition of our inadequacies.

- We are poor in spirit because we recognize that God's ways are higher than ours. We acknowledge that we are easily misled and incapable of saving ourselves. We know that we are utterly dependent on Him.

- We mourn because we have soft hearts that recognize our brokenness and the suffering in the world around us. We weep due to our inability to repair what is broken.

- We are meek because we realize that only God is worthy of praise and awe. We recognize that we aren't superior to our neighbors and that whatever good fortune we have comes from God.

- We hunger and thirst for righteousness because we see our own spiritual failings and recognize our need for God's cleansing.

- We are merciful because God is merciful, and we depend on that mercy.

- We try to be pure in heart because it draws us closer to the source of all purity.

- We are peacemakers because God made peace with us and loves our enemies as deeply as He loves us.

- We are persecuted and reviled because we recognize that the systems of this world are grounded in selfishness, tribalism, and hate. The kingdom of heaven seeks to change that system, not through political power but through radical and personal transformation.

Jesus' blessings are, perhaps, the most revolutionary sayings ever spoken. They turn on its head the basis of much of this world's values. Placing God and others before our own needs is the opposite of what we are taught. It's rarely something that is modeled by religion. Even when lip service is given to the values of

Jesus' kingdom, they are seldom practiced. They are seen as so impossible to embrace, as to be mere anecdotes. Sadly, often the same people who will become apoplectic if you suggest that Job's story was not written to be seen as a historical event seemingly reject these values. But, these values are the baseline of our faith. These were spoken to the most distant of Jesus' followers.

I want God's blessing on my life, and I have to admit that I haven't always been worthy of these blessings. Some have come relatively easy for me, but some have been really tough. I don't believe that God will refuse to bless those who fail in exhibiting these values. Still, I'm convinced that we will miss out on the blessing in this life if we utterly dismiss these principles.

While this ends our study of the beatitudes, the Sermon on the Mount continues. I ponder this Sermon because it gives me the clearest picture of Jesus that I have. I think that Peter said it best:

> *"Lord, to whom shall we go? You have the words of eternal life."* -- John 6:68 (NIV)

Whatever my faith is, I want it to be grounded in Jesus and his teachings. Everything else in my religion and beliefs is secondary to that.

Today's Verse:

> *"Blessed be the God and Father of our Lord Jesus Christ, the Father of mercies and the God of all*

comfort. He comforts us in all our affliction, so that we may be able to comfort those who are in any kind of affliction, through the comfort we ourselves receive from God. For just as the sufferings of Christ overflow to us, so also through Christ our comfort overflows. If we are afflicted, it is for your comfort and salvation. If we are comforted, it is for your comfort, which produces in you patient endurance of the same sufferings that we suffer. And our hope for you is firm, because we know that as you share in the sufferings, so you will also share in the comfort." -- II Corinthians 1:3-7 (CSB)

Day Fifteen: The Salt of the Earth

"You are the salt of the earth. But if the salt should lose its taste, how can it be made salty? It's no longer good for anything but to be thrown out and trampled under people's feet." -- Matthew 5:13 (CSB)

"Everyone will be salted with fire. Salt is good, but if it loses its saltiness, how can you make it salty again? Have salt among yourselves, and be at peace with each other." -- Mark 9:49,50 (NIV)

"Salt is good, but if it loses its saltiness, how can it be made salty again? It is fit neither for the soil nor for the manure pile; it is thrown out. Whoever has ears to hear, let them hear." -- Luke 14:34,35 (NIV)

Jesus loved to speak in metaphors. He rarely expressed his theology plainly. Instead, Christ painted a picture that required those who heard him to think about what he meant. *"He that has ears to hear, let him hear"* was a challenge to those who listened to him. Frankly, his use of metaphor both delights and frustrates me. There are times when my problem-

96

solving mind wishes he would just plainly make statements that were unequivocal, unambiguous, and left no room for interpretation. There are times when my poetic side falls in love with his stories and word pictures. Here is one of those occasions.

The phrase *salt of the earth* has become a common English phrase, which has simply come to mean *he's good people*. When we read this first precept of Jesus' coming after the blessings, it's easy to interpret it using twenty-first century English. Still, it's essential to try to put ourselves in the sandals of those seated on that hillside in the first century. There are numerous interpretations of what Jesus meant when he told the crowd, "*You are the salt of the earth.*" Being a metaphor, no one can honestly claim to know precisely what he meant. However, I think several good possibilities make sense.

Everyone agrees Jesus was saying that there was something spiritually valuable about the people he was addressing. They had some asset critical to the kingdom of heaven that they should recognize and value.

Let's take a quick look at salt. Today, we all take salt for granted. It's on our tables, and it's cheap, but our use of it today is far different than in Jesus' day. In ancient times, salt served many essential purposes that made it universally valued.

First, salt was a critical preservative of food. There was no refrigeration, food was seasonal, and people often traveled by foot. Salt was also an essential if minor, ingredient used in fertilizer. So, salt was both necessary for the creation of food and helping it to last. Because of this, salt was precious. In economics, demand and scarcity determine value, and salt was something universally required. Because of this, salt was even, occasionally, used as currency. We get our English word *salary* from the Latin word for salt -- *sal.*

Appreciation of salt existed long before that sermon. Salt was often used as a metaphor for wisdom in the Rabbinic literature of Jesus' day. Because of its value, salt was required as part of the ritual grain and burnt offerings -- Leviticus 2:13; Ezekiel 43:24. There are two mentions of the *covenant of salt*, which implied a perpetual covenant of friendship in the Old Testament -- Numbers 18:19; II Chronicles 13:5. Jesus would have been familiar with the economic value of salt and its place in Rabbinical teaching and temple sacrifices.

He would have also been familiar with some negative references to salt. He knew of the fate of Lot's wife, being turned into a *pillar of salt* because of her disobedience -- Genesis 19:26. He would have known that *salted land* was seen as desolate -- Jeremiah 17:6 and that conquering armies would sometimes sow land with salt to prevent re-habitation -- Judges 9:45. In fertilizer, salt has to be used in proper proportion. Too much will prevent crops from growing.

With that as background, Jesus here is saying that this is the ideal within the kingdom of God. However, it comes with a warning. Faithful followers of Jesus serve an essential purpose. We are to preserve and give life. Genuine followers of Jesus are valued, rare, and necessary. In the kingdom of God, our lives should assist Him in His purposes on Earth. We are called to spread the gospel's good news by drawing everyone to Jesus and sacrificially loving our neighbors. What did Jesus call his followers to preserve? The truth of God's loving and holy nature, His never-ending mercy for mankind, and a just and truthful world.

Jesus was no fool, though. He knew that many would falsely claim to be his followers:

> *"Not everyone who says to me, 'Lord, Lord,' will enter the kingdom of heaven, but only the one who does the will of my Father in heaven."* -- Matthew 7:21 (CSB)

I believe that it's to these *false sheep* that Jesus addresses the second part of this precept :

> *"But if the salt should lose its taste, how can it be made salty? It's no longer good for anything"* -- Matthew 5:13 (CSB)

What did he mean? True salt, Sodium Chloride -- NaCl, is a very stable compound. On its own, it is incapable of being anything but salt. There is only one way to remove its saltiness- by dilution. I think, here, Jesus is warning his followers of two equally insidious dangers. Both are forms of dilution, and we see them both corrupting Jesus' teachings today.

In Jesus' day and location, most salt came from mines around the Dead Sea- one of the saltiest bodies of water on the planet. It is ten times saltier than the ocean. However, according to *Barnes Notes on the Bible*, it wasn't uncommon for unscrupulous merchants to mix in other substances to increase the volume of the salt they sold. Gypsum, which is common around the Dead Sea, and other substances would be mixed in, diminishing the ability of the salt to do what was needed. This form of dilution presents a counterfeit product. Today, we see the same phony Christianity being peddled by unscrupulous televangelists, politicians, and partisans. They take American nationalism, politics, lazy thinking, greed, power, racism, fundamentalism, injustice, and fear and mix in just enough of Jesus to hawk it as Christianity. I think Jesus is telling them, "you have lost the true faith and are of no use to prosper the kingdom of heaven."

I believe that Jesus is also warning his sincere followers. He doesn't want us to water down the truth by thoughtlessly abandoning scripture, and Church history, simply because it conflicts with our world's culture. Scripture is not always clear. We need to account for context, view it in its totality, and consider who the scripture is directly addressing. We have to wrestle with it and not simply scrap it because parts of it make us uncomfortable. It's wrong to arrogantly claim to fully understand God's mind. Many on the Christian Right seem to do this. It's equally wrong to arrogantly dismiss scripture and two millennia of Christian study, interpretation, and wisdom. Many on the Christian Left do this.

Jesus came to bring the kingdom of heaven, and he calls followers who will join him in building a world which will:

"act justly and to love mercy and to walk humbly with your God" -- Micah 6:8 (NIV)

Like true salt was, in Jesus' day, faithful followers of Jesus are valued, rare, and essential to Christ's purposes today. He said:

"for many are invited, but few are chosen." -- Matthew 22:14 (NIV)

He is looking for followers who will join him in furthering the kingdom of God, and to do that, we have to avoid dilution from any source. Look to Jesus. Read his words. I know that I've wasted many years by allowing my faith to be diluted by lesser things. For what time I have left, I want to be undiluted, pure salt.

Today's prayer:

Heavenly Father,

You are the source of all that is good in the world, in my faith, and in me. Forgive me for the times when I have tried to smuggle in values and loves which have distracted me from seeking Your face. Give me eyes, and ears, to discern what is and what isn't from You. Use me to preserve, protect, and promote Your kingdom. Protect me from false teachers, and give me the courage to speak the truth, in love, and hold fast to the pure, holy, and uncompromising gospel.

Day Sixteen: The Light of the World Part I

"You are the light of the world. A city situated on a hill cannot be hidden. No one lights a lamp and puts it under a basket, but rather on a lampstand, and it gives light for all who are in the house. In the same way, let your light shine before others, so that they may see your good works and give glory to your Father in heaven." -- Matthew 5:14-16 (CSB)

Imagine a world where you stub your toe during the day, can't appreciate the beauty of a sunset, laugh at the smile of an infant, or avoid clear danger. Many live in such a world and have come to lean on other senses and skills to journey through life. It's hard to imagine how difficult it must be. Being born color-blind, I am aware that I can never fully appreciate the changing of the seasons or subtle color variations in paintings. I am aggravated by engineers who design everything to fit a binary Red-Green world. They should know that Red-Green color-blindness is the most common form of color deficiency. Except for times we want to sleep, we can all agree that light is a good and necessary thing.

Here, Jesus is continuing his precepts, using a metaphor to teach us about his kingdom. Speaking to his followers, he reveals their value and purpose by reminding them that they are essential. Previously, he described them as salt, and now he compares them to light.

Light certainly has a special place in God's Creation.

> *"And God said, "Let there be light," and there was light."* -- Genesis 1:3 (NIV)

As far as Creation is concerned, it was light that introduced us to our Creator, and it was God's first gift to us. It seems likely that something directly connects us to God's nature through the medium of light. Even the tiny points of light in the pitch black of the night sky cause us to think about eternity. Light guides us, warms us, provides the energy that produces our food, protects us, informs us, and reveals us. So, when Jesus tells us, his followers, that we are "*the light of the world*," it is no cliché or trite compliment. As with salt, he tells us of the essential role played by those who follow his teachings.

Note that Jesus didn't say, "You should be the light of the world." It isn't an aspiration to achieve or a goal. It is a statement of our identity by virtue of being adopted members of God's family. I think this concept of God's adoption of believers is tied to this teaching.

> *"But to all who did receive him, he gave them the right to be children of God, to those who believe in his name"* -- John 1:12 (CSB)

"When the time came to completion, God sent his Son, born of a woman, born under the law, to redeem those under the law, so that we might receive adoption as sons." -- Galatians 4:4-5 (CSB)

"he predestined us for adoption to sonship through Jesus Christ, in accordance with his pleasure and will." -- Ephesians 1:5 (NIV)

Note that this means if we fail to shine our light the world around us will be dark.

God's very nature is one of light. As adopted children of God, light is our birthright and our inherited nature. Jesus reminds his followers that they possess God's light-giving nature and have a critical role to perform in providing it. Obviously, he isn't saying that we are to emit photons of energy. He is using light as a metaphor. We are to perform a similar function to light. To people of faith, God has given the mandate to guide, warm, feed, protect, inform, and reveal. Just as light is the source of physical life on our planet, God tells us that we are to be a source of spiritual and physical life in our world. When people want to know the meaning of life, it is our calling to aid them in their finding the answers. Of course, that requires that we ask ourselves difficult, spiritual questions and wrestle with the answers. When people are emotionally and physically chilled, we are to warm them. When they are spiritually and physically hungry, we are to feed them. As adopted children of the Creator, this is our function- to be the light of the world.

When so many on our planet claim to follow God, why

is the world such a dark place then? Some of that darkness is indeed beyond our control. Even the brightness of the sun is dimmed by cloud cover and the earth's rotation on its axis, away from the sun's rays. If the world was populated by an adequate number of authentic people of faith, there would still be hunger, war, poverty, bigotry, ignorance, and hate. Salt doesn't block the eventual decay of food but merely delays it. Even in a world where every believer lived up to Jesus' teachings, darkness would still exist. However, what we see in the world today, is a Church that has too often lost sight of what God's light even is, much less genuinely and consistently reflects it. The world suffers needlessly because we fail to live our calling. This is largely due to organized religion's role in replacing Jesus at the heart of its identity.

Jesus is not telling his followers that they are independent sources of light. In fact, he makes it clear that he is the natural source of that light.

> *"Jesus spoke to them again:"I am the light of the world. Anyone who follows me will never walk in the darkness but will have the light of life."* -- John 8:12 (CSB)

> *"I have come into the world as a light, so that no one who believes in me should stay in darkness."* -- John 12:46 (NIV)

In Jesus' metaphor, we are less like the sun than we are the moon. In the dark, night of our world, when the earth has turned its back on the daylight, it is from the moon that we receive the sun's illumination, but the moon merely reflects. It doesn't, by itself, create light. In a sense, Jesus addresses us as if we were the moon, saying, "without you, God's light will not be seen. Reflect that light, as I have done."

Metaphorically, humanity has turned its back on God's light. All too often, instead of seeing the natural and pure glow of Jesus' reflection, they are confronted by a Church that is shining an inauthentic, artificial light. Harsh, neon, man-made laser lights will never draw anyone to Jesus. The phrase *in a bad light* seems appropriate to describe how much of the world perceives God because the light we are reflecting often doesn't find its source in our savior or the Creator. There are many authentically transformed believers. However, they exist amid a vast ocean of apostasy.

Tonight, walk into your bedroom and don't flip the light switch. Instead, contemplate how you can remove the darkness in the room. No vacuum cleaner, broom, law, or harsh word will drive the shadows away, yet that is how much of the Church responds to the world's culture. Many wrongly believe they can force the removal of what they perceive to be darkness. The only way to remove the darkness is to bring light into the room.

Jesus doesn't call his followers to establish laws that mimic our view of morality. He doesn't say, "You are the government of the world. Force people to follow your interpretation of the Bible." Like the darkness in your bedroom, he knows that no law can drive away the darkness. Instead, he reminds us that we are light. When we live out our adopted nature, as true children of God, we will reflect God's goodness, purity, and mercy. People hunger for that, even if they don't know it. I've spent far too much of my life in darkness. Moving forward and as honestly as I can, I want my face to seek God and reflect the light that He gives me.

Today's verse:

> *"Everything exposed by the light is made visible, for what makes everything visible is light. Therefore it is said:*
>
> *Get up, sleeper, and rise up from the dead, and Christ will shine on you."* -- Ephesians 5:13-14 (CSB)

Day Seventeen: The Light of the World Part II

"You are the light of the world. A city situated on a hill cannot be hidden. No one lights a lamp and puts it under a basket, but rather on a lampstand, and it gives light for all who are in the house. In the same way, let your light shine before others, so that they may see your good works and give glory to your Father in heaven." -- Matthew 5:14-16 (CSB)

Jesus has established that his followers are the light of the world, regardless of their obedience. Jesus goes on to point out the obvious. Light is only helpful when it is not covered up. Was Jesus encouraging his followers to make a public show of manufactured righteousness? He later makes it clear that this is what the Pharisees do:

"Whenever you pray, you must not be like the hypocrites, because they love to pray standing in the synagogues and on the street corners to be seen by people. Truly I tell you, they have their reward." -- Matthew 6:5 (CSB)

Was he calling us to public acts of righteousness?

Certainly not to receive recognition or praise. When Jesus went around healing, he didn't put up fliers beforehand, with the boast, "Come see me raise the dead." The loving and spectacular deeds that he performed were often done in public but never to receive applause. Doing good, showing compassion, loving the unloved was so much a part of his character that it would have been impossible for him to hide that away. He was motivated by concern for others. He was not motivated by any desire for people to see how godly he was.

Within the religious community, there is a stream that focuses on isolating from the world. The extreme version of this is seen by those who cloister themselves away in some desert commune. There, they have little contact with the outside world. Obviously, some good can come from spending time alone, in prayer, and in meditation. We see that Jesus often did this. However, these cloistered groups are operating under the false belief that the world is the enemy of their faith. In hopes of protecting their faith, they strictly limit their contact with the world.

To a lesser degree, this is what is practiced in many Conservative Christian communities. They don't live in communes, but they take their children out of public schools and only travel in circles with others who share their belief system. They often view *the world* as a threat to their faith. They have established a pseudo-Christian sub-culture, with their own radio stations, businesses with fish symbols on their cards, and Christian bumper stickers on their cars. They appear to share identical social and political goals, intending to mold themselves and perhaps, the world to fit their vision of how the world should be. Again, where there is some good in joining together for support, and prayer, is this *us against them* approach what Jesus intended?

When he announced the kingdom of God, Jesus wasn't attempting to isolate his followers from the rest of the world. While he spent time in the Temple, he spent far more time in public, with ordinary people. He didn't preach a distinction between the sacred and the secular. In his *priestly prayer*, Jesus talks about his vision for our connection with those outside the walls of the church:

> *"I have given them your word and the world has hated them, for they are not of the world any more than I am of the world. My prayer is not that you take them out of the world but that you protect them from the evil one. They are not of the world, even as I am not of it. Sanctify them by the truth; your word is truth. As you sent me into the world, I have sent them into the world."* -- John 17:14-18 (NIV)

Jesus does not call us to isolate ourselves from the world. He does not invite us to hate the world. What he does is say that we must be different. We must present a better way. Just as he came because of God's passionate love for the world, he calls us to love the world, and you can not love someone and simultaneously despise, fear, and avoid them. What Jesus does say is that the world is not our eternal home. As adopted sons and daughters, our citizenship is with God, and we are merely temporary guests here, in the earthly realm.

Jesus recognizes there is evil in this world and that persecution will come. He does not say that the world itself is evil. His prayer is that God will protect us from *the evil one.*

Many Christians have come to believe that the world is to be feared, that it will either corrupt our values or attempt to harm us. This is a lie that comes from "*the father of lies*" -- John 8:44. As a result, many of Jesus' followers have chosen to disobey or corrupt his message about shining our light. Often, instead of following Jesus' example of loving sacrificially, many have selected one of two paths: they have abandoned any meaningful connection with the world at large, or they have adopted a scheme to force the world, through political power, to fit a mold of their own design. This is absolutely not the mission that Jesus has summoned his followers to.

Consider whether the way you are dealing with the secular world aligns with Jesus' wishes. How do we know if we do? Fortunately, Christ gives us the rubric to ascertain that. Does your approach demonstrate the sort of good works that will cause people to "*glorify your Father who is in heaven*"? While the truth is that private prayer has never been forbidden in school, some believe we should pass laws that force public prayer in schools. Some want to criminalize behavior they believe to be immoral. Will that ever lead anyone to glorify God? I'm convinced this strategy is seriously mistaken and unwise. It will only result in justified contempt for religious hypocrisy. Also, we often overreact or base our response on lies. This is precisely what Jesus

111

condemned.

While we have a responsibility to love and care for our brothers and sisters in the faith, we need to take a page from the book of the early Christian Church. They lived simple lives of poverty, which they poured out to one another AND those outside their faith communities.

Our good deeds should flow from us naturally, not out of some attempt to gain recognition or increase church attendance. Doing good should be as natural as breathing. Because our connection with the world should mirror God's, we should love selflessly. Jesus commands us to love God and our neighbor. If people see our authentic and selfless faith, they will be more likely to glorify God and join Jesus in building God's kingdom. Micah describes what God requires from us.

> *"He has shown you, O mortal, what is good. And what does the LORD require of you? To act justly and to love mercy and to walk humbly with your God."* -- Micah 6:8 (NIV)

Today's challenge:

Take a moment, pray, and prepare a list of things that demonstrate the authenticity of my personal walk of faith and areas where I need to make changes. Include items that verify not only my love of God but also my care for those outside my *tribe*. Where am I shining Christ's light, and where am I casting a shadow?

Day Eighteen: The Law

"Don't think that I came to abolish the Law or the Prophets. I did not come to abolish but to fulfill. For truly I tell you, until heaven and earth pass away, not the smallest letter or one stroke of a letter will pass away from the law until all things are accomplished. Therefore, whoever breaks one of the least of these commands and teaches others to do the same will be called least in the kingdom of heaven. But whoever does and teaches these commands will be called great in the kingdom of heaven. For I tell you, unless your righteousness surpasses that of the scribes and Pharisees, you will never get into the kingdom of heaven." -- Matthew 5:17-20 (CSB)

L et's look, with honesty, at Jesus. There is something there to challenge, and possibly offend, the worldview of nearly everyone. Up to this point, we see a Jesus who appeals to a more liberal sense of the world. Blessing the poor, the humble, the persecuted, and affirming the value of all those who follow him. In this section, Jesus wades into seemingly more conservative waters. Here, he stresses the enduring importance of *The Law*. When I read this section, I am reminded that Jesus doesn't consider holiness optional for his followers. It is essential. In Jesus' vision of the kingdom, God doesn't look the other way when we sin. He doesn't grade on a curve. Those with a more liberal take on the world often major in God's grace, patience, and forgiveness. They may stress the Jesus who tells the woman, caught in the act of adultery, that he does not condemn her, but then they ignore the second half, where he tells her, "*Go now and leave your life of sin.*" -- John 8:11 (NIV)

In discussing the relationship between the Law, and Grace, what is most apparent is that there isn't a single, uniform agreement about it within the Christian community. We may look at the Ten Commandments -- Exodus 20:1-17 and think, "how complicated can it be." Unfortunately, the Pharisees had taken those commandments and other directions from Moses and the Prophets and manufactured hundreds of rules. By the third century, Jewish scholars were teaching that there were 613 commandments. There are likely as many opinions on how the Law applies to followers of Jesus today. What did Jesus mean by the Law and the Prophets, and what would he make of how many Christians today teach that "we are no longer under the Law?" At the same time, other Christians act like everyone is under judgment.

I have struggled with this question and have to confess that I have no authoritative answer. The only one with authority on this is Jesus. I don't look to other Christians, theologians, or even the Apostles to find the answer. They may provide some insight, but Jesus has the final word. I grew up being told that "the Law was for a previous Covenant, and since we are now under a new Covenant, it no longer applies to us." I think I understand this theological argument, but it seems to disagree with what Jesus is saying. What did Jesus mean by *the Law and the Prophets*? For example, was he saying that we shouldn't wear clothing made from different fabrics, which was part of the Mosaic Law -- Leviticus 19:19? Was he talking about those seemingly strange and arcane rules, or was he pointing to some underlying principle that was eternal and would not fade? I suspect that it was the latter.

Why would God tell Moses to instruct the Israelites to not mix fabrics? Why would He command him to not eat pork? Seems pretty absurd to my modern mind. The best explanation that I've heard is that fabrics shrink at different rates, so a shady fabric merchant might mix a cloth that shrinks along with one that doesn't in an attempt to defraud a client. If true, the point of the Law was to promote honesty and fairness. Its purpose was not to insist on some arbitrary rule. My grandmother used to say that the prohibition against pork was simply a health concern before we knew about Trichinosis.

I think that Jesus gives us some clues as to his intent here. Matthew tells us that a teacher of the Law asked Jesus about this. He asked:

"Teacher, which commandment is the greatest in

the Law?

Jesus replied, 'Love the Lord your God with all your heart and with all your soul and with all your mind.' This is the first and greatest commandment. And the second is like it: 'Love your neighbor as yourself.' All the Law and the Prophets hang on these two commandments." -- Matthew 22:36-40 (NIV)

Here, he points to God's heart, which sees beyond the external, to our truest nature.

"The LORD does not look at the things people look at. People look at the outward appearance, but the LORD looks at the heart." -- I Samuel 16:7b (NIV)

The Pharisees spent their lives cultivating an appearance of righteousness, but Jesus was no fan. Certainly, they followed the Law, at least externally and to the letter. Still, if the Law didn't specifically prohibit some evil, they had little issue with it. Jesus expressed his disdain for that sort of faux-godliness:

"Woe to you, teachers of the law and Pharisees, you hypocrites! You are like whitewashed tombs, which look beautiful on the outside but on the inside are full of the bones of the dead and everything unclean. In the same way, on the outside you appear to people as righteous but on the inside you are full of hypocrisy and wickedness." -- Matthew 23:27,28 (NIV)

The Pharisees would strictly command the people to not work on the Sabbath but had no problem with

116

merchants defrauding visitors to the Temple. They obeyed the letter but ignored the heart and intent of the Law.

I tend to think of the Law, as lights along a dark and winding road, at night. They are there to guide our path. They help prevent us from going off the road and harming ourselves or others. When Jesus came along, he pointed out that simply having those lights was not enough. A committed follower would both value those lights along the way and be a watchful and considerate driver.

I disagree with the commonly held view that the Law is no longer valid. Isn't believing that to call Jesus a liar? Jesus did not come to invalidate the Law, but he came to better illuminate our path.

It's reasonable to question a church or leader who is adamant about the importance of one Old Testament command while entirely rejecting a different one. So, what do we do with biblical commands that seem irrelevant or culturally difficult? As a follower of Jesus, if we simply ignore them, that seems wrong, but to insist on them or ignore how culture and history impact their meaning seems irresponsible and Pharisaical. According to the definitions set by the Pharisees, Jesus did not follow the letter of the Law. We see Jesus' disciples picking grain to eat on the Sabbath -- Matthew 12:1. When the Pharisees sought to attack his disciples for violating their rules about respecting the Sabbath, Jesus does not condemn his disciples. Instead, he defends them. Ultimately, he reminds the Pharisees that God *"desires mercy, not sacrifice"* -- Matthew 12:7. They focused on the external rule, but Jesus had mercy on his hungry disciples. On another Sabbath, he goes into the Temple and heals a man with a shriveled hand. The Pharisees wanted to claim Jesus was breaking the Law when he healed the man. Jesus asks them:

> *"Which is lawful on the Sabbath: to do good or to do evil, to save life or to kill?"* -- Mark 3:4 (NIV)

Again, the Pharisees missed the point of the Law. It's not about following a bunch of irrelevant rules to gain respect from the community or gain currency with God, It's entirely about loving God and neighbor. It's about our heart and our intent.

I won't say whether someone should or shouldn't observe a specific Mosaic command. Ultimately, it is something that we have to decide for ourselves. Still, it means nothing if it isn't motivated by our love of God or love for our neighbor. I've often thought it odd that we go to church on Sunday and then go out to eat afterward. By doing so, we put pressure on businesses to require their employees to work on Sunday. I wouldn't teach someone that God blesses our choice to ignore that commandment. Neither would I insist that it be followed to the letter. I would simply suggest considering why God required it and ask how we can honor God's underlying intent.

When Jesus says that our righteousness must exceed that of the Pharisees, I don't think that he's setting a very high bar. He clearly believed that most of the Pharisees were disreputable and not sincere followers of God. What concerns me is what he says later in this chapter:

> *"Be perfect, therefore, as your heavenly Father is perfect."* -- Matthew 5:48 (CSB)

Jesus was not the first to set this standard. It is stated in the same chapter, where God, through Moses, tells the Israelites to not mix fabric.

> *"Speak to the entire assembly of Israel and say to them: 'Be holy because I, the Lord your God, am holy."* -- Leviticus 19:2 (NIV)

Be perfect. Be holy. How is that possible? I think that the Apostle Paul says it clearly:

> *"for all have sinned and fall short of the glory of God."* -- Romans 3:23 (NIV)

I don't believe that the word, translated here as *perfect*, means that we never fall short of God's perfect desire for us. I don't think Jesus' command is some expectation that we will never sin. The English word perfect here comes from the Greek word *téleioi*, which means *complete*, that we should be equipped for our intended function. Still, I believe that Jesus is telling us that perfect holiness should be our desire and aim.

While achieving perfection in this life is impossible, note the reasoning behind the command. Jesus doesn't say, "Be perfect, so you won't go to hell." He is pointing to a remarkable statement- *"as your heavenly Father is perfect."* We are to make holiness and obedience our aim, because of who God is, and by extension, who we are, as His children. We are called to be like our Abba

Father. What good child of a good father doesn't want that? It's less an impossible commandment than it is a birthright.

Does the Law still apply to followers of Jesus? I think so, but it is a more meaningful and fuller Law than what the Pharisees taught. Our motivation should be to express our devotion, respect, and love for our Creator and His creation in everything we do. Some follow the old maxim, "I don't smoke, drink, or chew, and don't go with girls who do." Still, if our love of God and God's Creation (particularly our neighbors) is not what motivates us, then we're missing the point.

Today's prayer:

Perfect Heavenly Father,

Perfect in me, my love for You, and for all that You have created. Deliver me both from a life without guidelines and a life weighed down by guilt and senseless rules. Set me free to walk the path you have for me.

Day Nineteen: Murder

*"You have heard that it was said to our ancestors,
Do not murder, and whoever murders will be
subject to judgment. But I tell you, everyone who is
angry with his brother or sister will be subject to
judgment. Whoever insults his brother or sister, will
be subject to the court. Whoever says, 'You fool!'
will be subject to hellfire."* -- Matthew 5:21-22 (CSB)

As a young Christian, I learned the value of scripture memorization. I had little cards with selected verses on them. I was taught that memorizing those scriptures would change my outlook on the world and make God ever-present for me. There was some truth in that. We should *"Do your best to present yourself to God as one approved,"* -- II Timothy 2:15a (NIV). However, there is a problem with relying solely on this method of studying scripture. The second half of that verse states it: *"a worker who does not need to be ashamed "* -- II Timothy 2:15b (NIV)

In Jesus' encounter with the devil, during his temptation in the desert, we see that scripture memorization was not a problem for Jesus' adversary.

He could quote scripture with the best of them. That encounter teaches us a critical lesson- that we must not let a tree obscure our view of the forest. Jesus' adversary, while thoroughly knowing scripture, did not *accurately handle* it. No single verse or group of verses can stand on their own. They must always be viewed as a part of a whole. Even those selected verses I was given to memorize were selected by someone who decided, on their own, that those verses were more significant than others. They were often chosen to reinforce some selected theological doctrine. This choice, as all choices are, was based on a personal worldview and agenda. The same is true of my selection of verses here. In reading through what I've written, I notice that I reference many of these verses multiple times. Again, to some degree, that is a reflection of my own bias and personal values.

This brings us to this week's section, where Jesus is continuing with his discussion of the Law. As I stated previously, for me, this portion of the Sermon on the Mount is more challenging than the Beatitudes. While it all challenges me, I find myself struggling with this section because I am admittedly weak in the area of self-control and self-discipline. Much of the Law calls me to reign in my instinctually un-Christlike nature. The same is true for all of us. In this week's section, Jesus is building on his statement:

> *"Don't think that I came to abolish the Law or the Prophets. I did not come to abolish but to fulfill."* --
> Matthew 5:17 (CSB)

Here, he makes it clear that rather than doing away with moral law, God wants us to see beyond an external, structural morality. Rather than simply abstaining from outward disobedience, God wants us to have obedient and increasingly Christlike hearts. In this portion, Jesus uses the sin of murder as an example to make this point.

He recognizes that grievous sin, like murder, is the culmination of a slippery slope. The story of the world's first murder illustrates this. In Genesis, chapter four, we read of brothers Cain and Abel. Abel was a shepherd, and Cain was a farmer. They both brought an offering to God. It says Cain brought "*some of the fruits of the soil*" as an offering. However, Abel brought "*fat portions, from some of the firstborn of his flock*" -- Genesis 4:3,4. For some reason, God was pleased with Abel's offering, but not with Cain's.

"The LORD looked with favor on Abel and his offering, but on Cain and his offering he did not look with favor." -- Genesis 4:4,5 (NIV)

I think the wording explains why. While Abel's offering came from the *firstborn* and the *fat portions* (the best of the best), Cain seemed to only be going through the motions by giving *some of the fruits*. I don't believe that God really needed the gifts. He wanted to see their motivation. Abel was giving from his heart and out of appreciation and love for God. I suspect that is what pleased Him. It seems that God didn't sense this in Cain's offering. So, what was Cain's response to this? *"So Cain was very angry, and his face was downcast."*

-- Genesis 4:5. Instead of recognizing that his priorities were askew, Cain became angry and sad. God understands when we grow angry with him, as does a parent to a young child's anger. God simply asks Cain why he is angry. God goes on to give one of the first lessons on the Law, recorded in scripture:

> *"If you do what is right, will you not be accepted? But if you do not do what is right, sin is crouching at your door; it desires to have you, but you must rule over it."* -- Genesis 4:7 (NIV)

Here, God is not telling Cain that he will *smite* him if he doesn't give a good enough gift. Instead, he reminds Cain of the cost that sin demands from us. Certainly, his parents knew this all too well. God compares sin to a lion that is waiting in hiding to devour us, but that He has given us the authority to *rule over it*. Unfortunately, instead of listening to God and changing his heart attitude toward God and jealousy of his brother, Abel, Cain allows the anger to fester. It's not clear how much time transpires between God's discussion with Cain and the rest of the story. I suspect that Cain likely stewed in his anger for some time. He eventually surrendered to his heart's anger and made it flesh by murdering his brother. When God confronts Cain, he tells him:

"What have you done? Listen! Your brother's blood cries out to me from the ground." -- Genesis 4:10 (NIV)

God eventually responded to man's inability to control his anger by making murder one of the top ten things that He commands that we do not do. *"You shall not kill"* -- Exodus 20:13. The Hebrew word used here is

124

Retzach. In some versions, it is translated as *Kill*, but in others, it is translated as *Murder*. The word, however, does have other meanings as well. It can be used to describe some destructive activity, which breaks, or dashes to pieces. The book of Numbers clarifies that any killing outside of war is considered *Retzach*. If the killing is accidental, the person can flee to a *city of refuge* -- Numbers, chapter thirty-five.

Arguably, the Ten Commandments were interpreted as the basis for a legal, criminal, and civil relationship with this cardinal sin. While most governments don't legally codify each of the Ten Commandments, nearly all recognize, at least on paper, that murder is an act that can not be allowed. That our government allows behavior that results in the unjust deaths of innocents is a topic for another day. Still, universal respect for human life is not valued in much of our nation. This is true among both political worldviews. Sadly, our political parties have successfully created their own subsets of human life that they value and those that they don't.

While the legal code treated murder entirely as a criminal matter, Jesus here is reminding us that it is, inherently, a moral and spiritual matter as well. Additionally, I suspect he is pointing back to God's lesson to Cain when he murdered his brother. Jesus reminds us of the slippery slope that sin if left unchecked can develop into something worse. To address it, we must first correct our hearts.

Jesus reminds us that all people, even those who do

horrible things, are God-breathed beings with the potential for change and growth. Men and women are universally created with God's imprint on their being. We all come from Him and return to Him. We must remember that we are interacting with unique creations in our dealings with each other. God has a plan for each, hopes for their futures, and is the ultimate judge of their destiny. To some extent, the way we interact with God's Creation is a reflection of our relationship with Him.

To get this point across, I believe that Jesus is using the example of calling someone a bad name as being comparable to murder. I don't think he is making this rather extreme comparison because they are equally offensive (criminally or morally). He's pointing out that name-calling and murder both flow from the same source- our uncontrolled sin and selfishness. This is the very thing that God warns us to *rule over*. The issue is less the insult than it is the dangerous thing, which may lie behind it. Jesus is reminding us that anger is something we must control.

The word *Raca* -- Rhaka was an Aramaic slur, which is translated here as fool. It was an insulting term of utter contempt. It derives from the word meaning *to spit*. It suggested that the person was *empty-headed* and worthless. The word also had a second application for something combustible and to be burned. Gehenna was the place where trash was burned, outside the gates of Jerusalem. Jesus may be suggesting that if you call someone worthless and disposable, you may be predicting your own future.

Finally, I do NOT believe that Jesus is saying that it is always wrong to point out and confront foolishness, entrenched ignorance, dishonesty, and behavior that hurts others. Likewise, I don't believe that he is saying that anger is never acceptable. The Bible is replete with instances of just and righteous anger, and with good and godly people describing behavior as foolish and occasionally even referring to people as fools. Both Paul and James refer to certain people as fools -- I Corinthians 15:36; James 2:20. Jesus himself expressed anger (even violently, on one occasion, in John 2:15). He called a group of religious leaders *fools*.

> *"You blind fools! Which is greater: the gold, or the temple that makes the gold sacred?"* -- Matthew 23:17 (NIV)

This section is not intended as an excuse to ignore injustice. It doesn't give Christians a pass when they promote evil and provide tacit support for behavior that harms our neighbors and the gospel. There will be times when we must stand up and speak truth to power- to both political and religious power and the religious majority. Still, we must be on guard to not allow our righteous indignation, desire for justice or love for the mistreated to become an excuse for rude, snarky, and condescending statements or heartfelt disgust focused on any soul. These days, we may find ourselves talking with someone who claims to follow Jesus and loves the Bible, and yet patently promotes un-Christlike policies and views. They may defend policies that do substantial harm to the poor and to people of color. They may align with politicians who blatantly glorify greed and open violence (denying both Jesus and demonstrating profound ignorance of scripture). Even with all this, they may still falsely claim the spiritual high ground. In those instances, we may confuse righteous anger about the lies they embrace with hatred toward the person. I've certainly been guilty of that and am trying to do better and be more gracious.

Yes, speak the truth. Defend those being mistreated, and be passionate about it. However, don't allow that to turn into a cancer that rules over us. This verse has been used as a proof text to dissuade valid and needed criticism of other believers. Some habitually defend and promote policies and attitudes that do great harm to the gospel. That's not something that we should respond to with silence. The entirety of scripture provides a clearer understanding of what Jesus was communicating.

Today's verses:

"In your anger do not sin": Do not let the sun go down while you are still angry." -- Ephesians 4:26 (NIV)

"Do not be quickly provoked in your spirit, for anger resides in the lap of fools." -- Ecclesiastes 7:9 (NIV)

Day Twenty: Reconciliation

"So if you are offering your gift on the altar, and there you remember that your brother or sister has something against you, leave your gift there in front of the altar. First go and be reconciled with your brother or sister, and then come and offer your gift. Reach a settlement quickly with your adversary while you're on the way with him to the court, or your adversary will hand you over to the judge, and the judge to the officer, and you will be thrown into prison. Truly I tell you, you will never get out of there until you have paid the last penny." -- Matthew 5:23-26 (CSB)

Being a homeowner keeps me constantly busy. There seems to always be some need for repair or improvement. On more than one occasion, I've had to put a coat of paint on some piece of wood, only to discover that beneath the existing layer lies wood that has rotted. It's not enough to simply cover it up. Ignoring it won't make it go away. The rot demands that I look beyond the surface and address the decay. Once the wood rot has been carefully removed, I can patch it and paint it, knowing that the decay won't spread further. This is true of homes and most material possessions. It is also true of our thinking, our values, our beliefs, and our relationships.

In this section, Jesus is continuing his discussion of the Law, anger, and how we respond to conflict. Jesus was keenly aware of man's nature. Disagreement and conflict were issues he saw or experienced regularly. He received criticism from the religious leaders. He also delivered it. Even the perfect, loving, and kind-hearted Jesus was not immune to conflict. He could have chosen to stay in his carpenter's shop, limited his contact with the Pharisees, and avoided topics where their values and views diverged from his. It would have been easier. No one would have called him a trouble maker, contentious, or judgmental. He still would have experienced friction. But he didn't take that course. He spoke the truth, and that sometimes ruffled feathers.

While disputes were not foreign to him, Jesus never made conflict his goal. His goal was to point to God the Father, remind people of what God wanted, and speak the truth. Conflict was simply the anticipated consequence of exposing unpleasant facts. Jesus knew that, in the short term, following him would often lead to conflict.

> *"Do not suppose that I have come to bring peace to the earth. I did not come to bring peace, but a sword."* -- Matthew 10:34 (NIV)

Ultimately, I believe that Jesus' eventual goal was to bring peace- peace with God and peace between neighbors. However, there must be honesty, repentance, and healing before there can be lasting peace.

Jesus isn't saying that we won't have conflict. He knew that in both good and bad people, disagreements and hurt feelings come. I believe he is reminding us of a critical truth. It makes no sense to give your offering to God and seek His forgiveness if you have enmity with a neighbor and have made no effort to resolve that. The whole purpose of the ritual, *Korban* sacrifice, was to reconcile with God, but that is meaningless if we are holding a grudge against a brother.

Additionally, anger blinds us and makes us numb and unable to discern God's voice. In Jesus' view of the kingdom, our relationship with God is entwined with our treatment and response to our neighbor. He is telling us that making peace with our brother is more important than any religious act. If you have an unresolved issue with a brother, going to church can wait. It's OK to pray first, but pray about your next step in peacemaking, and go.

In the previous section, I talked about Cain and Abel. Here, that story seems even more pertinent. Both Cain and Abel attempted to give a suitable sacrifice to God, but God's preference for Abel's sacrifice resulted in Cain having hurt feelings and simmering anger toward his brother. Cain didn't try to have an open and honest conversation about his feelings with Abel. Instead of dropping what he was doing and attempting to make peace, Cain allowed his resentment to build to the point of a violent eruption. Here, Jesus is reminding us of the importance of dealing with anger promptly and not allowing it to fester.

What Jesus is saying is by no means unique. The importance of seeking peace is something that is often found in the scriptures. That peace should be our objective is expressed by the author of the Psalms:

> *"How good and pleasant it is when God's people live together in unity!"* -- Psalm 133:1 (NIV)

But, that unity will never exist by simply avoiding conflict and issues. It will only force the splinter to dig in more deeply. David knew that conflict was sometimes unavoidable. His discord with King Saul shows his genuine desire for peace and the reality that it takes two people to actually obtain it.

Paul reminds us:

> *"If it is possible, as far as it depends on you, live at peace with everyone."* -- Romans 12:18 (NIV)

Later in Matthew, Jesus even tells us that the way we forgive is how God will forgive us:

> *"For if you forgive others their offenses, your heavenly Father will forgive you as well. But if you don't forgive others, your Father will not forgive your offenses."* -- Matthew 6:14-15 (CSB)

Forgiveness and letting go of anger are critical to life in the kingdom of heaven, but that doesn't mean that conflict will cease to be an issue. You can faithfully forgive and still have conflict. You can love someone and still fail to reconcile with them. This is for two primary reasons:

First, sometimes, even when we honestly try to, we don't recognize that we are the ones at fault. Much conflict falls into gray areas, and our perception of the disagreement may not be correct. Perhaps, the other person was partially at fault, but our response to it was also wrong. I've had many conflicts where we both thought the other was responsible for the bad blood. In a situation like that, all we can do is honestly pray for God to open our eyes. We can ask Him to reveal if there:

> "is any offensive way in me, and lead me in the way everlasting." -- Psalm 139:24 (NIV).

We can speak to an objective third party and ask them to mediate. They may be able to reveal a truth that we don't see. Most importantly, we need to humbly recognize that we might share in the blame regardless of how right we think we were. The point is never to prove the other person wrong. The point is to lovingly come to a place of acceptance, even if we disagree on the specifics.

Second, the other person may not be willing to listen. They may not be ready for peace. This is especially true if we have been impatient, condescending, or self-righteous in our conversations. If we needlessly hurt someone's feelings, it makes reconciliation that much more challenging. It may take time, patience, and understanding to win them over. In a case like this, Jesus later gives us guidance on how to proceed:

133

"If your brother or sister sins, go and point out their fault, just between the two of you. If they listen to you, you have won them over. But if they will not listen, take one or two others along, so that 'every matter may be established by the testimony of two or three witnesses.' If they still refuse to listen, tell it to the church; and if they refuse to listen even to the church, treat them as you would a pagan or a tax collector." -- Matthew 18:15 (NIV)

When we seek to resolve conflict and be the peacemakers that Jesus tells us that God will bless, we must choose our battles wisely. We don't have to agree on every issue to live at peace with another. Seeking peace doesn't mean that we have to be silent about what we believe is true. Paul tells us:

"each of you must put off falsehood and speak truthfully to your neighbor, for we are all members of one body. In your anger do not sin. Do not let the sun go down while you are still angry." -- Ephesians 4:25,26 (NIV)

If it appears that even broaching the subject will only increase hostility, it may be wiser to take a break and walk away. Consider if it's the closest path to peace. While the verse is seemingly insulting, there is wisdom when Jesus says:

"Don't give what is holy to dogs or toss your pearls before pigs, or they will trample them under their feet, turn, and tear you to pieces." -- Matthew 7:6 (CSB)

Jesus is not suggesting that we demean people or call them dogs or pigs. He's pointing out the futility of offering wisdom to those who are unable or unwilling to appreciate it. We can disagree, but it must be done as kindly as possible while accepting the other person's decision. That acceptance doesn't even require that we respect their view, but respect that God allows us each free will to make our choices. Ultimately, all we can ask of ourselves and others is to seek God earnestly for the correct view.

In almost every disagreement, both parties are convinced they are in the right. Even if we believe that we are entirely correct, we should be the first to seek reconciliation.

> *"A gentle answer turns away wrath, but a harsh word stirs up anger."* -- Proverbs 15:1 (NIV)

One of the early Church fathers says:

> "But if it is he that hath done you the wrong, and yet you be the first to seek reconciliation, you shall have a great reward." -- Pseudo-Chrysostom

Jesus' message here is especially crucial for the world we live in today. We are in the middle of what has been described as a *Cold Civil War*. Significant segments of the country and much of the Church hold views that make no logical or moral sense to me. It seems uncivil, unsustainable, and un-Christlike. So, it's easy to let my tongue overrule God's prompting. On occasion, I've certainly been guilty of speaking without kindness, without consideration, and without humility. Even if my views were entirely correct, my words have unintentionally hurt feelings and erected barriers. Some of that has been unavoidable. Some tension would have come regardless of how diplomatic my words were. Most of what I have said has been motivated by my love of God, neighbor, reason, and truth. I still am partially at fault, and it's my responsibility to seek to restore and reconcile. God doesn't ask me to ignore injustice, dishonesty, bigotry, greed, or any other sin that harms others. However, He does ask me to address those issues as kindly and patiently as possible.

Today's thought:

If I see *rot* in my relationship with a brother, I can't just paint over it and pretend it will disappear. Relationships are complicated, but God's Spirit can restore relationships. God can and does change hearts. If I don't see the change in the other person, that's OK, but I must ensure that God has my permission to change me.

Day Twenty-one: Adultery

"You have heard that it was said, Do not commit adultery. But I tell you, everyone who looks at a woman lustfully has already committed adultery with her in his heart. If your right eye causes you to sin, gouge it out and throw it away. For it is better that you lose one of the parts of your body than for your whole body to be thrown into hell. And if your right hand causes you to sin, cut it off and throw it away. For it is better that you lose one of the parts of your body than for your whole body to go into hell." -- Matthew 5:27-30 (CSB)

Previously, Jesus showed that he not only affirms the importance of the Law, but he guides us to see beyond the mere legal commands. He began by addressing the Sixth Commandment *"you shall not murder"* -- Exodus 20:13. Society requires the prohibition against murder. Jesus uses this to reveal that the Law is the bare, spiritual minimum. It doesn't address the chain of events or thoughts that can lead to murder. The Law sees murder primarily as a criminal issue. It addresses the consequence, while Jesus wants to treat the cause. The Law looks at the symptoms. Jesus wants to cure the infection. Jesus shows that, at its heart, it is the result of unrestrained and unaddressed anger. The Law ignores the spiritual and moral foundation. Jesus continues emphasizing this point in his discussion of the Seventh Commandment-the sin of adultery.

All those listening to Jesus that day knew that adultery is prohibited. "*You shall not commit adultery.*" -- Exodus 20:14 would have been something they heard almost every Sabbath. While the Pharisees were often focused on the simple letter of the Law, Jesus is suggesting that we look deeper. I believe he is saying that the act of adultery is the culmination of coveting-intensely desiring and planning to obtain something at the expense of another. I don't believe that he is saying that appreciating beauty is wrong. I don't think that he is saying that having a momentary sexual attraction is wrong. I certainly don't believe that he is saying that intense sexual desire, for the right person, at the right time is wrong. Scripture tells us that Jesus, himself, knew temptation, just as we are tempted. This would suggest that there is no human temptation that he didn't have to resist.

> "*For we do not have a high priest who is unable to empathize with our weaknesses, but we have one who has been tempted in every way, just as we are —yet he did not sin.*" -- Hebrews 4:15 (NIV)

So, I don't believe that he is speaking about either a passing or legitimate desire. He is addressing the active

138

pursuit of something which God has not given us. In the verses above, the phrase *look at a woman lustfully* is translated from the Greek words *pros-* meaning *in order to*, and the Greek word *Epithumeo*. *Epithumeo* is an active verb, combining *Epi-* meaning *upon*, and *thumeo-* meaning *passionate desire*. This word is commonly translated as *to covet* and doesn't implicitly mean a sexual desire. Combined, this phrase expresses an active desire and intent to satisfy some passion for an object that isn't ours.

Additionally, our understanding of the sin of adultery today appears to be different from the standard view when Jesus was addressing it. At that time, the religious leaders viewed adultery as a form of theft- stealing another man's wife. The charge of adultery was, in their view, less about sexual immorality than about damage to the husband. It was seen as a social and legal wrong that required compensation. Their motivation was clearly misogynistic, in that it was considered adultery if a man stole another man's wife, but it wasn't treated as adultery if the married man had sex with an unmarried woman. Also, typically, it was the woman who suffered the consequence instead of the man. Consider Jesus' intervention at the stoning of the *woman caught in the act of adultery* -- John 8. Note that adultery takes two people, but the religious leader only brings the woman for punishment. I think this false view is part of what Jesus was confronting. While it may be true that the Seventh Commandment was specifically addressing adultery as a man stealing another man's wife, I believe that Jesus is broadening the issue to consider the role our hearts play.

Jesus is not equating the act of adultery with a passing appreciation or normal sexual desire. I don't think he was even equating the mental coveting with the act. He says that the man who looks at a woman with lust has "*committed adultery with her IN HIS HEART.*" He doesn't say that he has actually committed adultery. While he notes the importance of how an uncontrolled thought can lead to a sinful act, I don't think that he is saying that one is equal to the other. I believe he is simply pointing to the slippery slope of our human nature. I think the story of David, Bathsheba, and Uriah best illustrates this.

In II Samuel chapters eleven and twelve, we read a tragic and shameful chapter in the life of King David. It tells the story of how he actively conspired to take the wife of one of his soldiers, Uriah. David sees a beautiful woman from a distance. The fact that she is bathing indicates that anything beyond a passing glance will lead to temptation. As he looks at Bathsheba, he not only is attracted, but he sends a servant to find out who she is. A passing glance becomes a concrete desire. Perhaps, he watched for too long, but so far, has he done anything wrong? When the servant returns and tells David that Bathsheba is the wife of his faithful soldier, Uriah, David has a choice. He could appreciate that Uriah has a beautiful wife and let the healthy attraction end there, or he could do what he did. He sent for Bathsheba and had sex with her, and she became pregnant. Bathsheba was likely entirely innocent in this. This is an ancient example of *Me Too*, where a powerful man used his authority to essentially rape a vulnerable woman.

Appreciating her beauty was fine and normal. Wanting to find out who she was, was acceptable. He had not yet stolen Uriah's wife. Still, a dangerous seed was planted when he decided to have Bathsheba brought to him, knowing she was married. Likely, he justified that he just wanted to talk with her, but deep down, he had already decided. Of course, one sin often leads to another, and David orchestrates events to take the life of faithful Uriah in battle so that the King can have Bathsheba. In chapter twelve, we read about the repercussions of that choice in David's life.

So far, I've addressed this through a mostly academic lens. But, sex, coveting, adultery, and desire are primal forces that can overwhelm, cause tremendous pain, derail God's plan for people's lives. No Greek word study can heal any of that. I'd like to address this from a more human and terrestrial point of view.

Firstly, men of my generation came of age during the birth of Playboy. Nearly all forms of media taught us one manufactured view of sex. It also sold another manufactured view to women, but I'll leave that to someone else to address. As boys, we obsessed over Barbara Eden's midriff, were deluged with images of impossibly beautiful women, over-romanticized and sexualized fantasies, and were taught to view women as objects. Even knowing that women are unique souls, created in God's image, the lessons that the media and our culture taught us have certainly done tremendous harm- to ourselves and those we love. For many men, the soil of our upbringing has distorted our view of women and of sex. The hedonism of my generation has led to the easy availability of internet pornography and sexual addiction. While I won't focus on that here, neither can I see any good coming from it.

Our culture's portrayal of sex has been schizophrenic-promoting it through glorified hedonism while also devaluing it. It has been presented as both a climactic everything and a trivial physical act. Our culture recognizes few boundaries. There is a predictable counterpoint from those on the other end of the extreme. The Religious often equate sex and sin. For them, sex is mostly boundaries. The puritanical response to sex, while it may seem godly on the surface, is no less a distortion of God's plan.

Man didn't invent sex. It was always part of God's plan to meet mankind's need for intimacy and connection and not merely intended as a route to procreation.

It seems clear that God doesn't want us to be sex-obsessed slaves with an insatiable appetite. Neither does He want us to be prune-faced kill joys who equate all pleasure with depravity. He didn't intend sex to be either an idol or a monster. Some have given sexual sin a promotion. They treat it as the worst of sins. They obsess over controlling the sex lives of others.

I see both extremes as equally harmful. As in most things, a middle ground is usually the most healthy and wise course. Neither Hugh Hefner nor a castrated Origen reflect God's desire for us. I seriously doubt that Jesus' imagery of plucking out an eye or cutting off a hand was offered as a serious response to temptation. I speculate that he was merely using a word picture to illustrate the supreme importance of our souls. For all who claim to interpret scripture literally, it seems few have followed in Origen's footsteps, which is good. A genuinely literal interpretation of scripture would render a congregation of amputees and blind eunuchs.

Secondly, while David did much worse than almost any sexual sin- murder to get what he wanted, even that was not greater than God's grace. This man who did such a nauseatingly selfish, and evil thing, is someone God describes as a "*man after my own heart*." -- I Samuel 13:14; Acts 13:22. While the Mosaic Law required a life for a life. Nathan reveals to King David that God will forgive him and spare his life. Later, David recounts God's grace for him when he writes:

> "*Blessed is the one whose transgressions are forgiven, whose sins are covered. Blessed is the one whose sin the LORD does not count against them and in whose spirit is no deceit.*" -- Psalm 32:1,2 (NIV)

While God does fully forgive and cleanse David, there were, and are, consequences when we do evil, ignore God, and harm others. In David's case, the prophet Nathan tells David that "*Now therefore, the sword will never depart from your house.*" -- I Samuel 12:10 (NIV) Note that later, God won't allow David to build His

143

temple because of that:

> *"But God said to me, 'You are not to build a house for my Name, because you are a warrior and have shed blood."* -- I Chronicles 28:3 (NIV)

God seems outraged by David's involvement in war and the harm he did to Bathsheba and Uriah. He says virtually nothing about David's sex life. Eight wives resulted in mostly silence. War seemed to be a more significant concern to God. Doesn't much of the Church's obsession with sex seem to have those concerns swapped?

In the end, Jesus reminds us that while temptation is common to us all, allowing our minds to linger, and obsess can easily lead us to surrender to that desire. I've previously quoted pastor Tim Keller with a statement, which I believe sums up much of what Jesus is saying in this section on the Law:

> "It (idolatry) means turning a good thing into an ultimate thing."

Desire is a healthy and natural part of life and can be good. It's human to want a safe, comfortable, and healthy life. It's right to ask God to give us the means to have *our daily bread.* God understands our need to be loved, to not be alone and our desire for a healthy sex life. Even desiring more than we have is perfectly fine. The problem is when that desire becomes an obsession. We get off track when what we want is more important to us than God or others, and we become willing to scrap everything else for the object of our desire. We

144

run into problems when we are unwilling to accept that God might shut the door on that desire. It stops being healthy and becomes coveting. It becomes idolatry, and no idol can ever give us lasting peace or true joy.

Today's questions:

While it's unlikely that any of us have golden idols that we worship, it is important that we consider where our true affections lie. What things, both good and bad, are competing for our heart's devotion? What things do I struggle with that I know are evil? What is my plan to allow God the liberty to free me from those things? What good and healthy things have I promoted to become my ultimate thing? What things, values, dreams, or desires drive me daily, more than simply loving God and my neighbor?

Day Twenty-two: Divorce

"It was also said, Whoever divorces his wife must give her a written notice of divorce. But I tell you, everyone who divorces his wife, except in a case of sexual immorality, causes her to commit adultery. And whoever marries a divorced woman commits adultery." -- Matthew 5:31-32 (CSB)

"The Lord God said, "It is not good for the man to be alone. I will make a helper suitable for him." -- Genesis 2:18 (NIV)

Marriage is a wonderful idea, and God knew what He was doing when He sanctified it. That said, it reminds me of the following quote:

"It is easier to start a war than to end it." -- Gabriel Garcia Marquez

The first recorded marriage was personally arranged by God, in a place where there were no stresses. Yet, it still resulted in what must have been the greatest argument in the history of marriage. It came with unimaginable pain, sorrow, and loss. They saw one son murder his brother. So, it becomes clear that even the best of marriages can go through difficult times. When it works, as God desires, it is a beautiful, comforting thing and a shadow of our promised union with our Creator. When it doesn't work, it can seem unbearable. As long as partners have been uniting to build lives together, forces have worked to challenge those unions. Some of that was touched on in the last section. In the previous verses, Jesus warned us about coveting- wanting something that isn't ours. In an early collection of wisdom from the Church Fathers, the *Glossa Ordinaria* says, "The Lord had taught us above that our neighbor's wife was not to be coveted, He now proceeds to teach that our own wife is not to be put away." So here, for those of us who are married, Jesus encourages us to appreciate what we do have.

In Jesus' day, much like ours, divorce was prevalent. As with other topics, he begins by addressing the current thinking and the Mosaic Law. When he says, *It has been said*, Jesus is pointing us back to Deuteronomy Chapter twenty-four, verse one. There, Moses outlines various laws regarding how followers of God should treat one another. On the issue of divorce, he says:

> *"If a man marries a woman who becomes displeasing to him because he finds something indecent about her, and he writes her a certificate of divorce, gives it to her and sends her from his house..."* -- Deuteronomy 24:1 (NIV)

First, notice the word *if*. This verse is not a command. It is a conditional clause for what is to follow. Next, we see the primary aim of this passage is not about the divorce

147

but is meant to prohibit remarriage to the same woman after divorce. Verse one simply points to the legal necessity for the divorcing husband to give a Certificate to his wife. It's possible this legal requirement was intended to provide the couple with time to reconsider and reconcile. Since it was a legal document, it is possible it was not meant to be immediate. The certificate also allowed the woman to remarry. Being a single woman in that culture promised an almost certain life of poverty or prostitution. This verse permits but does not promote divorce. It simply provided a minimal guideline for this unfortunate human event.

When Jesus was addressing this issue, there was debate over what constituted acceptable grounds for divorce. Much of that debate hung on what Moses meant when he said that if the husband was displeased and found something *indecent* in his wife, he could divorce her. Here, the English word indecent, translated from the Hebrew word *ervâh*, literally means a shameful, disgraceful, exposed, unprotected thing, or nakedness.

The word is also used elsewhere, which might give us a better idea of its meaning. In Deuteronomy chapter twenty-three, verses nine through fourteen, Moses lays out requirements for life in a military camp. In this situation, lives are at stake, and order must be maintained. Since they were to see God as their commander, following His rules was essential to win the battle and stay alive. In that environment, they depended on God's presence. In this section, the soldiers are instructed that latrines should be dug OUTSIDE the camp. They are aware that God is in the camp with them and wants nothing *unclean* there. I suspect this had more to do with His concern for health issues than some aversion to the digestive system that He had created. The word unclean here is the same word used in Deuteronomy chapter twenty-four, verse one. The word is not directly tied to sexual indiscretion. Additionally, since Mosaic Law also prescribed that adultery was punishable by death, it's unlikely that this word was associated with adultery. Instead, it's saying that in the event the wife did something so offensive to God, violated basic required standards of decency, and endangered the safety of the home, in that case, divorce was permitted. It was not suggesting divorce based on a whim or displeasure about a petty concern.

The two most common rabbinical interpretations of this verse were promoted by Jewish scholars Beit Hillel or Beit Shammai. The school of Hillel was more liberal and permitted divorce for truly minor offenses, such as burning a meal. In contrast, the school of Shammai was generally more conservative and said that a husband was only permitted to divorce his wife for some significant wrong. The Pharisees in Jesus' day largely supported Hillel's view and even amplified it. We later see this in a confrontation between Jesus and the Pharisees:

> *"Some Pharisees came to him to test him. They asked, "Is it lawful for a man to divorce his wife for any and every reason?"* -- Matthew 19:3 (NIV)

In this sermon, Jesus is likely speaking to this debate, and he seemingly comes down on the side of Shammai. Remember that in Jesus' day, Israel was a pretty misogynistic, male-dominated society (as was Rome, though less so, and almost every culture of the day). While limiting divorce to instances of adultery, I don't think that Jesus was suggesting that spouses stay in a home where they are being abused. I also don't think that, apart from adultery, divorce was never allowed. I think he was doing what God did with most of His commands. He was protecting the innocent. Under Hillel's view, a woman's security could have been destroyed in an instant, and vows meant nothing.

Note that, in Jewish culture, only the man could initiate divorce. Still, we see that it did happen because Roman culture allowed that. This is mentioned in the book of Mark:

"and if she divorces her husband and marries another man, she commits adultery." -- Mark 10:12 (NIV)

This is an excellent example of how the author's audience impacts what is written. Matthew addresses a predominantly Jewish audience, where women couldn't initiate a divorce. In contrast, Mark addresses the Gentile, Roman world, where women could initiate a divorce. Matthew chose to not mention the instance where Jesus said this, perhaps because a Jewish audience would not have understood this.

It's true that God prefers to spare people the pain of

150

divorce. It's not because He wants people to suffer in bad marriages, but because He recognizes the harm from divorce. Divorce causes intense emotional pain, especially if one partner doesn't want the divorce. It can cause tremendous financial difficulty. When children are involved, the harm can last a lifetime. That doesn't mean that He doesn't care about the damage that can happen to people in a bad marriage. His dislike of the one doesn't mean that He approves of the other.

This brings me to my experience with divorce. When I was six, my father moved from our home in Virginia to Florida. I don't know the whole truth of why that happened. Still, I'm sure that there was plenty of blame to go around, but except for one or two very brief visits, I didn't see my father again until I was twenty. I eventually restored a relationship with my Dad, but I often wonder what life would have been like if he had remained a part of my childhood. Divorce from a spouse doesn't have to mean a divorce from the children, but it often does. At best, it makes parenting far more complicated and increases the chances of the children living in poverty. My Dad's absence may have been part of the reason that Mom was often not physically present, rarely affectionate, and why we were almost always hungry. In my case, divorce meant that neither parent was what I thought I needed. Only God knows if it was what I truly needed, but it left a hole in my self-image that impacted much of my life.

As a young man, I wrote a song about the cyclical nature of divorce called *Time to Change Partners*. The song was about the effects of divorce on children and how the failure in one generation can continue into the next. The words of the chorus are:

"It's time to change partners again.
We just can't go on living like we're living.
Everyone's taking, and nobody's giving.
We'll just have to start once again,
leave behind the years of our commitments.
The children will grow to understand in time."

In a case of life imitating art, not long after I wrote those words, I rushed into marriage with a woman I met when I was in seminary. At the time, I had no business getting married. I was still struggling with deficits from my childhood. I was immature, had no financial stability, no support structure, and had some significant spiritual questions that I needed to address. However, that hole in me was gnawing at me, and I had deluded myself into believing that marriage would fix what was broken. As I've quoted before, making a good thing into the ultimate thing is idolatry. Idolatry never promotes peace or joy. I won't say anything bad about her. I take ownership of my ultimately selfish choice to marry when I knew I was not equipped to provide adequately. The result of that choice was five years of fighting, anger, grief, and turmoil. Counseling failed to improve things, and eventually, she decided to move out and file for divorce. I wanted to stay in counseling and didn't want her to leave, but I had no legal or practical way of stopping it. I hold no ill will and continue to pray for her, though we've had no contact since the divorce.

As much as I believe that divorce is not a good option, sometimes it is the best remaining option. Paul says:

"If it is possible, as far as it depends on you, live at peace with everyone." -- Romans 12:18 (NIV)

I believe that this expectation also applies to marriages. It takes two whole people for any relationship to work, and regardless of my efforts, it wasn't enough. Only God knows what the last thirty-five years would have been like for either of us if that marriage had not dissolved. Short of the miraculous, however, I can't see any good or contribution to God's kingdom, having come from remaining. Like the quote at the start of this, marriages, like wars, are far easier to start than end. The best way to reduce divorce is to prevent bad marriages in the first place. Developing considerate, stable, and mature people with reasonable expectations will do far more to prevent divorce than anything that happens after the ceremony is over.

I would like to speak about how the Church too often deals with people who are divorced. Soon after my wife left me, I was at the church I was attending, and a dear brother approached me and said:

"If you had loved her the way that Jesus loves the Church, she wouldn't have left you."

That was painful to hear, and it was certainly true that I didn't love her as much as Jesus loves us. I wasn't aware that his comment was really coming from a place of

153

naivety and simplistic thinking. A year later, I became aware of that when he came to me to apologize after his wife left him. I could honestly grieve with him, in his loss, and look past his earlier comment.

I had pastors tell me I had to resign myself to remaining single for the remainder of my life. About six months after the divorce, I went to the church that my ex-wife attended and asked the pastor if he would mediate an attempt to, at least, build an amicable friendship. That's when I learned that she had already remarried. Even after learning that she had remarried, I found that being divorced seemingly made me a second-class citizen in the church I was in. The Singles Sunday School class I attended announced that divorced people would no longer be allowed. They didn't take the circumstance into account or show much grace to hurting people.

Ultimately, I grew enough to deal with the deficits that had hindered my first marriage. I was fortunate enough to meet and marry a woman who has become my best friend and companion for the last thirty years. God's grace looked past my initial failings, an unwise union, and gave me a second chance. When Jesus addresses this issue and clearly discourages divorce, he doesn't do it in a vacuum, where abused, neglected, or harmed spouses are expected to suffer in silence and simply accept it. He certainly doesn't relegate people who have been divorced to some ecclesiastical purgatory. More importantly, the totality of scripture shows God's heart for children who have experienced profound loss because their parent's marriage failed. My mother was a choir director in a large church. I don't remember a single instance where an adult in that church stepped in to provide the sort of adult guidance or attention that was missing and I desperately needed. That is partly why I was a pretty angry agnostic until I was eighteen when God began salvaging and restoring the wreck of my childhood.

God wants us to value our spouses enough to recognize that when trials, temptations, and frustrations come, we value them and our promises enough to genuinely follow Paul's admonition to endeavor, as far as it depends on us, to live at peace with them. God desires that we not damage them, ourselves, or the gospel, by running away when times are tough. God only asks us to do our part, as faithfully and lovingly, as we can.

Today's promises:

For those who have experienced pain, shame, loss, heartache, or loneliness, because of the failure of frail, and imperfect human relationships, know that:

God longs to be the loving father that you never had:

> *"A father to the fatherless, a defender of widows, is God in his holy dwelling."* -- Psalm 68:5 (NIV)

God is there to be as close as a spouse to you:

> *"For your Maker is your husband – the Lord Almighty is his name"* -- Isaiah 54:5 (NIV)

God will never leave you:

"Though my father and mother forsake me, the L<small>ORD</small> *will receive me."* -- Psalm 27:10 (NIV)

And ultimately, God will restore what has been lost and comfort you:

"He will wipe every tear from their eyes" -- Revelation 21:4 (NIV)

Day Twenty-three: Oaths

"Again, you have heard that it was said to our ancestors, You must not break your oath, but you must keep your oaths to the Lord. But I tell you, don't take an oath at all: either by heaven, because it is God's throne; or by the earth, because it is his footstool; or by Jerusalem, because it is the city of the great King. Do not swear by your head, because you cannot make a single hair white or black. But let your 'yes' mean 'yes,' and your 'no' mean 'no.' Anything more than this is from the evil one." --
Matthew 5:33-37 (CSB)

Jesus tells us that it is truth that will set us free -- John 8:32. He says this because most people are not free, and most are not consistently truthful. While this section of Jesus' sermon is perplexing, what he addresses is pretty understandable. Our spiritual lineage began with a lie, and dishonesty has plagued us since the Garden.

"We can easily forgive a child who is afraid of the dark; the real tragedy of life is when men are afraid of the light." Plato

Living honestly doesn't come cheap. Honesty is always more expensive, in the short term than dishonesty. For example, a cashier might give you too much change back from your purchase or, an opportunity arises to use a questionable tax benefit. Perhaps, you find a wallet on the sidewalk or, it's easy to sneak a peek at your neighbor's test. You may realize that you were wrong about something, but you don't want to admit it. Telling the truth can be painful and will typically leave you with less cash in your pocket. Daily, we encounter opportunities to speak the truth, shade it, or outright corrupt it.

Robin Williams said of those in politics:

"Politics: *Poli*, a Latin word meaning *many* and *tics* meaning *bloodsucking creatures*."

Politicians, of all people, are viewed as dishonest. Yet, along with many business leaders, they are typically those with the most money, attention, and power. Jesus knew this and wasn't naive, but he didn't come to promote the kingdom of this world but to build the kingdom of heaven. In his economy, honesty truly is the best policy. That's what is at the heart of this portion of his message on that hill.

Oaths are often mentioned in scripture and not prohibited, yet Jesus seems to be saying that they are bad. Jesus knew these scriptures well:

"Fear the Lord your God, serve him only and take your oaths in his name." -- Deuteronomy 6:13 (NIV)

He knew that while oaths were permitted, there were specific requirements in how to use them. Oaths and Vows, taken in God's name, were bringing God into the bargain. Jesus is emphasizing how serious this was.

"You shall not misuse the name of the Lord your God, for the Lord will not hold anyone guiltless who misuses his name." -- Exodus 20:7 (NIV)

As a young man, I needed to purchase my first clunker of a car. A good friend agreed to cosign the loan with me. If I had reneged on my commitment to repay that loan, it would have reflected poorly on my friend and fallen to him to pay what I owed. When someone swears by God's name, they are essentially asking God to cosign that claim. For that reason, scripture is clear about how we should approach and treat our vows:

"When a man makes a vow to the Lord or takes an oath to obligate himself by a pledge, he must not break his word but must do everything he said." -- Numbers 30:2 (NIV)

"If you make a vow to the LORD your God, do not be slow to pay it, for the LORD your God will certainly demand it of you and you will be guilty of sin. But if you refrain from making a vow, you will not be guilty. Whatever your lips utter you must be sure to do, because you made your vow freely to the Lord your God with your own mouth." -- Deuteronomy 23:21-23 (NIV)

It's clear that when we make a vow to God and do so falsely, it is an insult to God's character.

"Do not swear falsely by my name and so profane the name of your God. I am the Lord." -- Leviticus 19:12 (NIV)

Additionally, Jesus was also aware of how the Pharisees and the Jewish people were misusing those verses. It was not uncommon, in those days, for business people to make vows. Instead of swearing to God, they would swear by something else- perhaps their parents, children, homes, the temple, or heaven. An entire legal system had been set up to determine which vows were legitimate and which weren't. The religious court might rule that a vow sworn on the city of Jerusalem was not valid, and the debt did not need to be repaid. This was the equivalent of making a promise with your fingers crossed behind your back.

As we have seen, Jesus is no fan of hypocrisy or dishonesty- especially when it robs the poor. We see elsewhere that Jesus confronts the Pharisees over this very thing.

"Woe to you, blind guides! You say, 'If anyone swears by the temple, it means nothing; but anyone who swears by the gold of the temple is bound by that oath.' You blind fools! Which is greater: the gold, or the temple that makes the gold sacred? You also say, 'If anyone swears by the altar, it means nothing; but anyone who swears by the gift on the altar is bound by that oath.' You blind men! Which is greater: the gift, or the altar that makes the gift sacred? Therefore, anyone who swears by the altar swears by it and by everything on it. And anyone

160

who swears by the temple swears by it and by the one who dwells in it. And anyone who swears by heaven swears by God's throne and by the one who sits on it." -- Matthew 23:16-22 (NIV)

It is in this environment that he makes these statements. I don't believe that he is saying that it is never acceptable to make an Oath or a Vow. Firstly, vows were explicitly allowed in scripture, with restrictions. Secondly, there are many situations where people are required to take an oath or make a vow. Examples are committing to a marriage, protecting the Constitution, upholding an office, and telling the truth under penalty of perjury. Some have interpreted this section to mean that Jesus has prohibited all oaths. He does say, *"do not swear an oath at all,"* yet there are numerous instances after this when oaths were made and considered appropriate. Paul certainly made some informal vows by bringing God's name into claims about his behavior.

"God, whom I serve in my spirit in preaching the gospel of his Son, is my witness how constantly I remember you." -- Romans 1:9 (NIV)

"I assure you before God that what I am writing you is no lie." -- Galatians 1:20 (NIV)

Still, there are also vows following this that didn't go well. It wasn't long after Jesus' sermon that the Apostle Peter made a vow, that he broke (to his shame):

"But Peter declared, "Even if I have to die with you, I will never disown you." And all the other disciples

161

said the same." -- Matthew 26:35 (NIV)

Perhaps the most obvious broken vow came in the days of the early Church. The story of Ananias and his wife Sapphira occurred when the new believers had to band together simply to survive. Much like soldiers sacrificing for the group's safety, the early Church found itself under constant threat. It's likely given the animosity against them, by the formal religious community, that finding work was difficult. They addressed this by forming a communal group -- Acts 4:32-37. In this environment, they willingly chose to forgo personal ownership of any property. Instead, they gave it to the group for their own survival and the spread of the gospel. While this was a form of communism, it seems that entering into the agreement was entirely voluntary. It was, however, a form of a vow to share ALL things in common.

While it was assumed that everyone who had agreed to this would add everything to the common pot, Ananias went to sell a piece of property. However, he secretly chose to keep a portion of the proceeds for himself. His wife, Sapphira, was fully aware of this deception. While all the others gave all that they had, Ananias lied and only gave a portion. He was not only dishonest, but he also stole from the group by doing this. The result of his deception is described below:

> *"With his wife's full knowledge he kept back part of the money for himself, but brought the rest and put it at the apostles' feet. Then Peter said, "Ananias, how is it that Satan has so filled your heart that you*

162

have lied to the Holy Spirit and have kept for
yourself some of the money you received for the
land? Didn't it belong to you before it was sold? And
after it was sold, wasn't the money at your
disposal? What made you think of doing such a
thing? You have not lied just to human beings but to
God." -- Acts 5:2-4 (NIV)

Ultimately, what Jesus is pointing to here is the utter shame that human society requires we take oaths. In a world where telling even painful truth was the norm, oaths would be unnecessary. Sadly, we live in a time when truth is a uniquely disrespected virtue. That this seems especially prevalent in so much of the Church is even more concerning. We claim to follow Jesus, who described himself as *The Truth*. If our savior is the very embodiment of truth, then truth should be at the core of what it means to be a Christian. On that count, we need to do better.

If a young child confidently states that "two plus two equals five," we think it's cute. If that child grows to be an adult who continues to make that claim, it's no longer acceptable. They can insist that "people have different opinions." Still, if their opinion is contradicted by studied mathematicians, their opinion is simply a lie. Before we pass along rumor, opinion, or conspiracy, Jesus calls us to lives that reflect truth. If some topic is controversial, I believe the rule should be to thoroughly and objectively investigate it or be silent. If the rumor, in any way, might cause harm to another, scripture calls us to deal with that individual directly and not spread lies.

As to the application of this, I have a few points. First, there is a difference between lying and failing to accomplish something you fully intended and endeavored to accomplish. A young man saying, "I mowed the lawn" but hadn't, is far different from promising to mow the lawn but being delayed by something unavoidable. We should always do our best to follow through on our promises, but we don't always succeed. God is gracious, but the expectation is that we will do our best to honor our commitments.

Secondly, I genuinely believe that the best way to fully honor our promises is to know our own limitations. A person who earns $20,000 a year will almost assuredly be incapable of repaying a home loan for $400,000. Hopefully, they are aware of that (though certainly, the lender should be aware). If that person mistakenly thinks they earn far more than they do, they will likely fail to honor that vow. In the last section, we spoke about divorce. We enter into marriages by making a vow. In most marriages, both partners genuinely believe they will honor that vow. Unfortunately, many enter into that vow without adequately knowing either their potential partner or themselves. I may have a suspicion about some theory posited by physicists but I recognize that I am entirely unqualified to disagree. No person who got an average grade in High School biology is qualified to call a person with a doctorate in infectious disease and decades of experience a liar. To do so is not only ignorant and dangerous. It is an example of arrogance. If we feel strongly enough to disagree then we need to return to school, do the work and respectfully consider our own limitations.

Being honest with others and with ourselves requires us to occasionally choose the more painful of available paths. It also requires us to allow God to search our hearts to reveal our true natures. Until we have done that, we should not make promises that we are likely to break. Honesty is a sign of maturity- both spiritual and emotional maturity.

Suppose you have a dishonest leader. They don't search and challenge their own character. They repeat things that they haven't personally investigated and verified. They falsely assume that they can repeat it if they hear something from another believer or their favorite media source. They readily share questionable information and present it as fact. They refuse to acknowledge their mistakes and correct them. They ignore the central importance of honesty or fail to keep promises. In that case, they aren't ready to be a leader. You should pray for them. You should love them, but you should not follow them.

Today's thought:

Be brave enough to choose to live a life of honesty. In the economy of God's Kingdom, you can take that to the bank.

Day Twenty-four: An Eye for an Eye

"You have heard that it was said, An eye for an eye and a tooth for a tooth. But I tell you, don't resist an evildoer. On the contrary, if anyone slaps you on your right cheek, turn the other to him also. As for the one who wants to sue you and take away your shirt, let him have your coat as well. And if anyone forces you to go one mile, go with him two. Give to the one who asks you, and don't turn away from the one who wants to borrow from you." -- Matthew 5:38-42 (CSB)

At this point, do we see a pattern starting to emerge? After he completed his list of blessings, in the Beatitudes, and his comparison of true faith to salt and light, Jesus said:

"Don't think that I came to abolish the Law or the Prophets. I did not come to abolish but to fulfill." -- Matthew 5:17 (CSB)

If we don't know what he meant by this statement, he goes on to explain. What follows, beginning in verse twenty-one, is a series of corrective statements. We refer to these as Jesus' *antitheses*. Each antithesis follows the same pattern- *it was said, but I tell you.* Let's review these:

- *"You have heard that it was said to our ancestors, Do not murder, and whoever murders will be subject to judgment. But I tell you..."* -- Matthew 5:21 (CSB)

- *"You have heard that it was said, Do not commit adultery. But I tell you..."* -- Matthew 5:27 (CSB)

- *"It was also said, Whoever divorces his wife must give her a written notice of divorce. But I tell you..."* -- Matthew 5:31 (CSB)

- *"Again, you have heard that it was said to our ancestors, You must not break your oath, but you must keep your oaths to the Lord. But I tell you..."* -- Matthew 5:33 (CSB)

and the current antithesis:

- *"You have heard that it was said, An eye for an eye and a tooth for a tooth. But I tell you..."* -- Matthew 5:38 (CSB)

In each of these antitheses, Jesus tells his listeners that their understanding of these issues is way off. An antithesis -- *Anti-* meaning *against* and *thesis-* meaning a *proposition, or statement,* can mean either something that is the direct opposite of something else, or at least a contrast, or opposition between two things. I don't believe that Jesus is entirely contradicting the *has been*

167

said statements but is, in fact, clarifying them.

Consider, for a moment, the source of these *has been said* statements. Jesus is not saying "secular, humanist, atheist culture has said, but I tell you... " In most cases, he is directly referring to Old Testament scripture. So, he isn't correcting worldly people or atheists. He is either correcting the scriptures themselves or the flawed understanding of them by religious leaders. I believe that it is the latter. In clarifying these Old Testament verses, he is not abolishing the Law and Prophets. Instead, he puts them into context, clarifies, and fulfills them by giving them their full, foundational meaning. Jesus was aware that it was common for religious leaders to claim an authoritative understanding of some scriptures. He makes it clear that they are not the experts they make themselves out to be.

With today's antithesis, this is a crucial concept. This particular *has been said* points back to numerous Old Testament verses, where God gives the Israelites their criminal and civil legal code.

> *"But if there is serious injury, you are to take life for life, eye for eye, tooth for tooth, hand for hand, foot for foot, burn for burn, wound for wound, bruise for bruise."* -- Exodus 21:23,24 (NIV)

> *"Anyone who injures their neighbor is to be injured in the same manner: fracture for fracture, eye for eye, tooth for tooth. The one who has inflicted the injury must suffer the same injury."* -- Leviticus

24:19,20 (NIV)

"The rest of the people will hear of this and be afraid, and never again will such an evil thing be done among you. Show no pity: life for life, eye for eye, tooth for tooth, hand for hand, foot for foot." -- Deuteronomy 19:20,21 (NIV)

In reading these Old Testament passages, to me, they are seemingly barbaric. How can a loving and merciful God say *show no pity*? In what Jesus goes on to teach, is he saying that God was wrong in saying this? Again, understanding context, history, and culture are essential.

In reading these verses, I think of the scene from the movie *The Untouchables*. Sean Connery's character, Jim Malone, explains to Kevin Costner's character, Eliot Ness, how to rid the world of the notoriously vicious gangster, Al Capone. Speaking of Capone, in the scene, Malone says:

> "He sends one of yours to the hospital. You send one of his to the morgue. That's the Chicago way!"

Malone is taking the first part of the Old Testament teaching- that there can be legal punishment for criminal behavior. However, he is ignoring the main point of those verses. It may be *the Chicago way*, but it isn't God's way. The response must be proportional. There has always been criminal behavior in man's history, and often the punishment didn't match the crime. Someone steals a loaf of bread, and they lose a hand. Someone is arrested for a relatively minor offense

169

and spends decades in prison. A refugee legally applies for asylum at the wrong location, and their children are taken from them. These are the abuses that God, in the Old Testament, is addressing. In a sense, in the Old Testament, God, through the hand of Moses, is addressing man as we are. In the New Testament, God, through the life of Jesus, is addressing man as He wants us to be. In the Old Testament, God was providing minimal, legal guidelines for the nation of Israel. He prohibits both criminal behavior and man's use of criminal punishment to enact vengeance. He establishes the law against stealing and prohibits torture in response. Again, God establishes that the sentence can not be worse than the crime under His criminal code.

What Jesus does, though, is to remind us that those Old Testament laws did not reflect God's intent for His Kingdom. Those verses often were emphasized, while verses about mercy and forgiveness were ignored. They were laws for Man's Kingdom, not God's. For Man's Kingdom, God established prohibitions against criminal behavior and promoted just punishment within the legal system. Here, Jesus is addressing our response to injustice within the kingdom of God. Instead of taking someone to court who has stolen from you, perhaps forgiveness is a better option.

One of my fondest memories of my early days as a new follower of Jesus occurred during the Summer of 1975. Along with other Christian college students, I spent the Summer in Virginia Beach, Virginia, as part of a

Summer Project with Campus Crusade for Christ. There, we found local Summer jobs during the day and spent our off-hours, either talking to people on the beach about Jesus, having Bible Study, or praying. We rented two houses, one for the about thirty guys and one for the thirty or so girls. Having thirty college guys sharing a house for the Summer was both challenging and a lot of fun. One day, we met a young homeless man (back when homelessness was far less common in America). We invited him to come and stay with us, till he could find a place. That first evening, we invited him to join us at a different location, where we were to have a Bible Study. He told us he needed to rest, so we left him to sleep. The study ended early, and we headed back to the house and found that he had gone through each of our personal belongings and stolen most of our cash. Imagine his shock when we walked in the door before he had made his escape, and we discovered what he had done. Here he was, one skinny, hungry, tired guy, in a room with thirty healthy, well-rested, and well-fed young men. Some were quite tough-looking. I assume he thought that the best case would be for us to call the police, but he likely feared a severe beating. Instead, what happened is what I would call a God moment. We each said:

"Keep the money. It's yours. That was just extra spending money, meant for fun. You need it more than we do."

He was clearly shocked and relieved. I don't have a clue whether that act of forgiveness and kindness had any lasting impact on him, but it confirmed the power of the gospel to me. Forty-seven years later, nothing I would have bought with that money would still be with me, but that memory is always there to challenge and encourage me.

When Jesus tells us that God's desire for us is to *turn the other cheek* or to *give to the one who asks*, is he telling us to be naive doormats or spineless? I believe that it's quite the opposite. When we restrain our natural desire to respond in anger or to punish someone who has harmed us, we are both showing great courage and strength. When we hold our earthly possessions loosely, they become less treasured, and other treasures take their place. Does Jesus ever want us to protect ourselves or our belongings? Of course, he wants us to be good stewards and show common sense, but I think that is a decision we each have to make. Still, if our natural response is to protect ourselves, in the same way that those without faith do, aren't we simply announcing that earthly concerns are what we treasure, and our faith is mostly artifice? The *Prosperity Gospel* is the false idea that worldly wealth is God's promised reward for living as its church leaders dictate. Any church that promotes that is preaching something that is definitely not the gospel. Neither is it true. A church where the American gun culture is fostered, without at least some minimal consideration, should question whether the words of Jesus are welcome there. These are issues that should be wrestled with and challenged. All too often, it is culture rather than scripture and godly wisdom that churches listen to.

God has ordained governmental authority to enforce minimal standards of ethical behavior. God sees us as we are- too often unjust, inconsiderate, fearful, angry, and greedy. Jesus reminds us that *it has been said* is not the goal line. It is merely the starting line.

Today's verse:

"And let us run with perseverance the race marked out for us, fixing our eyes on Jesus, the pioneer and perfecter of faith." -- Hebrews 12:1,2 (NIV)

Day Twenty-five: Love Your Enemy

"You have heard that it was said, Love your neighbor and hate your enemy. But I tell you, love your enemies and pray for those who persecute you, so that you may be children of your Father in heaven. For he causes his sun to rise on the evil and the good, and sends rain on the righteous and the unrighteous. For if you love those who love you, what reward will you have? Don't even the tax collectors do the same? And if you greet only your brothers and sisters, what are you doing out of the ordinary? Don't even the Gentiles do the same?" -- Matthew 5:43-47 (CSB)

So much of what Jesus said was, to my mind, intentionally vague. He loved to hide truths through his use of parables, imagery, and phrases. This left it up to the listener to dig to determine what Christ really meant. Sadly, religious folk often come along to claim that their interpretation is what he actually meant, and any disagreement is treated as heresy. Perhaps, he was talking about this in his parable of the treasure, hidden

174

in the field -- Matthew 13:44. At times, I really wish he had just been clear and stated things in ways that left no room for misinterpretation. I wish he had provided an explicit formula for many things, like the precise requirements for entrance into heaven, an understandable explanation of the Trinity, a Christology class on his own nature, and relation to the Creator God. It would have been nice to hear his opinion on the *culture war* issues of today. While he provides blurry hints, clues, and references to many of these things, he rarely came out and defined things, like an auto mechanic or a plumber. Perhaps, his hope was that he would get us to think about these things and approach them as if searching for treasure. Sadly, genuine thinking and open-minded discussion on issues of religion or politics rarely yield dividends. Maybe, when he spoke of the *narrow gate* -- Matthew 7:13, he was recognizing that very few would be willing to do the painful and difficult work of challenging their own view of the world in order to adopt Jesus' view.

That's why this, the last of Jesus' antitheses from the Sermon Mount, is so refreshing and unique. It is impossible to misunderstand. As people who claim to follow Jesus, we can and do, disagree about what he meant on many issues. On this issue, Jesus left no room for us to pervert what he is saying. Before anything else, if we claim to follow Jesus, we are to love everyone, including those we see as enemies. Of course, Jesus is calling upon a truth that was echoed in the Old Testament:

"Do not seek revenge or bear a grudge against anyone among your people, but love your neighbor as yourself. I am the Lord." -- Leviticus 19:18 (NIV)

As he often did, Jesus appealed to life in a very different moral economy than we are used to. In the world's kingdom, we don't love our enemy. In that kingdom, we survive and prosper by utterly destroying them. There are laws against murdering our enemies, except during the seemingly endless wars that provide cover for State-sanctioned murder. But, there are no laws against destroying your enemy through legal means. Politicians, talking heads, and some religious zealots have built careers promoting fear and hate of those they claim to be their enemies.

While some have fully embraced the worldly kingdom's visible hatred of their enemy, most are far more subtle about it. They oppose the things they believe that their enemy loves. If it *triggers* their enemy, even if it's costly to themselves, they will oppose it. They promote social and political policies that place their enemy at a disadvantage. When they see their enemy in need, they ignore that need and secretly celebrate. At best, they may help, but make sure to point out that *they brought this on themselves.*

Jesus turns this idea on its head. He doesn't say:

"Hey guys, walk it back a bit. Maybe keep the insults private."

He doesn't say:

"We have to have a strategy. If you show kindness to them, they'll let their guard down, and then we can subdue them."

He doesn't see love as a strategy. He simply says:

"But I tell you, love your enemies and pray for those who persecute you," -- Matthew 5:44 (CSB)

Why? Not because you'll show them that you're a better person than they are if you do it. He makes it clear that the reason is *"that you may be children of your Father in heaven."* -- Matthew 5:45 Again, he reminds us of our birthright as children of our Creator. He is reminding us of the kingdom of heaven and telling us to make a choice.

On the surface, a verse by the Apostle Paul seems to get this wrong:

"On the contrary: If your enemy is hungry, feed him; if he is thirsty, give him something to drink. In doing this, you will heap burning coals on his head. Do not be overcome by evil, but overcome evil with good." -- Romans 12:20,21 (NIV)

Paul is actually quoting a verse from Proverbs 25:21,22. It's almost as if he was mimicking Jesus and saying, *"You have heard it said, but I tell you."* However, earlier, Paul said:

"Love must be sincere. Hate what is evil; cling to what is good." -- Romans 12:9 (NIV)

The love that Jesus, and Paul, are referring to is a genuine, authentic, and supernatural love. It isn't meant to be grudging, tactical, or half-hearted. God's intent for us is to love our enemies fearlessly, selflessly, and with our whole hearts.

Clearly, that's a huge ask. How can we truly love someone who has hurt us or others? Some hurts are small and understandable. A person we are dating breaks up with us. Someone gets a promotion we thought that we deserved, and they didn't. A neighbor throws a loud party and is inconsiderate. I don't believe that these everyday slights are what Jesus is calling us to aspire to forgive. That sort of forgiveness is simply part of being a civil human being and an expression of maturity. I think Jesus is speaking to actions which, by human standards, we may see as unforgivable.

Last time, I mentioned an incident from the early days of my faith, where a young man stole from us- a group of young believers. While I saw God's hand in moving us to uniformly forgive the young man who stole the money, it was not a difficult hurdle to jump. While it was a form of betrayal, there was no long relationship, and what was stolen was relatively insignificant. What we did was what most any decent person should do. It was an ordinary act of grace that seemed extraordinary because of how rarely grace is exhibited.

The sort of forgiveness of an enemy that I believe Jesus was addressing is seen in acts of extraordinary grace provided when it seems humanly impossible. For example, those members of the Rwandan Tutsi
178

community who forgave members of the Hutu tribe, responsible for the murder of family members, during the Rwandan genocide. A survivor of Auschwitz forgives a Nazi guard. A woman forgives a relative who sexually abused her as a child. A church calls for forgiveness for a young man whose racism and violence claimed the lives of some of its members.

When I consider what Jesus was commanding here, a particular story of supernatural forgiveness springs to mind. It took place in the Pennsylvania Amish countryside. When I remember it, it reminds me that Jesus' command to love our enemies is as powerful and odd today as when he spoke it. In October 2006, Terri Roberts' son, Charlie, walked into a one-room, Amish schoolhouse and shot eight of the ten young girls there. He killed five of them and then shot himself. Two of the girls had asked that they be shot, but the others be spared. Their act of incredible selflessness and heroism still moves me.

The response of the local Amish community followed the economy of the kingdom of heaven rather than the economy of the world's kingdom. They could have been lost in a season of rage. They could have expressed vitriol toward the shooter, his parents, family, and the society that created the killer, made the weapon easily available, and failed to protect their children. It would have been understandable if they had vented their anger at God, who allowed this horrendous act of senseless brutality. I think that we all would have seen the humanity in that and understood. Instead, the community chose to take seriously Jesus' commandment to love their enemy. The grandfather of one of the murdered girls called for forgiveness. He said:

"We must not think evil of this man."

Another said:

"He had a mother and a wife and a soul, and now he's standing before a just God."

A third said:

"I don't think there's anybody here that wants to do anything but forgive and not only reach out to those who have suffered a loss in that way but to reach out to the family of the man who committed these acts."

Putting their faith into action through amazing grace and forgiveness, they visited the shooter's widow, family, and parents. While they were grieving their own tremendous loss, they weren't blind to the pain that the shooter's family was experiencing. They weren't demanding God to punish the shooter. Reportedly, one Amish man held the sobbing father of the shooter for an hour. They joined to support them at their son's funeral.

Some attacked them for responding this way, suggesting they couldn't have truly loved their children if they could forgive so easily. What they got wrong is that there was nothing easy in that forgiveness. Their grief and loss were real and deep, but they knew that forgiveness did not rob them of their right to mourn or take anything from the children they had so tragically lost. The undeserved and supernatural grace that they showed was not only a testament to the authenticity of their faith but honored the memory of their children. Of the thousands of American children who have died from senseless gun violence since that day, those eight children are uniquely remembered because of the supernatural Kingdom response to an oppressively evil act.

These days, this teaching is weighing on me and challenging the solidity of my own faith. In no time, since the Civil War, has our nation been so divided. There are two sides, two takes, on nearly every issue. Even after the campaign signs go down, the different paths are still traveled and well marked. What is most distressing, though, is not that we simply disagree, but it's the way that we disagree.

Very few listen, and even fewer approach these disagreements with humility, a desire to learn, or understand. I'm not simply pointing at others. I've certainly been guilty at times of venting my anger, speaking too hastily, being condescending, or being stubborn. I've always attempted to be open to hearing compelling evidence for an opposing view. Still, I've rarely had success in finding agreement. Our desire to be proven right, win the argument and defeat those we see as our enemies have hobbled us. It has brought our government to a standstill. For many of our political leaders, the common good is no longer the goal. Defeating the other side and retaining power is what seems to matter, even if society is harmed in the process. It has infected our communications, broken familial and brotherly connections, and done seemingly irreparable harm to the witness of the Church.

These days, if you want to simply tell someone how great God's love is for them, you have to strain out the countless images of angry and ignorant rhetoric that they connect to any discussion of God.

We live during a time where those we view as the *enemy* seem to be everywhere. The rationale, motivation, and even humanity of the other tribe seem alien to us. Also, the stakes involved in our disagreements might have dire and irreparable consequences. It becomes increasingly challenging to love my enemy. This is especially painful since I used to see some of them as friends. Occasionally, I hear someone say something I'm convinced is ignorant, false, harmful, selfish, hateful or, destructive. They may support, promote, and implement behaviors that I believe harm individuals or the collective good. At times like this, a part of me simply wants to call them out and turn over tables. I can see Jesus, in the Temple Courtyard, whip in hand, driving them away... but is that what Jesus called me to do?

Jesus had both the right and the temperament to cleanse the Temple Courtyard, but do I? I think I have neither. As is too often the case, my mouth sometimes demonstrates a lack of discipline. I don't think that I'm alone in that. While I have seriously studied, thought, and prayed over the issues that divide us, I am not Jesus. I have to admit that I could be mistaken in some of these things. Unfortunately, few who hold opposing views express any doubt, humility, or grace in their approach. This makes it even more disappointing and annoying and causes me to dig my heels in even deeper. That doesn't give me license to respond in anger, self-righteousness, or think evil of them. I am left realizing that I can only go to God with this:

Today's prayer:

Dear God,

We, Your creation, often treat You and Your creation with disrespect and treat truth as a flexible commodity to be used for our purposes. Too often, we give an ear to dishonesty, ignorance, and arrogance. We quarrel and harvest our disgust of those with whom we disagree. God, help us to place our trust in Your hand and Your plan for what You have created.

Help us correct our own thinking, soften our own hearts, and sharpen our ability to think, learn, and grow. As we fail to properly steward the resources of creation that You have entrusted to us, help us tend our own garden. Help us forgive and have patience for those who litter theirs, and recognize that Your sovereign hand will, in Your timing, renew all things. Help us to forgive supernaturally and love unconditionally. Let us see our enemy, as a brother, created in Your image, not defined by their views, and worth far more than we realize.

Day Twenty-six: Be Perfect

"Be perfect, therefore, as your heavenly Father is perfect." -- Matthew 5:48 (CSB)

The first Greek letter that most of us ever heard was the letter Pi. The concept represented by that letter is mentioned relatively early in our study of mathematics. There is something fascinating about the number which Pi represents. Suppose you begin writing the correct numerals, adding one correct subsequent digit for every second, of every day, for the entirety of your life. In the end, you would still not even be remotely complete or successful in fully recording it. You can never perfectly represent it on paper. You can only grow closer.

Throughout high school, I exercised for hours every day. I earned seven varsity letters and was captain of the Cross Country team. I poured myself into these sports, but I only won a single wrestling match in four years of trying, and I was far from the fastest member of our Cross Country team. My efforts never resulted in success, much less perfection.

I was, at times, an excellent student. I graduated from one college summa cum laude, but I nearly repeated two grades before high school and was a C- student in my first two years of college. My emotional flaws were a limitation that nearly derailed my academic endeavors. Even when I excelled, some concepts eluded me, and I was never the perfect student.

When I fell in love with Jesus, my life changed profoundly. Decades have passed since then. There have been periods where I diligently tried to live a Christlike and holy life, as well as periods where I was far from that goal.

The very concept of perfection is like the concept of Pi. Even if you never cease doing your best, it's unlikely that you will ever be the best at anything. To attempt to grasp perfection seems ludicrous. To think I could be as perfect as God sounds insane. That's why, over the years, when I've read this verse, it's left me feeling lost and an utter failure. It's also made me question whether we should even take this challenge seriously.

When Jesus said,

> *"It is easier for a camel to go through the eye of a needle than for someone who is rich to enter the kingdom of God." -- Mark 10:25 (NIV)*

his disciples questioned how anyone could be saved. Jesus' reply was simple:

> *"With man this is impossible, but not with God; all things are possible with God." -- Mark 10:27 (NIV)*

185

What surprises me is that the disciples saw giving up earthly treasures as impossible but didn't see Jesus' challenge to be perfect, like God, as infinitely more impossible. While embracing a life of poverty is certainly within the realm of possibility, it's hard to see how being perfect, like God, is something that any mortal could achieve.

It seems clear, then, that I've misunderstood what Jesus was saying. So, what word did Jesus use here? When we read the words be perfect, most of us read an English translation and think of what the word perfection means today. Jesus' challenge was presented in Aramaic and recounted, by Matthew, likely also in Aramaic. At some point, the Aramaic was possibly translated into Hebrew and then into Greek. The thousands of fragments of that Greek translation have resulted in countless translations since, including the English version above. The Greek word translated *perfection* here was *teleioi* or *teleios*. It is a multifaceted word that has many, often related, meanings. That word was used quite a bit in the New Testament and throughout the Roman world. Commonly, it could mean something which is finished or completed. It could also be used to mean mature, fully grown, or adult. Additionally, it could mean infinite or omnipotent. As a noun, *telos* can mean an accomplished goal. The Greek word *teleo* was often used to denote that something had finished, as when Jesus had finished teaching something-- Matthew 7:28; Matthew 13:53. Jesus' use, on the cross, of *tetelestai* (often translated *It is finished*, or *paid in full*) is related to the word used here. It signified that he had completed his work and that accounts were paid entirely and closed.

Many other New Testament scriptures use some version of this word. Here are just a few:

> *"And let endurance carry out its intended purpose (teleion), so that you may be mature (teleioi) and complete, lacking in nothing."* -- James 1:4 (Mounce Reverse Interlinear)

> *"Brothers, do not be children in your thinking. Rather, in evil be infants but in your thinking be adults (teleio)"* -- I Corinthians 14:20 (Mounce Reverse Interlinear)

> *"And do not be conformed to this world, but be transformed by the renewing of your mind, so that you may discern the will of God, what is good and acceptable and perfect (teleion)"* -- Romans 12:2 (Mounce Reverse Interlinear)

In these verses, we don't see this word meaning that we can succeed in all things or without fault, error, or sin. In these uses, the word means to thoroughly apply some good thing to the point of completion. Also, the entirety of scripture makes our flawed state clear. Never does scripture address God's Creation as being on par with the Creator. Even in the Garden, before the Fall, Adam and Eve were not as holy, powerful, knowledgeable, correct, or mature as God. Since that time, God clearly acknowledges our frailty.

"for he knows how we are formed, he remembers that we are dust. The life of mortals is like grass, they flourish like a flower of the field." -- Psalm 103:14,15 (NIV)

"for all have sinned and fall short of the glory of God." -- Romans 3:23 (NIV)

Luke recounts a similar, seemingly unattainable, challenge from Jesus:

"Be merciful, just as your Father is merciful." -- Luke 6:36 (NIV)

Here, Jesus is saying something similar, but I think that it provides more context. In this challenge, Jesus sounds like what an adult might say to a young child, "Eat your veggies, like your father does." There is no expectation that the child will be as mature, strong, consistent, or capable as the father in a challenge like that. The father is simply given as a positive example to follow and emulate. No loving parent would say, even to a grown child:

"You have grown to be a good person, but you're not as good as your mother. Your Mom is perfect."

In this verse, Jesus is simply saying that we should also aspire to be merciful in the same way God is merciful. None of us will ever match, much less surpass, God's mercy. God will never envy our ability to show mercy. Shakespeare pointed to this when he said:

"The quality of mercy is not strained;
It droppeth as the gentle rain from heaven.

188

Upon the place beneath. It is twice blest;
It blesseth him that gives and him that takes." -- *The Merchant of Venice*, William Shakespeare

Shakespeare knew that God was the source of all mercy. Jesus reminds us here to emulate the source, our heavenly Father, the always merciful. There is something of the image of God in all of us that we need to nurture. In a sense, both of these verses are pointing us to that reality. Jesus is reminding us to love God and to aspire to follow His example.

As we look at the context of this, in the last verse of the first portion of this sermon, Jesus provides a clue as to what he means. *"Be perfect, therefore, as your heavenly Father is perfect"* -- Matthew 5:48. The word that gives context here is *therefore*. In a sense, Jesus is finishing, completing, resolving everything that he has taught up to this point. Jesus is reminding those *"with ears to hear"* -- Matthew 11:15 to consider the nature of those who God will bless. He blesses humility of spirit, remorse, repentance, a desire for righteousness, mercy, purity, the pursuit of peace, and acceptance of difficulties. This is currency in the economy of God's Kingdom. Jesus reminds us to become mature, complete, and embrace those things.

He is saying:

"don't simply hear my words and walk away. You have heard religious leaders say one thing, but I tell you something radically different. Put my words into practice. Consider the intent behind the Law and let

189

these values make you complete."

All the things that he has said are goals for us to strive for and are also qualities of our Heavenly Father. God will bless those who demonstrate the qualities above because they are aspects of His nature. When we are humble, we follow in our Creator's footsteps. When we seek peace, we are doing what our loving Heavenly Father is doing. While God doesn't feel remorse, He mourns the difficulties and pain we choose for ourselves.

No, we'll never be perfect, in my current thinking of the word. In 1976, Nadia Comaneci earned the first-ever perfect 10.0 score at an Olympic game. Her incredible work ethic, and passion, combined with gifted genetics, earned her that place in history. She is now fifty-nine years old. It's unlikely she could do most of the things that she did back then. I suspect there were competitions before and after those games where she was far from perfect. No one is perfect. God doesn't expect perfection from any of us. His expectation for us is that we, with our whole heart, seek the truth, seek to know Him, and seek to follow His example. This is best illustrated through the life and words of Jesus. I will never be perfect. Some days, I'm barely good. However, I want to be complete, mature, and finish the race to be more like Jesus and more like my patient and merciful Heavenly Father. I can never write the complete number of Pi. If I could, Jesus would be at the beginning and at the end of it.

Today's prayer:

Abba Father,

Help me to reject the voices that tell me that I have failed, that I am unworthy, that I don't measure up. Help me to see Your grace as the freeing force that it is. Remind me that you don't see, judge, or value, as the world does. You see to the core of my heart, which both comforts and terrifies me. Continue to call me to Yourself, to whittle away the rough edges, to expose the harm that I may bring on myself and others, to humble me, heal me, and complete me.

Day Twenty-seven: Consider Jesus' Audience

"When he saw the crowds, he went up on the mountain, and after he sat down, his disciples came to him.
Then he began to teach them, saying:" -- Matthew 5:1-2 (CSB)

This brings us to the end of Matthew, chapter five, the first of three chapters that we refer to as The Sermon on the Mount. I think it's good to go back and consider the setting and the audience. It's equally important to place ourselves in that audience.

There was no stenographer there, recording his every word, so he may have said other things that day, as well. Perhaps, children were playing loudly, and a disciple asked the mother to take them somewhere else. Maybe, Jesus stopped them and asked the mother to bring the children to the front -- Matthew 19:13,14. Perhaps, it was a hot and dry day. People were becoming tired and thirsty, which led Jesus to tell the story of Lazarus' torment of thirst after having lived a life of immense wealth -- Luke 16:19-31.

Take a look around, and consider those who are in the crowd. Next to you stands a young man who has grown up being told about David's kingdom. He has been led to believe that those were *the good old days*. He came to hear Jesus because he hoped that Jesus would set about restoring that purportedly idyllic time. In reality, those days were far from perfect, but the troubles of the day, and the passing of time, make them seem perfect. He hoped Jesus would become king and kick out the Romans. Instead of hearing the words of a political and military leader, he hears about the values and importance of God's kingdom. His anger against the occupying Roman army drives him far more than anything which Jesus has said.

Off to your right stand a group of powerful, impressively dressed, and stern-looking men. They reflect confidence and subtle disdain for what Jesus is saying. These men have built comfortable lives of privilege, respect, and control by claiming to be the arbiters of their religion. They claim to know how to earn God's approval. Creating rules to strictly follow are their stock and trade. They avoid directly confronting Jesus. Instead, they feign interest and pretend that spiritual things are what they care about. Their true goal is one of protecting their positions of authority. It is no longer apparent if they ever embraced genuine faith out of a desire to know their Creator and reflect His character. Prideful bias, unfounded confidence, and fear are tools they use to control those who listen to them. Jesus' words reflect a living and vital faith centered on the values of God's kingdom. These men have chosen cold, lifeless, and rigid religion, concerned only with man's kingdom.

The Pharisees maintain their power, in part, by working with the group of men who stand off to your left. Surrounding you stands the military might of the Roman Legion. Officials of the Roman government scan the crowd. They look for anyone, any word, or anything that might challenge the region's control and dominance. They note the young man standing to your right. They know him to be a Zealot, a political hothead, who considers himself a patriot. Jesus knows that, in the next fifty years, irrational fanaticism and misplaced patriotism, led by zealots like him, will lead to the destruction of the nation and the dispersion of its Jewish inhabitants. Most of the Roman officials aren't here to consider God's kingdom, but only to preserve control of their own.

Far behind you, to your left, laying on a mat, is an old Jewish man who has regularly attended his local synagogue. He has rigorously followed the customs he has been taught. He believes every word those around him have told him about the nation, the Romans, his religion, and God. He wants to know God, but he has rarely questioned what he has been taught. He has simply ingested his Rabbi's teachings and those of his father and father's father. He has always lived in poverty and is angry about the state of his existence. He is hoping that Jesus will make his *golden years* more comfortable and cure the pain in his hip. He hopes Jesus will punish those he blames for life's difficulties. If he would listen to Jesus' words, he could be transformed, but Jesus' words contradict much of what he has been taught. While he does consider the life to come, he is more concerned with the days and months ahead.

In front of him stands the Rabbi who instructs him. He started out his ministry loving God and wanting to live a righteous life. Over the years, the world's brokenness has jaded and distracted him and led him to look for someone to blame for the state of his country and the absence in his neighborhood of his measure of righteousness. He has rarely questioned or challenged his own faith. This pattern of unexamined faith has been transmitted to those he teaches. Increasingly, he spends less and less time encouraging those in his care to seek God, justice, and mercy. He has become focused on his dislike of the tax gatherers, Samaritans, Romans, sinners, and the foreigners he blames for his community's broken state.

Far behind you, down the hill, sit the women, the lepers, the outcasts, and the Samaritans. It's ironic that the ones who most have to strain to hear Jesus' words are the ones who genuinely desire to hear him. To get here, they had to subject themselves to insults from others in the crowd and choose between being there or earning just enough for the evening meal. While the wealthy, the respected, the powerful, the religious, and the loudmouths occupy the space physically closest to

Jesus, I suspect that Jesus' blessings were meant, primarily, for those in the back. Perhaps, the antitheses were directed toward those in the front. Corrections for those the world rewards and blessings for the less fortunate, who recognize their need for God's mercy.

Scattered throughout the crowd, you may see Jesus' closest disciples. Some are listening intently, while others may be trying to answer questions from the curious. While his words excite them, they are only beginning to understand what he's saying. They have heard Jesus mention these things multiple times, yet it never gets old. Daily, they are filled with joy by simply being around Jesus. There are days when the things he says make perfect sense and other days when they are left scratching their heads, questioning their meaning. Like everyone there, they have concerns, aches, and pains. Some are bone-tired and just want to take a nap. Some are impatient. Most have false expectations of what Jesus has planned. They see a messy, angry world and simply wish that Jesus would change things. They want him to take control and kick out the Romans and the Pharisees. Like most there, they are still focused on a different kingdom than the one Jesus is preaching.

If you look around the world today, you will see that we share much in common with the audience that occupied that Jerusalem hillside about 2,000 years ago. We are not that different. We find many of the same groups vying to get Jesus' approval today or to use Jesus for their own purposes. As it was then, today, our world is divided between those who have and those who don't.

I see a bit of myself in each of those groups. While I would like to think that I am one of the eager listeners and avid followers if I'm honest, I recognize that I'm not always a faithful disciple. I don't know Jesus' face, but like his disciples, something about him stirs my heart, creates a longing, and gives me joy. There are days when, like the Pharisees, I am too quick to judge and falsely think I know more than I do. Like much of the crowd, there are times when the call of the physical, carnal, and material obscure my view of Jesus. Like the zealot, I am tempted to think that I am wise and strong enough to fix the world through political, social, or cultural activism. Like the Centurion soldier, I can be too motivated to control. In contrast, God wants me to let go and simply try to understand, listen, and appreciate.

As we listen to Jesus' words, I hope you will join me in considering just how much we share with these different groups. Can we see where Jesus was addressing us individually? Only God's Spirit can open our eyes to see our true selves.

> *"I keep asking that the God of our Lord Jesus Christ, the glorious Father, may give you the Spirit of wisdom and revelation, so that you may know him better. I pray that the eyes of your heart may be enlightened in order that you may know the hope to which he has called you, the riches of his glorious inheritance in his holy people, and his incomparably great power for us who believe."* --
> Ephesians 1:17-19 (NIV)

Today's prayer:

Dear God,

Help me recognize when I am like the Pharisees, who knew religion but didn't know You. Help me to leave my sinful, selfish baggage behind and start anew with You. Let me recognize that you came preaching the kingdom of heaven instead of a political plan for the kingdom of man. Help me be open, honest, and willing to hear what You desperately want to teach me. Give me ears to hear and eyes to see.

Day Twenty-eight: Hypocrisy

"Be careful not to practice your righteousness in front of others to be seen by them. Otherwise, you have no reward with your Father in heaven. So whenever you give to the poor, don't sound a trumpet before you, as the hypocrites do in the synagogues and on the streets, to be applauded by people. Truly I tell you, they have their reward. But when you give to the poor, don't let your left hand know what your right hand is doing, so that your giving may be in secret. And your Father who sees in secret will reward you.

Whenever you pray, you must not be like the hypocrites, because they love to pray standing in the synagogues and on the street corners to be seen by people. Truly I tell you, they have their reward. But when you pray, go into your private room, shut your door, and pray to your Father who is in secret. And your Father who sees in secret will reward you. When you pray, don't babble like the Gentiles, since they imagine they'll be heard for their many words.

199

Don't be like them, because your Father knows the things you need before you ask him." -- Matthew 6:1-8 (CSB)

"Whenever you fast, don't be gloomy like the hypocrites. For they disfigure their faces so that their fasting is obvious to people. Truly I tell you, they have their reward. But when you fast, put oil on your head and wash your face, so that your fasting isn't obvious to others but to your Father who is in secret. And your Father who sees in secret will reward you." -- Matthew 6:16-18 (CSB)

Back in my early bachelor days, I liked to begin the morning with a bowl of Cap'n Crunch and a package of Pop-Tarts. Sadly, those days are gone. These days it's typically a cup of yogurt and a piece of fruit. On one recent morning, I selected a plum that was in the refrigerator. I'm not a huge fan of fruit, but plums tend to be sweet, and that's always a plus. As I sat down to eat and go through my emails, I picked up this beautiful, seemingly delicious treat and took a bite. What confronted me was less like a delicious breakfast than a trip to the landfill. While it was beautiful on the outside, on the inside, it was foul. Instead of traveling to my stomach, it went to the trash.

Bad things can camouflage themselves in attractive packages. Rotten fruit is simply one example. My first car, a 1962 Ford Falcon, was a thing of beauty. Shiny and black on the outside, and a crushed blue velvet interior. As lovely as it was, it went through a quart of oil every thirty miles. I drove from Virginia to New

Hampshire in the summer of 1975 and used up four gallons of oil. The very first song I ever wrote was a love song to that car. Part of the chorus to *The Ford Falcon Farewell Fanfare* read:

"Gonna' send that car to heaven.
Gonna' send to the Lord,
'Cause I figure if He can save me,
He can surely save a Ford."

My point here is that what is on the outside doesn't always reflect what's inside.

I've previously pointed to a favorite verse:

"The LORD does not look at the things people look at. People look at the outward appearance, but the LORD looks at the heart." -- I Samuel 16:7b (NIV)

Abraham Lincoln is quoted as saying:

"You can fool all the people some of the time and some of the people all the time, but you cannot fool all the people all the time."

Even that seems to be a falsified claim, as we have no evidence that he said it. While people are often fooled, no one can fool God. Jesus was well aware of this. He was frustrated with religious leaders who trumpeted a good outward demonstration but had no spiritual authenticity.

As we begin chapter six of Matthew, Jesus continues with his sermon. Most of the first quarter of this chapter deals with one issue- hypocrisy. This isn't a new topic for him. Much of his mission was to confront hypocrisy and demonstrate the difference between genuine faith and counterfeit religion. The Pharisees were experts at the latter. Today's Pharisees still are.

In the verses above, he confronts those who wear a mask of righteousness but have no authentic desire for God. Ever the diplomat, Jesus called them:

> *"whitewashed tombs, which look beautiful on the outside but on the inside are full of the bones of the dead and everything unclean."* -- Matthew 23:27 (NIV)

He points to several issues where phony *believers* make public shows to gain some earthly advantage. Specifically, he talks about those who give charity, pray or fast. Jesus makes it clear that there is no eternal benefit to an intentionally public exhibition of these things.

He isn't criticizing the acts themselves. Anyone who wants to live a kingdom life should make these things a part of their day.

- Sharing from our abundance with others is a central message throughout scripture.

> *"Whoever is generous to the poor lends to the Lord, and he will reward them for what they have done."* -- Proverbs 19:17 (NIV)

> *"If anyone has material possessions and sees a brother or sister in need but has no pity on them, how can the love of God be in that person?"* -- I John

3:17 (NIV)

- The importance of prayer is expressed throughout scripture and in Jesus' own life.

"The Lord is near to all who call on him, to all who call on him in truth." -- Psalm 145:18 (NIV)

"Devote yourselves to prayer, being watchful and thankful." -- Colossians 4:2 (NIV)

"But Jesus often withdrew to lonely places and prayed." -- Luke 5:16 (NIV)

- Regular fasting was also something that scripture and Jesus encouraged. It was often associated with prayer. It was particularly connected to the act of repentance.

"Yet even now," declares the Lord, "return to me with all your heart, with fasting, with weeping, and with mourning." -- Joel 2:12 (NIV)

"When I heard these words, I sat down and wept. I mourned for a number of days, fasting and praying before the God of the heavens." -- Nehemiah 1:4 (CSB)

No, Jesus encouraged and modeled these things. What he opposed was the counterfeit motivation behind much of what he saw. Was he saying that we should never openly fast, pray, or give? In the previous chapter, Jesus seems to encourage public acts of righteousness when he said:

"In the same way, let your light shine before others,

so that they may see your good works and give
glory to your Father in heaven." -- Matthew 5:16
(CSB)

If people see our *good deeds*, isn't that a public display? Is Jesus contradicting himself here? No. The problem he was confronting was not the presence of the light or righteous acts. He was addressing the motivation. When Jesus prayed, it wasn't to draw attention to himself. He prayed because he depended on God for strength and insight. When Christ fasted, he did it to draw closer to God and as the natural result of his dedication to his Father God. Jesus fasted to redirect his focus from man's kingdom to the kingdom of heaven. When he healed or fed the poor, he did it because he had compassion for them. Jesus took the light God gave him, and he shone it where it would do the most good. He drew attention to the power and love of God as well as God's mercy for those who were needy. He drew attention to the transformative work of faith. He drew attention to the dangers of religion.

We live in what some call a *post-Christian* world. In response to this, many Christians have promoted legislating public acts of faith. They demanded we place God's name on our money. They insist that a representation of the Ten Commandments be hung in our courthouses. They seek to enforce public prayer in schools, courts, and public places. I find it ironic that these same people are incensed if the government enacts minimal charity. I don't know the motivations behind these demands, but they do more harm than good.

I was a school teacher for a decade, and I prayed nearly every day there. I know other teachers who also did. It saddens and frustrates me when I hear someone claim that "God has been kicked out of school." God is omnipresent. There has never been a governmental force capable of banning God from any place. The only thing that has been prohibited is forcing prayer on any student. These protestations about America becoming *godless* are often based on lies and half-truths. God gives us free will. Many ignore this. They don't see the folly in attempting to enforce their personal moral code. If God wanted to enforce His will, He could. More critically, they misunderstand the mission they have been given. Jesus never asks us to demand external signs of our religious culture. He commands us to be agents of restoration and transformation. We don't do that through legislation. If that had been Jesus' plan, he could have done that long ago.

Jesus came to bring faith because faith gives life. It sets people free. While he was here, he battled cultural and institutional religion. He knew that rules and laws will never change the heart. He was aware that without changed hearts, his kingdom's objectives would never be met.

Today's verses and thought:

"Is not this the kind of fasting I have chosen:
to loose the chains of injustice
and untie the cords of the yoke,

205

to set the oppressed free
and break every yoke?
Is it not to share your food with the hungry
and to provide the poor wanderer with shelter
when you see the naked, to clothe them,
and not to turn away from your own flesh and
blood?
Then your light will break forth like the dawn,
and your healing will quickly appear;
then your righteousness will go before you,
and the glory of the LORD will be your rear guard."
-- Isaiah 58:6-8 (NIV)

Many in the Church overreact to what they believe is a post-Christian America. I have an observation and a promise.

First, America has never been a Christian nation. People who make that claim are either ignorant of our nation's history or of kingdom priorities. America's policies and values have never been the values of the kingdom of heaven. Additionally, nations have no soul. A nation's policies do reflect the spiritual motivation of a nation's citizens though. I won't go into our nation's history here, and it's not my intent to criticize America. There are worse countries and better ones, but only people have souls. Only souls can follow Jesus. Let's leave our nation's destiny to God but seek truth, common sense, and decency as citizens of this earthly kingdom.

Second, read through Isaiah, chapter fifty-eight, and ask yourself:

"What is more likely to make your neighbors turn to Jesus? Enforcing a law to make people pray or doing what God says?"

If we genuinely believe that the gospel is good news and want others to see that, this passage gives us a blueprint. What would happen if we instituted biblical justice, freed the oppressed, fed the hungry, clothed the naked, and welcomed those who come to us? I believe God's light would shine, lives would change, and the Church would flourish. Only then will there be healing and righteousness here. It will never shine from forced prayer or politically legislated religion.

Pray without ceasing, give selflessly, take a break and fast. Don't do it to get a pat on the back. Do it because you want to be like your heavenly Father and because you love your neighbor.

Day Twenty-nine: How to Pray

"Don't be like them, because your Father knows the things you need before you ask him.

Therefore, you should pray like this:
Our Father in heaven,
your name be honored as holy.
Your kingdom come.
Your will be done
on earth as it is in heaven.
Give us today our daily bread." -- Matthew 6:8-11 (CSB)

After chastising the Pharisees for how they pray, give charity, and fast, Jesus now explains how we should pray. This lesson doesn't come from a freshman in the college of prayer. Jesus was a master of prayer. While the Pharisees only pretended to connect with God, Jesus never disconnected. In everything he did, he listened to God for direction and the faith to implement it. His life reflected the power that can come from consistent and prayerful dependency.

Everyone seems to have a positive comment to offer about prayer. Even the most secular will *send warm thoughts* and extol the benefits of meditation. Many say "I'll pray for you" as a segue to end the conversation and escape hearing about someone's troubles. There are books, movies, apps, and conferences dedicated to learning how to pray. We gather for prayer meetings and say grace before meals.

While Jesus *prayed without ceasing* -- I Thessalonians 5:16, it seems more likely we cease without praying. With its seeming popularity and abundance of resources, I would think that unceasing and effective prayer must be an everyday thing. However, if that's the case, why don't Jesus' followers today look more like Jesus? Didn't he promise,

> *"Very truly I tell you, whoever believes in me will do the works I have been doing, and they will do even greater things than these, because I am going to the Father."* -- John 14:12 (NIV)

I don't think he was only referring to miraculous works. I think he was promising that we would reflect God's character, just as he did. While there are many beautiful and faithful followers, it's rare that we *move mountains* -- Mark 11:23, either figuratively or literally. Far too often, instead of moving them, we erect them. It would be difficult to argue that any of us are doing *greater things* than Jesus. I can't provide an authoritative explanation for this discrepancy, but I have a suggestion on where to start. We should listen less to self-proclaimed prayer warriors. Instead, we should go back and examine Jesus' model.

There have been volumes written about Jesus' instructions on prayer. I will only talk about the points which strike me. The Greek word for pray is *proseuchomai*. This comes from *pros*, meaning to face toward, and *euchomai*, meaning to speak out or vow. With authentic prayer, we always metaphorically face God and speak to Him directly. We refer to this section of the sermon as The Lord's Prayer. Most Christian churches recite the prayer. With all of our divisions, it seems to be a constant that binds us together. Still, I don't believe Jesus is giving us a script to parrot. Instead, he provides a blueprint to follow. He doesn't tell us, "say these words." He tells us this "is how you should pray." I agree with C.H. Spurgeon, who said:

"I believe that this prayer was never intended for universal use."

A shorter version of this prayer is recorded in Luke 11:2-4. This was when one of his disciples said:

"Lord, teach us to pray, just as John taught his disciples." -- Luke 11:1 (NIV)

Jesus gave this prayer example to his disciples and to the masses on the hillside. It was intended as an example and invitation for everyone, not just the select few.

Just before the prayer, Jesus says:

"your Father knows the things you need before you ask him." -- Matthew 6:8b (CSB)

210

Nothing that we take to God will surprise Him. He isn't dependent on our information. This conversation with God is more for our benefit than for His. Since He already knows what we need, then why even pray? Can't God just address the need? Sometimes, He does, but the primary reason we should take our needs to God is to correct our hearts. We'll discuss this more later.

Jesus begins by saying:

> *"Our Father in heaven, hallowed be your name."* -- Matthew 6:9 (NIV)

I find this to be remarkably telling. He is pointing to a seeming paradox. We are to come to a God who is both a loving father and someone infinitely powerful. The word father here is *Abba*. It is an Aramaic word. It is still used today between Jewish and Palestinian fathers and their children. Some have translated Jesus' use of it to mean *Papa* or *Daddy*. Others say that it has a more formal meaning, like *sir*. I suspect that it means both the informal and the formal. If you tie the second half of the verse to the beginning, you won't read it as "Our Papa, who is just my bud." Neither would you interpret it as, "Our stern commander, who I will obey out of fear." This phrase expresses both sincere affection along with respect. Also, this isn't Jesus' prayer to his father. He is telling us this is how we pray to our heavenly father. He doesn't say, "God is my father, but He isn't yours." He says, "*Our Father.*" In some sense, we share sonship with Jesus. Jesus is our savior, but he is also our brother.

"For the one who sanctifies and those who are sanctified all have one Father. That is why Jesus is not ashamed to call them brothers and sisters, saying: I will proclaim your name to my brothers and sisters; I will sing hymns to you in the congregation." -- Hebrews 2:11-12 (CSB)

Jesus distinguishes that the prayer is addressing our *heavenly* Father. We have no choice in who our earthly father is. Is the same true for our heavenly Father? Some suggest that God is only father to those who believe. I won't argue the point, but it's clear that God's desire is to adopt all of us. Anyone who sees God as Father is an adopted child of God. All that Jesus requires here is to address Him as Father. Jesus doesn't list prerequisites that must be met before praying to God as our heavenly Father. We simply need to accept that He is and go to Him.

Upon addressing our Father God, Jesus reminds us of who we are addressing. He tells us how we are to approach Him:

"Hallowed be your name." -- Matthew 6:9 (NIV)

The English word translated *Hallowed* means holy. Jesus is saying that the name of God is holy. It is to be honored. The Greek word for *hallowed* is *hagiazo*, from the root *hagios*, which means set apart, holy, or sanctified. Jesus instructs us that the object of our honor is the name of God. While we value our name, the name of God has a far greater significance. This was made clear when God said,

"You shall not misuse the name of the Lord your God, for the Lord will not hold anyone guiltless who misuses his name." -- Exodus 20:7 (NIV)

The Hebrews took this literally and felt that utterning the name was disrespectful. I suspect that He was less concerned with the combination of phonemes than with how we represent Him to the world. We are tasked with the business of being ambassadors for Christ -- II Corinthians 5:20. If we are ambassadors to a nation, what is most likely to get us fired? I suspect that it would be misrepresenting the nation's intent or aiding an opponent. Too often, Christ's ambassadors do both. If we genuinely *hallow* God's name we will correctly represent Him to the world around us and guard against promoting evil. Of course, this means that we have to actually consider and study to ensure we know Him. Prayer, study, discussion, and critical thinking skills should all be employed to ensure we are correctly representing Him.

This first part of Jesus' prayer is addressed vertically toward God. It is focused explicitly on adoring and appreciating the love and majesty of our heavenly Father. In the second part, Jesus makes a connection between God's kingdom will for His creation and His desire to heal and transform the kingdom of man:

"Your kingdom come. Your will be done on earth as it is in heaven." -- Matthew 6:10-9 (CSB)

The connection between God's plan and man's reality is through our relationship with God and His creation.

213

The values of the kingdom of heaven and the kingdom of man are entirely different. God sees the pain that we bring on ourselves by our rebellion and selfishness. *"Jesus wept"* -- John 11:35 because God weeps and empathizes with our pain. Many interpret this *coming kingdom* as some future hope. They see it as some New Earth promise. They suggest that it is an expression of longing for God to establish His future kingdom. God indeed has a long-term plan to resolve and restore what we have broken. However, in the present, He wants us to join Him in living out His kingdom values today. As Jesus expressed in the previous chapter, to the world, we are salt and light. By living as God desires, we can be a part of God's establishing His will on earth. To pray that God's kingdom would come is simply to invite God and join Him in His mission to transform the world. We assist this transformation by living out Jesus' kingdom values of loving God and neighbor. Later in this chapter, Jesus says,

> *"But seek first the kingdom of God and his righteousness, and all these things will be provided for you."* -- Matthew 6:33 (CSB)

This is how we are to join God in bringing His kingdom to earth. We do this when we, above all, seek Him and His value of justice, mercy, and humility.

However, there is a danger with this concept of promoting God's heavenly will on Earth. If we don't know His will and love His will, we are likely to use His name to justify doing our will. This is the opposite of *hallowing* His name. Throughout the ages, people have

214

done this very thing. So many monstrous acts have been done by people who think they are enforcing the will of God. One of Bob Dylan's earlier songs addresses this. In the song, he recounts our young nation's many wars. He ends each verse referencing how we justify killing with the song's title- *With God On Our Side.*

We are to pray that God's kingdom will be given flesh in our neighborhoods. However, we must approach this cautiously. Those who attempt this often employ an earthly strategy instead of a heavenly one. Instead of authentically modeling God's kingdom in our lives and treatment of others, we try to force change through political involvement. There are times when, as dual citizens of heaven and earth, we may join with a political goal. We should always exercise wisdom and caution when we do that. We should always confirm that the cause we defend genuinely demonstrates love of God or neighbor. Suppose we are confident that the cause we support is godly. In that case, we must be satisfied that our strategy to accomplish that goal doesn't promote or defend some other evil. You may believe that a law purportedly intended to limit theft is godly. If implementing that law empowers a policy that protects injustice, then that strategy is not righteous.

God's kingdom will never be built through force or law. When we adopt an unrighteous strategy, the result is that the kingdom of man corrupts us. Eventually, we are the ones who need to be rescued. Jesus did more to establish the kingdom of heaven on Earth than any other person. Did he accomplish this through culture wars, spreading fear and half-truths, or seeking influence with Pontius Pilate? If he didn't take that approach, we should have a very good reason to travel a different route.

Next, Jesus moves from praying for God's general will for creation to seeking God's provisions in our own lives.

> *"Give us today our daily bread."* -- Matthew 6:11 (CSB)

By praying this prayer, we recognize an essential truth. We are dependent on our Creator. In this conversation, there is only one God, and it's not me. While we are to not be lazy, no amount of work ethic will ever remove our dependency on God.

This verse provides some crucial financial planning advice. We are not asked to go to God for future provision. God has a plan for that, and we should wisely be good stewards of what He has provided. On this, see Jesus' parable of the Three Servants -- Matthew 25:14-30. He is saying that we should not be anxious about next month's income. Prepare, yes, but don't worry. God calls us to the peaceful application of common sense. Daily, we should pray for our present needs. What about praying for more than I need? The word here is translated as *daily*, which presents the notion of what is essential, not surplus. Praying for a private jet doesn't seem to be in line with this.

One issue, though, is that the word may be improperly translated. The Greek word used is *epiousios*. While it is

216

translated as *daily*, it appears nowhere else, either within or outside scripture. It is only found in these two verses. There is a different word that is typically translated as *daily*. From the root segments of the word- *epi*, which means super, and *ousia*, which means substance, we get a new word that literally means *supersubstantial* or most *essential* (more than substantial... transcending substance). Possibly, this means "today, give me bread which transcends substance." Jesus did use this analogy when he said:

> *"I am the bread of life. Whoever comes to me will never go hungry, and whoever believes in me will never be thirsty."* -- John 6:35 (NIV)

I suspect that Jesus is saying that, daily, we should pray for our essential physical and spiritual needs.

A story in the Old Testament provides a good illustration of how a person of faith should approach economics. In Exodus, chapter sixteen, we read about Moses and the Hebrew refugees. They escaped from Egypt about six weeks earlier and are wandering through the Sinai Peninsula. They have quickly forgotten how poorly they were treated in Egypt. They are hungry and growing angry. Since they lack their *daily bread*, God tells Moses that He will provide what they need. He doesn't promise to give them what they want, only what they need. Each night, God sends quail for them to have meat. Each morning, except for the Sabbath, He sends manna to eat. Manna is curious. It literally means *What is it?* When I was in school, I had a few meals where I've asked that question. There is actually a plant in the region known as the Rimth Shrub -- Haloxylon salicornicum. At night, insects eat the plant's sap, which is known as honeydew. Their digestive systems leave a residue that contains sugar. Once that hardens, it forms white granules. This is still used for food in some parts of the Middle East.

God tells them that they are only to gather enough for the day. Except for the Sabbath, what they collect will spoil. They are told to not store up but to depend on God for provision. They are told how much to gather:

> "This is what the LORD has commanded: 'Everyone is to gather as much as they need. Take an omer for each person you have in your tent.'
>
> The Israelites did as they were told; some gathered much, some little. "And when they measured it by the omer, the one who gathered much did not have too much, and the one who gathered little did not have too little. Everyone had gathered just as much as they needed." -- Exodus 16:16-18 (NIV)

Note that in God's kingdom economy, everyone gets the same share. You don't find some who have too much and some who don't have enough. While I don't believe communism is being taught here, it's clear that unbridled capitalism is not God's intent. Still, some of this group decide to disobey God's instructions and go out to gather more than they were supposed to. Does God respond by applauding their industrious drive? This is what happens:

> "However, some of them paid no attention to

218

Moses; they kept part of it until morning, but it was full of maggots and began to smell. So Moses was angry with them." -- Exodus 16:20 (NIV)

Wouldn't that be a nice verse to read before a meal? I'm not sure that we can determine hard and fast rules, but I do see some basic principles revealing themselves here. First, God wants us to depend on Him for our daily needs. When we move beyond needs to wants, we have to proceed with caution. God may be perfectly fine with something we have our eye on. The question is whether that thing is competing with God for our affection. If it might draw us away from Him, I don't see God answering that prayer. Second, when we focus exclusively on our wants but entirely ignore the needs of our neighbors, we will get a result similar to the manna above. It will decay and stink. Jesus was correct that *"the poor you will always have with you"* -- Matthew 26:11. That was not intended as an excuse to ignore economic injustice.

Today's thoughts and verses:

We have a heavenly Father who loves us more than any earthly father ever could. We should face Him daily and have a heartfelt conversation. While He loves us, we should not approach God without regard. We depend on Him. He wants to provide for our daily needs. If God has provided for our physical and spiritual needs, should we keep those blessings to ourselves, or should we share them? Do we want the kingdom of heaven to be manifest in the world around us? If we do, we must first know and love God's will. His word gives us both an objective and a strategy, but He must be the foundation.

> *"Unless the LORD builds the house, the builders labor in vain.*
> *Unless the LORD watches over the city,*
> *the guards stand watch in vain.*
> *In vain you rise early and stay up late,*
> *toiling for food to eat—*
> *for he grants sleep to those he loves."* -- Psalm 127:1,2 (NIV)

Day Thirty: Forgiveness

"And forgive us our debts, as we also have forgiven our debtors. And do not bring us into temptation, but deliver us from the evil one. For if you forgive others their offenses, your heavenly Father will forgive you as well. But if you don't forgive others, your Father will not forgive your offenses." -- Matthew 6:12-15 (CSB)

"And whenever you stand praying, if you have anything against anyone, forgive him, so that your Father in heaven will also forgive you your wrongdoing." -- Mark 11:25 (CSB)

"And forgive us our sins, for we ourselves also forgive everyone in debt to us. And do not bring us into temptation." -- Luke 11:4 (CSB)

Verses twelve, fourteen, and fifteen address a topic that Jesus spoke of often, forgiveness. These verses present a challenge to the modern view of God. We often speak of God's love as unconditional. I believe that is true. Still, while God doesn't place conditions on loving us, we can erect barriers that prevent us from receiving God's love. Here, and elsewhere, Jesus

221

connects how we forgive others to how God forgives us. We previously looked at the parable of The Unforgiving Debtor. In that passage, Jesus expresses this truth this way:

> *"So also my heavenly Father will do to you unless every one of you forgives his brother or sister from your heart."* -- Matthew 18:35 (CSB)

Jesus ties our being forgiven to how we forgive. In Matthew's recounting above, the conditional phrase is *But if you do not*. In Mark's gospel, Jesus uses the conditional word *so*, meaning *in order that*. Still, Luke provides a third recounting with no conditional clause. It simply assumes that we will forgive others.

There is little doubt that God desires to forgive each of us. However, circumstances can interrupt that forgiveness. Consider a drowning man who will not let go of some weight that is dragging him under. That man must first release his grip on that weight to be rescued.

I think the physiological process of respiration powerfully illustrates this concept of *reciprocal forgiveness*. From the first moment after birth to our final seconds, what is the thing that signifies we are alive? It is the act of breathing. *Respiration* is an absolute essential for life. The scientists among you can correct my simplistic understanding of the process. We inhale oxygen. More precisely, it's seventy-nine percent nitrogen, twenty-one percent oxygen, and trace gases. That oxygen is used to support metabolism and provide energy to our cells. Still, breathing is complex. It is not simply inhaling life-giving oxygen. It encompasses *ventilation*, which is the inhalation and exhalation of breath. We breathe in O2 and breathe out the byproducts of metabolism- carbon dioxide. CO2 is a waste product. It is toxic to us if it is not expelled. Respiration also consists of *perfusion*. This is the movement of those gases in the blood and between tissue and cells. It is a beautiful but complex process. If any single component of that process fails, the result can be fatal.

Ventilation illustrates the first concept of reciprocal forgiveness. Imagine you find someone who isn't breathing, and you stop to give CPR (again, I'm simplifying). Assume you breathe life-giving oxygen into their lungs, but they don't exhale. What is the result? First, they have no more capacity in their lungs for oxygen. They will get that first lungful of O2. It will eventually be replaced by CO2. The lack of oxygen causes a condition known as *hypoxemia*. Second, the CO2 will continue to build up. This is a condition known as *hypercapnia*. Either of these conditions, if severe enough, can result in death. Hypoxemia paints the first picture of reciprocal forgiveness. Like holding on to a breath, if we hold on to anger, resentment, rage, and a sense of victimization, we allow no room for God to give us His forgiveness. Our spiritual lungs have no capacity for it. Additionally, hypercapnia demonstrates that our unwillingness to let go of resentment is toxic. Even if we receive oxygen or forgiveness, if we don't expel the CO2 or anger, the toxicity will take its toll on us.

The second illustration is perfusion, where the gases are

exchanged with the cells. Even if our lungs are working, if gas is not exchanged between the lungs with blood being carried to the cells, the eventual result is death. In Matthew 18:35 above, Jesus talks about forgiving *from your heart*. Like perfusion, it's not enough to ignore the one who has wronged you. A superficial response of *whatever* is like breathing without any benefit to the cells. The forgiveness that God desires is to entirely let go and release them from any debt. True forgiveness is never superficial.

But why is forgiveness even necessary? Why does God care if I can't stand someone who is a crook, liar, bully, or unkind? Let's start by asking what God wants us to forgive. In Matthew 6:12, we are commanded to forgive *debts*. In Luke 11:4, we are commanded to forgive *sins*. Jesus likely stated these concepts many times and in Aramaic. We don't know precisely what word he used, but the writers of the gospels knew him and translated it both ways. I suspect that Jesus said to forgive both debts and sins. Let's look at debt first. A similar form of the word for debt is used by Paul:

> *"Let no debt remain outstanding, except the continuing debt to love one another, for whoever loves others has fulfilled the law."* -- Romans 13:8 (NIV)

In this verse, debts are not referring to a financial obligation. Jesus may be telling us to forgive a monetary debt, clear harm, or even a failure to do the moral and charitable thing. I believe that it is all three.

Why do we resist forgiving? Why do we cling to a

lifetime of resentment? What is the foundation for a grudge we tightly grasp? It is the sense that someone has abused a right we believe is ours. It's often the sense that "I deserved better than this."

When we bear a grudge, refuse to forgive, or harbor resentment, it is because we claim ownership of some right or privilege. We scream, "no one had the right to do this to me." While that may be true, this thinking has some implications to ponder. How we respond to injustice is at the heart of God's nature and plan for His kingdom. God's rights are limitless. While God passionately loves us, He allows injustice to happen. He permits us to connect with people who mistreat us or simply fail to do what we believe we deserve. When we hold on to bitterness, who are we really blaming? Aren't we blaming more than the person who wronged us? We are blaming God for the things we view as injustice. We wrongly think if we don't correct injustice against us, no one will.

God understands when we are angry with Him. He's not a fragile soul who can't handle honest anger, frustration, or our confusion. I think God would prefer we have an open conversation with Him about our anger than for us to try to exist without Him. Also, He cares about how we are treated. When injustice or unkindness is visited on us or others, He is right there. The problem occurs when we refuse to take those issues to Him with trusting hearts. If we hold on to hate, it means that we don't trust God to heal us. Imagine a snake bites you, and you arrive at the ER, clutching that snake. The doctor assures you that it is safe to let go.

They will capture the snake so it won't bite you again. If you refuse to let go, what are you saying? You are saying, "I don't trust you to keep me safe." You may be more focused on harming the snake than on receiving treatment.

None of this means we should use our trust in God as an excuse to ignore genuine injustice. He saw injustice, and it so offended him that it was impossible to ignore his anger. He spoke out. He stepped in and stopped the crowd from stoning the woman -- John 8. He took action. He didn't simply go into the Temple and ignore what was going on outside. He didn't forget about the poor being swindled with an escapist praise song. No. Neither did he hold a grudge or blame God for those abuses.

Did Jesus forgive the money changers or the Pharisees? He clearly forgave those who crucified him -- Luke 23:34. I believe that forgiveness was meant for the Pharisees as well as the Romans. If ever there was someone who could justly claim that his rights were being violated, it was Jesus.

> *"He was oppressed and afflicted, yet he did not open his mouth; he was led like a lamb to the slaughter, and as a sheep before its shearers is silent, so he did not open his mouth."* -- Isaiah 53:7 (NIV)

Today's thoughts and challenge:

If Jesus can lay down his rights and forgive, what right do we have to hold on to resentment?

Think about the people who have wronged you. It's

likely the list is long. Jesus says:

> *"For he causes his sun to rise on the evil and the good, and sends rain on the righteous and the unrighteous."* -- Matthew 5:45 (CSB)

Acknowledge that the harms and injustices you've experienced were not a result of God punishing you. The laws of the physical universe are broken. We all experience unfair and unkind treatment. While God doesn't cause the pain, He will bring good out of it if we let Him.

Take your list and go to God with it. Tell Him how you have been hurt. Perhaps you daily feel the pain of those injuries. Listen for God's heart of compassion for you in response to your story. Imagine each of those injustices as a chain and give that chain to God. Tell God that you forgive those people. As monstrous or cruel as their actions were, recognize that God knows them. They are unique creations with some imprint of their Creator, no matter how faint. Acknowledge that they *are dust* -- Psalm 103:14. As you recognize their humanity and God's sovereign, restorative plan, He will break each chain and free you. I am confident of that.

Day Thirty-one: Temptation

"And do not bring us into temptation, but deliver us from the evil one." -- Matthew 6:13 (CSB)

"And do not bring us into temptation." -- Luke 11:4 (CSB)

This will be my third attempt at deciphering the meaning and implications of this verse. As we come to the end of Jesus' model prayer, we encounter a verse that demonstrates the importance of correctly handling *the word of truth* -- II Timothy 2:15. Like few other verses, this one is uniquely difficult to understand if we consider what Jesus is saying. If you were to read this verse by itself, it might suggest one concept. If considered against the entirety of scripture, it may be something entirely different.

As with so much of scripture, I began this study confident that the verse meant one thing. As I studied more, I started to think it meant something else. Scripture, if read honestly, can leave us uncomfortable and even confused. This isn't always the case, but if we read enough of it and examine it critically, it will eventually force us to stop and reconsider. At times, an honest follower of Jesus must wrestle with the meaning of scripture. We may be called to reevaluate our understanding of God's nature. We may be forced to correct our worldview. We may have to simply admit, "I'm not certain I understand exactly what this means." When we arrive at the latter conclusion, I think it's most important to avoid accepting flimsy answers. They only provide a false sense of closure but provide an unstable foundation. It's better to live in the tension of acknowledging our lack of understanding than to delude ourselves and others by trying to pretend we understand things we don't. We must always allow room for God to correct our understanding.

Our English translations of this verse may give the impression that Jesus was suggesting God is in the habit of enticing us to sin. You could walk away believing God was some mischievous force. Of course, this runs counter to everything Jesus has told us about our Heavenly Father.

Consider the Garden of Eden. God puts newly birthed humanity into this place. He only prohibits one thing. They are not to eat the fruit from the *Tree of the Knowledge of Good and Evil*. That's fair enough. If there had been no outside meddling, would Eve have taken that first bite? I don't know. However, the entry of the serpent changes the equation. It's commonly assumed that the serpent was the Devil. The question this raises is, "why did God allow the serpent to be there?" Since this was prior to man's fall, was temptation even a possibility? God could have banned the serpent from the Garden, just as He's banned mankind from returning. This last verse of the Lord's Prayer brings this question into focus. If God hates sin and loves us, why does He allow us to be tempted?

I reject the notion that God prompts, even by proxy, people to sin. That view paints a picture of God as some supernatural Venus Flytrap. Elsewhere in scripture, we are told:

> "When tempted, no one should say, "God is tempting me." For God cannot be tempted by evil, nor does he tempt anyone." -- James 1:13

That seems clear, but what about other verses that I will address later? Some give the indication that God is at least tacitly involved in the process of temptation. What do we do with this apparent contradiction? Perhaps it's because translations are never perfect. Jesus spoke these words in his native language of Aramaic. Those words were likely recorded in Aramaic. Next, they may have been translated into Hebrew and then into Greek. Much later, they were translated into English. We don't have the Aramaic, Hebrew, or original Greek texts. We have numerous early fragments, which give us confidence in the majority of the original Greek translation. Even if we know the precise word spoken, translations will always require context. Luke doesn't include the "deliver us from evil" phrase in his recounting. This serves to further confuse us.

Because of the verse in James and questions about the

translation, there is tremendous disagreement about what Jesus meant by "*lead us not into temptation.*" In 2017, Pope Francis opened a can of worms when he said of this verse:

> "This is not a good translation. It's not about letting me fall into temptation. It's I, the one who falls, not Him pushing me toward temptation, so as to then see how I fall. No, well, a father won't do that. A father will immediately help you pick yourself up. Satan is the one leading you into temptation. That's Satan's task." -- Pope Francis, 2017

He suggested the translation, "Do not let us fall into temptation." In 2019, the Catholic Church adopted that translation. There is valid criticism as to whether the Pope's translation was accurate to the Greek texts. The larger issue for me is logical consistency with other verses.

Let's start by taking a closer look at the verse. The verse in Matthew is made up of two phrases. *Lead us not into temptation,* and *deliver us from evil* (or *the evil one*). It's important to note that those two phrases are connected with the conjunction *but.* This presents a contrast that ties the two phrases together. It might be read, "Do not lead us into temptation, but instead, deliver us from evil."

There are four keywords in this verse that may help us understand it better:

Lead, temptation, deliver, and *evil.* Let's look at each individually:

The word translated as *lead* comes from the Greek *eisenenkēs*. It means *lead, take,* or *bring into*.

The word translated as temptation comes from the Greek word *peirasmon*. It means *test, trial, affliction,* or *temptation*. The same word is used in the verses below:

> "and even though my illness was a trial to you, you did not treat me with contempt or scorn." --
> Galatians 4:14 (NIV)

> "You are those who have stood by me in my trials."
> -- Luke 22:28 (NIV)

The word translated as *deliver* comes from the Greek word *rhysai*. It means to *deliver* or *rescue*. The same word is used in the verse below:

> "What a wretched man I am! Who will rescue me from this body that is subject to death?" -- Romans 7:24 (NIV)

The Greek word *poneros* is translated as *evil* (or evil one.) It can also mean wicked.

So, this phrase could mean, "Do not bring us into trials or afflictions. Instead, rescue me from anything outside Your will for me."

Many stories in the Bible address trials, difficulties, and temptations. I want to briefly point to a few as a launching pad for further study of the issue:

The story of Job is considered by many to be the oldest book in the Bible. It also seems to most directly address

232

the conflict of the presence of evil in the world and a good God who allows it. It also gives an example of how God participates in the process. In the story, Job is a godly and wealthy man. He has a large family and an ideal life. *The Accuser* (possibly Satan) goes to God to accuse Job. He says that Job is only godly because of how much God has given Job. Unlike the Accuser, God knows Job's heart and the authenticity of his faith. God allows the Accuser limited freedom to attack Job. Satan kills Job's family, destroys his property, and inflicts him with disease. His religious friends come to him with easy answers and no compassion. Their intervention only adds to his suffering. The beauty of Job is in its honesty. While Job begins praising God, like all of us, he is flawed and fragile. Eventually, he despairs. He wishes that he had never been born, and he lashes out at God. God's response to Job's accusations is blunt. God reminds Job who God is and who Job is. While God is not fragile or defensive, He confronts Job with reality. He asks Job:

> *"Will the one who contends with the Almighty correct him? Let him who accuses God answer him!"* -- Job 40:2 (NIV)

Job acknowledges God's sovereignty and his own dependency. He repents for blaming God for his troubles. God restrains the attacks of the Accuser and restores what Job has lost, and blesses him with far more.

In this telling, did God participate in the painful things that Job and his family members experienced? Not

233

directly. God didn't directly prompt any pain or loss. Did God request Satan to harm Job? No, Satan challenged the validity of Job's faith and said it wouldn't last without God's continued material blessing. Did God allow it? Yes, though He did place limits on what Satan could do. Job's pain was at the hand of God's enemy and at the request of God's enemy. While Satan's agenda was to harm Job and insult God, what was God's motivation? I suspect that God was protecting Job's eternal possessions by letting him lose his earthly possessions. While Satan would have liked to continue tormenting Job, God intervened. He stopped the torment and restored and healed Job.

Jesus knew more about temptation than any of us. In fact, Matthew records almost the exact words about Jesus' experience with temptation:

> *"Then Jesus was led up by the Spirit into the wilderness to be tempted by the devil."* -- Matthew 4:1 (CSB)

God did not tempt Jesus. Temptation is something that the Accuser or this world's momentum of evil promotes. Unlike Job, Jesus never blames God. He is never despondent or angry. He places complete trust in his Father. We are told that Jesus is not only aware of how we are tempted but that he was tempted *in every way*. I'm grateful my temptations and trials are far more limited.

> *"For we do not have a high priest who is unable to empathize with our weaknesses, but we have one*

who has been tempted in every way, just as we are
—yet he did not sin." -- Hebrews 4:15 (NIV)

Jesus' temptation didn't stop when he left the desert. Throughout his life, he experienced more in the way of trials than anyone. He was tempted to avoid the crucifixion. Unlike Job, who had no control over the trials he was experiencing, Jesus could have prevented the trials. When Peter tries to intervene with violence, Jesus says:

"Or do you think that I cannot call on my Father, and he will provide me here and now with more than twelve legions of angels?" -- Matthew 26:53 (CSB)

So, where did Jesus' temptation come from? Whether in the desert or on the cross, was it God who caused those things to happen? The Devil had his own agenda. In both cases, Jesus could say to the Accuser what Joseph said:

"You intended to harm me, but God intended it for good to accomplish what is now being done, the saving of many lives." -- Genesis 50:20 (NIV)

I think that what has confused me with these verses is the meaning of the Greek word *peirasmon*. The English word temptation gives the impression of drawing us to sin. However, the Greek word can also mean trial. What is the difference between a temptation and a trial? The difference is in the intention and result. While God doesn't tempt us, He does allow us to be tested through trials. His intention in testing us is not to harm us or

235

make us miserable. It is to strengthen our faith. However, temptation comes with a very different intention. Its intent is not to strengthen us. It is to destroy us. Temptation may come directly from the Devil. This was the case with Job and Jesus. We can also find ourselves tempted because we don't recognize the danger of sin. It is a slippery slope. It's very easy to fall into temptation when we regularly walk along the rim of the precipice. Consider this verse:

> *"Consider it pure joy, my brothers and sisters, whenever you face trials of many kinds, because you know that the testing of your faith produces perseverance. Let perseverance finish its work so that you may be mature and complete, not lacking anything."* -- James 1:2-4 (NIV)

Here, trials are seen as something positive. They aren't positive because we enjoy them. They can be positive when we allow them to strengthen our faith and dependence on God. The line between trials and temptations can become blurred. Trials can result in temptation. We can become so disheartened from a trial that we are tempted to take a shortcut that God has prohibited. God will never directly tempt us, but He may directly test us. Again, His purpose is to benefit us and His kingdom. The Devil will both tempt us and give us trials. In both cases, his intent is to harm us and thwart God. The Devil's hope is that temptation and trials will cause us to forsake God and despair. When the Devil met Jesus in the desert, he confronted Christ with both temptations and trials. He actively attempted to entice Jesus to sin. He utterly failed.

I think that Jesus' temptations provide a vital truth. Temptation is not sin. Jesus was tempted far more than any of us will ever be. While I won't state this with absolute certainty, you can not be tempted with something that doesn't appeal to you. Satan could wave a bowl of sauerkraut under my nose all day. It would never be a temptation because I can't stand the stuff. If Jesus was truly tempted *in every way*, it implies that Jesus was given the burden of desiring things we might find detestable. No matter the wickedness of the desire or temptation, Jesus did not sin. He remained spotless because he never allowed any of those temptations to threaten his obedience to God. While temptation is not sin, continuing to put ourselves in circumstances of temptation may be.

David prayed a prayer very similar to the first part of today's verse.

> *"Do not let my heart be drawn to what is evil*
> *so that I take part in wicked deeds*
> *along with those who are evildoers;*
> *do not let me eat their delicacies."* -- Psalms 141:4
> (NIV)

Fortunately, Jesus' prayer didn't end with our petition to God asking us to not be led into trials or temptation. Whether the draw to temptation or trials comes from the Accuser, from our own spiritual flaws, or with God's permission, Jesus' prayer doesn't end there. He continues with the solution to the danger and fear that

237

comes with temptation and trials. We should also ask God to *deliver us from evil*. Trials and temptation will come. God intends us to grow from those difficulties. His desire is to rescue us.

Whether it was Job's suffering, Jesus' crucifixion, the loss of a child, the death of a friend, God is not the source of that pain. However, He is the only one who can bring good out of it.

God does allow pain, suffering, injustice, and heartache. Man's natural tendency is to blame God for the horrors we experience and see around us. Yes, God could intervene and prevent every ill and injustice. For some reason, He doesn't. I won't provide some flimsy argument to explain why. I will only point to God's character. I believe that is most clearly modeled by Jesus.

You may interpret this passage and its underlying issue differently than I do. It does raise many difficult philosophical and spiritual questions. I only scratched the surface. I've deleted more than I've written on this topic. I encourage you to wrestle with this on your own. While trials and temptations play a role in God's plan for us, they are only a small part of that plan. Most often, when it comes to leading us, this is His desire:

> *"He leads me beside still waters. He restores my soul. He leads me in paths of righteousness for his name's sake."* -- Psalm 23: 1-4 (ESV)

I've talked to so many who struggle with pain and loss. Like most of us, they ask questions that I can't fully answer. Why does God allow pain and suffering? In an attempt to address this problem, I wrote a song called *The Strength to Go On*. Below is one of the verses.

"For all of you who question the goodness of God, remember He died for a world which was flawed and His love for you is so great that His own Son not sparing, expresses His caring."

Today's verse and challenge:

"No temptation has overtaken you except what is common to mankind. And God is faithful; he will not let you be tempted beyond what you can bear. But when you are tempted, he will also provide a way out so that you can endure it." -- I Corinthians 10:13 (NIV)

When we come into contact with hurting people, the last thing they need is for us to be like Job's friends. They don't need some pithy scripture verse or insincere promise to pray for them. They need us to listen to them. They need us to make ourselves available to be there to walk with them. For me, it's hard to not attempt to fix the problem, but these are problems only God and time can repair. Do genuinely pray for them, but show them you care by listening to them for indications for what they need. If others are there immediately, don't forget them when the crowds have forgotten. A true friend is far more helpful and healing than anything else.

Day Thirty-two: Treasures in Heaven

"Don't store up for yourselves treasures on earth, where moth and rust destroy and where thieves break in and steal. But store up for yourselves treasures in heaven, where neither moth nor rust destroys, and where thieves don't break in and steal. For where your treasure is, there your heart will be also." -- Matthew 6:19-21 (CSB)

The story goes that John D. Rockefeller was asked by a reporter, "How much money is enough?" Rockefeller is stated as responding, "Just a little bit more." At the time, Mr. Rockefeller's individual net worth was about 1% of the entire US economy. He owned 90% of all the oil and gas industry at the time. Today, Mr. Rockefeller can't purchase a single thing. His entire real estate holdings are the six feet of dirt that rest upon his dwelling.

David describes the poverty and foolishness of those who trust in wealth:

"Do not be overawed when others grow rich,

when the splendor of their houses increases;
for they will take nothing with them when they die,
their splendor will not descend with them." -- Psalm
49:16.17 (ESV)

The world has been mired in a pandemic that has made countless homeless and destitute in the last year. This only adds to what was already an epidemic of poverty. The Homelessness Research Institute estimates there is a current need of $11.5 billion to supply the additional beds needed solely for those rendered homeless by the pandemic. During that same period, Forbes and the Institute for Policy Studies Program on Inequality say that America's billionaires have increased their wealth by $1.2 to $1.8 trillion. There would be zero hesitancy to use that surplus to fund that need if our nation wasn't enslaved to runaway greed. Instead, the wealthy continue to push to pay less in taxes. You would think that the Church would be a driving force to request a more equitable system. Sadly, it is often one of the greatest opponents of economic equity. I am reminded that greed is an appetite that will never be satisfied.

"Greed is a bottomless pit which exhausts the person in an endless effort to satisfy the need without ever reaching satisfaction." -- Erich Fromm

This is nothing new. While humans have often shown significant generosity and selflessness, those with the most power tend to protect greed. They also are adept at teaching the masses that *Greed is good.* They falsely present it as a net positive for society. Tragically, some wrongly see possessions as an indicator of God's favor.

Jesus was aware of all of this. He lived in a time much like ours. The vast majority fell into the classification of impoverished. A small minority hoarded most of the resources, and some found themselves between the two extremes.

Jesus would have been familiar with this verse:

> *"Whoever loves money never has enough;*
> *whoever loves wealth is never satisfied with their*
> *income.*
> *This too is meaningless."* -- Ecclesiastes 5:10 (NIV)

Not many years after Jesus spoke these words, the Apostle Paul wrote:

> *"For the love of money is a root of all kinds of evil,*
> *and by craving it, some have wandered away from*
> *the faith and pierced themselves with many griefs."*
> -- I Timothy 6:10 (CSB)

Paul could have added that "they pierced others with even more grief." I'm amazed at how we seem to have rejected this warning. When Jesus found someone who had committed adultery, his response was calm compassion and forgiveness. When he encountered wealthy Pharisees, who ignored the troubles of the poor, he showed unrestrained contempt. When he found merchants cheating the poor, he turned over tables. Much of the Old Testament reflects God's love of the poor and command to enact just laws that reflect mercy.

Still, Jesus here is talking about more than economic injustice. That was of great concern to him, but he is pointing to an even more fundamental truth in this verse. The things we most value possess our hearts. We don't possess them.

Jesus begins by pointing to the fleeting value of this world's treasures. In the kingdom of man, the maxim is, "He who dies with the most toys wins." The economy of the kingdom of heaven turns this falsehood on its head. In God's kingdom, we are valued for our service to others rather than by satisfying our wants. Consider how the following verses contradict the economy of this world.

> *"Instead, whoever wants to become great among you must be your servant."* -- Matthew 20:26 (NIV)

> *"For whoever wants to save their life will lose it, but whoever loses their life for me will find it."* -- Matthew 16:25 (NIV)

Think, for a moment, of something that you desperately longed for years ago. As a young boy, I dreamed about owning a mini-bike. I would fantasize about riding one through our neighborhood. I would practically drool over catalogs that had pictures and details about them. If my desire for one of those toys had been met, I might have had some temporary fun, or I may have broken some bones. Undoubtedly, that vision of unbridled joy would have, long ago, been scrapped, rusted, and forgotten. I was too young to see that mini-bike as an idol back then, but I don't have that excuse today. Since then, countless idols have stolen my heart and distracted me from more important things. In nearly every instance, if I had possessed that item of affection, it would likely have only given me heartache. Even the longing for those things did nothing but rob me of more valuable loves.

Jesus is not saying that owning things is inherently wrong. He is saying that being owned by our possessions is dangerous. The more tightly we grip this material world, the more securely it binds us.

Earlier in my life, I experienced periods of poverty. As a child, I knew what it meant to be hungry. After college, I spent a brief time where I lived in my car. I remember living from paycheck to paycheck. A steady diet of Ramen noodles and frozen burritos was my idea of eating well. I haven't forgotten how a full-time job wasn't enough to support even the humblest of lifestyles. Today, my life is far different. My financial state is less uncertain. In both instances, love of the material was equally a temptation. When I was poor, it was easy to believe that money would solve all my problems. Today, it is easy to see money as my security. In both circumstances, the solution to my worries and trust in security can be misplaced. Yes, having few material needs seems freeing, but does wealth provide lasting freedom? Just as when Jesus spoke these words, external circumstances can drain our bank accounts. Living in a nation without universal health care means that a catastrophic illness can send any, except the obscenely wealthy, into bankruptcy. In fact, it does. Two-thirds of all bankruptcies in our country claim medical bills as the prime contributing factor. Whatever our economic success, only God's sovereignty provides lasting security.

244

Recently, we discussed the Hebrews wandering through the desert and how God provided for them daily. That taught the value of depending on God for provision each day. That doesn't mean that we should be irresponsible or unwise. God gives each of us talents and gifts. How we use those resources is an indication of our priorities, self-control, and wisdom.

> *"For which of you, wanting to build a tower, doesn't first sit down and calculate the cost to see if he has enough to complete it? Otherwise, after he has laid the foundation and cannot finish it, all the onlookers will begin to ridicule him, saying, 'This man started to build and wasn't able to finish.'"* -- Luke 14:28-30 (CSB)

Consider an immature and undisciplined young person. They often have limited discretionary income. Still, they may have a bit available that slips through their fingers. Instead of saving some of that and wisely investing it, they spend it on something that has little lasting value. In economic terms, the concept of delayed gratification is essential in investing. A mature follower of Jesus will develop the discipline to save for later. Apart from money, we each have strengths that are valuable to God's kingdom. If you have more time than money, consider how you can invest that time and energy to build the kingdom.

Whether we have economic need or excess, there are principles that we should honor. We should recognize that what we have is not ours. God has loaned all of our abilities, strengths, and possessions to us. They are not intended to serve our wants. God intends for us to use

245

them to further His kingdom. Within reason, we can enjoy the harvest He has provided, but we need to recognize that we are spending His money and gifts.

While Jesus warns us about the temporal nature of material things, he reminds us of possessions that will never fade, decay, or lose value. He reminds us to consider what our true loves are. In the following parable, Jesus shows us an important truth. Anything which has true and lasting value will require sacrifice.

> *"The kingdom of heaven is like treasure hidden in a field. When a man found it, he hid it again, and then in his joy went and sold all he had and bought that field.*
>
> *Again, the kingdom of heaven is like a merchant looking for fine pearls. When he found one of great value, he went away and sold everything he had and bought it."* -- Matthew 13:44-46 (NIV)

Yes, God's grace is offered to us freely, but we can never fully benefit from it until we recognize its value. Truth can never be ingested without real hunger for it.

Why should we sacrifice a thing of known value for an unknown? I have empirical evidence of the smile that a new car will bring. I only have faith that sacrificing something today will produce eternal rewards. Blaise Pascal posited an argument about this. It is known as *Pascal's Wager*. A much-simplified definition of it goes like this.

> "A rational person should live as though God exists and seek to believe in God. If God does not exist, such

a person will have only a finite loss (some pleasures, luxury, etc.), whereas if God does exist, he stands to receive infinite gains (as represented by eternity in Heaven) and avoid infinite losses (eternity in Hell)." -- Blaise Pascal, *Columbia History of Western Philosophy*, page 353

This concept is seen in Jesus' Parable of the Rich Fool.

> *"But God said to him, 'You fool! This very night your life is demanded of you. And the things you have prepared whose will they be?'*
> *That's how it is with the one who stores up treasure for himself and is not rich toward God."* -- Luke 12:20-21 (CSB)

While I agree with Pascal's argument, I don't think that Jesus was saying that the kingdom of heaven will only benefit us after death. I think he is acknowledging the benefits of the kingdom of heaven on this side of the grave as well. When he moves into his discussion of worry soon, I believe this is one of the benefits of having a right relationship to wealth.

Part of the future promise that Jesus gives is expressed in the following verse:

> *"Heaven and earth will pass away, but my words will never pass away."* -- Matthew 24:35 (CSB)

A return on investment by your stockbroker comes with no guarantees. Jesus promises dividends that we can trust.

In wrapping up this section, I want to briefly address

thoughts about the relationship between wealth and the Church. Throughout history, the Church has received justified criticism for her affection for material wealth. There have been times when the Church contributed significantly to showing love to our neighbor and promoting economic justice. Much of the Old Testament focused on justice for the poor, the hungry, and the refugee. Jesus regularly chastised the wealthy and showed an affinity for the poor. The early Church actually embraced a form of extreme socialism. Still, the verse I hear most often is:

> *"If anyone isn't willing to work, he should not eat."*
> *-- II Thessalonians 3:10 (CSB).*

God does not condone idleness, but most of those living in poverty in our nation are not idle. Many work multiple jobs and are still in poverty.

While Mother Teresa may have abandoned all earthly possessions to serve the poor, the Church that sent her is undoubtedly one of the world's wealthiest institutions. I used to attend a mega-church that was not far from the *Crystal Cathedral*. The church had many beautiful people. The sermons were good, and the people were friendly. It had a huge campus of buildings, with gyms, a book store, and a coffee shop. There's nothing inherently wrong with those things, but I wonder whether we really counted the cost. The church was in a middle to upper-class neighborhood. Still, you didn't have to drive far to find people who were homeless or living below the poverty level. In 1953, then-President Dwight Eisenhower gave a speech where he stated the following:

> "Every gun that is made, every warship launched, every rocket fired signifies, in the final sense, a theft from those who hunger and are not fed, those who are cold and are not clothed."

There may be some value to those warships. There may be some value to church coffee shops and gyms. Still, we must question whether these things are simply robbing the Church of a greater mission. In the American Church, it's estimated that only five percent of churchgoers actually tithe. When there are calls for the government to provide an adequate safety net for the millions of working poor, the refrain is often, "That's not the job of the government. That's the Church's job." That refrain is, at best, met with a flaccid response. If we can't even fully tithe we certainly aren't capable of doing what the government is eminently better equipped to do.

The American Church is wealthy. There's no doubt about that. Unfortunately, our nation is one of the most financially inequitable nations in the world. The top 20% own 86% of the nation's wealth. If the Church put all of its resources together, it's unlikely that we could erase all inequity. Still, we could make a significant impact in loving our neighbor and demonstrating the power of our faith. However, how should the world view the Church when we provide relatively little to those in need outside the Church walls? What should they think of us when the vast majority support political views that turn a cold shoulder to the poor being robbed and provide cover to those doing the robbing? Will they consider the gospel if they are told they are poor because they are lazy when most are not? Is the only way to get them to consider Jesus to lie to them and promise them financial prosperity if they give to some religious group?

One of the clearest indicators of the health of our faith is how we deal with money. This is true of individual believers, individual churches, and the universal Church. Churches typically receive tax-exempt status. The argument is that churches are good for society. If a required test had to be passed for a church to qualify, what do you think the result might be? If the people in the neighborhood around your church were asked if its presence was a clear positive for the community, what do you think the response might be? The world needs the Church to be salt and light in the arena of economics. I believe that Jesus demands it.

Today's verse and question:

> *"Therefore, put to death what belongs to your earthly nature: sexual immorality, impurity, lust, evil desire, and greed, which is idolatry."* -- Colossians 3:5 (CSB)

Yes, the Church should discourage immorality, but especially to those inside its walls. So, why do we focus so much on what we perceive as sexual immorality outside our community and then entirely ignore and sometimes even defend greed?

Day Thirty-three: Money

"The eye is the lamp of the body. If your eye is healthy, your whole body will be full of light. But if your eye is bad, your whole body will be full of darkness. So if the light within you is darkness, how deep is that darkness!

No one can serve two masters, since either he will hate one and love the other, or he will be devoted to one and despise the other. You cannot serve both God and money." -- Matthew 6:22-24 (CSB)

"The Pharisees, who were lovers of money, were listening to all these things and scoffing at him. And he told them, "You are the ones who justify yourselves in the sight of others, but God knows your hearts. For what is highly admired by people is revolting in God's sight." -- Luke 16:14-15 (CSB)

If you were a young person in the late 1960s, the teenagers you met might seem strange. They may have had long hair, wore bell-bottom pants, and said some things that seem odd today. They may have said that something was *far out* or *groovy*. In the 1980s, the teenagers may have said that something was *totally rad* or *tubular*. Today, if you hear someone say that something is *groovy*, it sounds odd and dated. Still, even the youngest today recognize that it's a compliment. The word originated from jazz slang in the 1930s. It originally meant that jazz players were *tight* and played as one, in the *groove*. By the 1960s, the word *groovy* meant that something was fashionable. Eventually, it simply meant that something was really good. Today, it's rarely used. The question is, what will people think the word means in a thousand years? By then, will the word have become so infrequently used that its original meaning will have been lost?

This illustrates one of the challenges in understanding scripture. Language is not static. Even if we have the original words, those words often include idioms that change. Combine that with a speaker like Jesus, who seemed to often use phrases and imagery with multiple possible meanings, and you are likely to have disagreements as to their meaning. Disagreements and discussions are helpful. Prohibiting valid interpretations is never good. In these following three verses, you find plenty of healthy debate. That debate is beneficial when it is driven by grounded insight and study.

In the three previous verses, Jesus addresses money. He compares earthly treasures' temporal and fleeting nature to the eternal treasures he wants us to seek. Now, he seems to give us whiplash in verses twenty-two and twenty-three before returning to the temptation of earthly wealth in twenty-four. Here, context is your first clue. Why would he talk about money for three verses, the eye being a lamp, and then return to money? One possibility is that he isn't changing the subject.

In verses twenty-two and twenty-three, Jesus presents this odd-sounding picture of the eye as a lamp. He compares two different pictures of the light from the lamp. A strict rendering of the Greek is not particularly helpful.

"The lamp (*Lychnos*) of the body is the eye. If therefore the eye of you is clear (*haplous*), whole body of you full of light will be."

The Yoda-like Greek paints a strange picture. It seems evident that Jesus is using some sort of metaphor here. Numerous scriptures use the body to illustrate some spiritual concept -- I Corinthians 12, Ephesians 4. I think the critical words here are *lychnos* and *haplous*. *Lychnos* means *lamp*. Many interpret this verse as a warning to not consume unwholesome things. While that is true (to a point), that is not the purpose of a lamp. A lamp is focused outward, not inward. It does inform us of the world, but it also emanates from us. Jesus often used the symbolism of light, and it was typically an outward carrier of the kingdom. The word *haplous* has been translated in numerous ways. It can mean clear, sound, simple, uncomplicated, singleness of purpose, generous, or healthy. When used with the word for *eye*, it can be translated as *good-eye*.

Jesus is drawing a comparison between the eye and a

253

person's spiritual health. However, that comparison isn't particularly clear. This has resulted in several different interpretations. Many see this as a statement about the importance of developing a godly worldview. How we see the world affects our loves, motivations, and actions. This may have been what Jesus was saying, but that seems to stray from the topic of money. Another view is that haplous means single-minded or single-eyed. Perhaps Jesus was saying we should be single-focused on pursuing God's kingdom and kingdom principles. There is some context support for this view because, in the following verse, he talks about the folly of serving two masters. The concept of being single-focused would tie to that. Another interpretation that seems to fit the context and idiom focuses on the meaning of the *good-eye* and the *evil-eye*. It appears that in Jewish culture, even to this day, there is the use of the term *good-eye* to mean generous and *evil-eye* to mean stingy. In the context of money, this last interpretation makes the most sense to me. Jesus is telling those listening that they should seek eternal treasures. In the context of this, he may be saying, "the thing which most demonstrates your spiritual health is to be generous. A stingy person is far from the kingdom." Scripture is clear that much, if not most, sin springs from the love of money.

> *"For the love of money is a root of all kinds of evil, and by craving it, some have wandered away from the faith and pierced themselves with many griefs."*
> -- I Timothy 6:10 (CSB)

I suspect that Jesus meant at least two things with this metaphor about light and the eye. He may have been telling us that we should love God and neighbor more than possessions. Additionally, we should have a single-minded focus on developing a worldview based on the kingdom of God instead of the kingdom of man.

He emphasizes both in verse twenty-four. Bob Dylan famously sang about this in his song, *Gotta Serve Somebody*. In the song, Dylan makes plain the truth that we all serve someone. Some may serve power and money. Others may serve pleasure and comfort. Others may serve political and cultural values. Still, some may serve God. Ultimately, the only question is who we will serve, not whether we will serve.

If you've ever worked in a job where you had more than one supervisor, and they disagreed, you know that it is impossible to have more than one master. Jesus tells us that you can't serve both God and money. The word translated money is *Mamona* or *Mammon*. *Mamona* was an Aramaic word that meant riches. It likely derives from the concept of *something that one trusts*. While Jesus was explicitly addressing money and treasures, Mammon can be any idol that we treasure.

I dare say that even the godliest among us have struggled with idols. For some, it's the golden calf of materialism and an over-reliance on ensuring our security. For others, it's an overwhelming desire to be liked, an unchecked ego, or any number of other false and unfaithful loves. When we try to love God but expect Him to compete with those idols, we are the ones who lose. God won't participate in that sort of competition. The Bible is replete with stories of idols. It's also full of stories of the sadness and pain they bring on us. I think the story of Judas is one of the most powerful illustrations of this.

Most people view Judas as pure evil, but I think they get it wrong. I think the reality was far more complex. People have speculated about Judas' motivation in handing over Jesus. Scripture suggests that greed and demonic influence may have been what prompted Judas. It also records that Judas repented of his action. I suspect that Judas loved some version of Jesus. He followed Jesus for three years. It was not a life of luxury, ease, respect, influence, or power that attached him to the other eleven. There must have been some genuine affection there and admiration for much of what Jesus taught. Sadly, Judas had some idol competing with Jesus for his affection. Perhaps Judas wanted something from Jesus that wasn't part of Jesus' mission. Maybe he was angry that Jesus didn't lead a populist revolution. Maybe he was upset about his poverty while the Pharisees were wealthy. Jesus wanted to do God's will. Judas thought that he knew better. Judas was engaged in a battle between the kingdom of God and the kingdom of man. If Judas thought that he could coerce Jesus into fighting for both, he was wrong. Judas didn't understand either kingdom. His love for the kingdom of God and Jesus were sacrificed to his love of the kingdom of man. That split allegiance was his undoing.

Today's thought and challenge:

Judas was not unique. Today, the world is full of potential Judases. Daily, we are confronted with the choice of following Jesus or something else. All too often, we choose a different master. We may demonstrate our spiritual weakness by being stingy. We may opt for judgment over grace. We may allow tribal propaganda to overwhelm our commitment to truth. Perhaps we permit our cultural, racial, political, or ideological worldview to corrupt Jesus' image. Whenever we do this, we are following in Judas' footsteps. This doesn't damn us as evil, but we should be wary. When we serve a different master, the result is never good. Jesus will never be a cheerleader for our culture wars, ethnic identity, political, or economic class. We simply reveal our idols when we attempt to kidnap Jesus and conscript him into our ideological conflicts. He will never defend our love of power, money, or privilege. Following Judas' folly will produce nothing but shame and loss. Tragically, it also harms our mission to live out the gospel. It destroys our ability to be salt and light. Search for the real Jesus. Love your neighbor and God generously. Take some time and ask God to search your heart. In what ways have you transformed your image of Jesus to coexist with your earthly treasures?

"Your word is a lamp for my feet, a light on my path." -- Psalm 119:105 (ESV)

Day Thirty-four: Worry

"Therefore I tell you: Don't worry about your life, what you will eat or what you will drink; or about your body, what you will wear. Isn't life more than food and the body more than clothing? Consider the birds of the sky: They don't sow or reap or gather into barns, yet your heavenly Father feeds them. Aren't you worth more than they? Can any of you add one moment to his life span by worrying? And why do you worry about clothes? Observe how the wildflowers of the field grow: They don't labor or spin thread. Yet I tell you that not even Solomon in all his splendor was adorned like one of these. If that's how God clothes the grass of the field, which is here today and thrown into the furnace tomorrow, won't he do much more for you — you of little faith? So don't worry, saying, 'What will we eat?' or 'What will we drink?' or 'What will we wear?' For the Gentiles eagerly seek all these things, and your heavenly Father knows that you need them. But seek first the kingdom of God and his righteousness, and all these things will be provided for you. Therefore don't worry about

tomorrow, because tomorrow will worry about itself. Each day has enough trouble of its own." -- Matthew 6:25-34 (CSB)

Throughout much of Jesus' sermon, he has addressed the relationship between money and faith. He has shown how greed is like a cancer that will stunt our spiritual growth. He's reminded us that earthly treasures are not a foundation that we can trust. He has warned us that when we seek earthly treasures, they can become another god competing for our soul. Up to this point, he has mostly pointed out the potential evil associated with consumption, greed, and selfishness. He has addressed how excess is not what God desires for us. His use of *therefore* connects what he is about to say with what he has just said. Now, he points to a more challenging aspect of our relationship with money. Not only can we become obsessed with getting more and more, but we can also be consumed with how we will meet our most basic needs. We can wrongly look to money to provide future security. It's one thing to take advantage of others to purchase a yacht. God clearly detests that. What about when we have difficulty sleeping because we aren't sure how we will pay this month's rent? That is an understandable human response to insecurity. I believe that God recognizes that.

Everyone worries because lack is a sad reality. So, what is so wrong with worry? As a young man, I didn't live what most would call a fast life. I was never a party animal. While I couldn't have been described as a thrill-seeker, I did enjoy driving fast. There was an amusement center near where I lived that had scaled-down models of Formula One race cars. I don't really know how fast they were, but they felt fast. They were low to the ground and accelerated quickly. I would go there on weekend nights, put on a helmet, and try to live out the famous movie line, "I feel the need... the need for speed." I would go as fast as I could and avoid the brakes like they were a snake. No matter how much I skidded or spun, I never felt fear. It just made me feel alive and happy. However, put this wannabe speed junkie in the passenger seat of a Honda Civic with a driver I don't know well, and I'm stepping on my imaginary brake and clinging to the door handle. So, why was I fearless in the first situation but shaking in the second? I trusted my own ability to drive, but I didn't trust the other person's ability to drive. That is at the heart of all worry. Worry represents a lack of trust.

Like my need for speed, I find it easy to trust my own ability to provide my daily bread. I don't always fully trust God's willingness and ability to provide it. How many times has God been *behind the wheel*, and I'm stomping on my imaginary brakes and asking Him to move over?

This section of verses is not particularly difficult to understand. There is little doubt about what Jesus is saying. We should not worry about having our needs met because worrying won't help. Worrying simply demonstrates a lack of faith in God's care. Worry makes it impossible to focus on anything else. It isn't productive. The challenge here is applying it and how seriously we take his command to not be anxious.

There is a difference between worry and wisely considering our decisions and learning from our mistakes. If you go to Vegas and lose your shirt by gambling, worrying won't help. However, wisely learning from your mistake and not repeating it is something a person of faith should do.

There's no prosperity gospel message in what Jesus is saying. He is not talking about worrying whether we'll get the latest toy or fancy house. That should not be a concern in the first place. As followers of Jesus, we should live lives of simplicity. Jesus makes no promise that we should trust God for our excess. Excess is most often a hindrance to our faith. Here, Jesus is saying we should not even worry about our most basic needs.

Jesus isn't telling us to not apply wisdom or to be poor stewards of our skills and assets. He isn't telling us to be foolish or lazy because God will fix it. If you look at his analogy of the birds, they seem pretty busy. Birds don't simply sit in their nests, mouth open, waiting for God to feed them. God has set in motion a world that can provide for our basic needs with proper stewardship. Still, those needs are only met with specific requirements. The birds must go out and get the worm. The worm rarely goes to the bird.

What sort of anxiety was Jesus warning us to avoid? It's understandable and even prudent to consider how we will pay our bills. He is warning against a form of worry that debilitates us and occupies our every waking thought. I have, at times, struggled with panic attacks. They seem to have no logical foundation. If I am set to get an MRI, I will likely experience mind-numbing terror. When I am in the grip of that fear, I am incapable of thinking about anything else. The fear subdues and overwhelms everything. That sort of fear is unconscious. However, I don't think Jesus is talking about our natural fight or flight response. God has programmed that for our defense. However, I believe it points to the reality that holding on to fear, anxiety, and worry prevents us from moving forward or acting productively. To be wary of danger is wise and biblical. To allow fear or worry to control us reflects a lack of trust in God. Jesus told his disciples to be wary.

> *"I am sending you out like sheep among wolves. Therefore be as shrewd as snakes and as innocent as doves. Be on your guard;"* -- Matthew 10:16,17a (NIV)

The word there defined as shrewd means to be wise, prudent, intelligent, or wary. In Jesus' command for us to not worry, he is not asking us to be careless. Trusting in God's sovereignty is not a license to be foolish. We should trust God for our health, wealth, and family, but we should not test Him by acting without wisdom:

> *"Do not test the Lord your God as you tested him at Massah."* -- Deuteronomy 6:16 (CSB)

There is a tension between blind, passive trust in God and prudent wisdom that prompts action. I think this tension is expressed in the story of Gideon, which we read in the Book of Judges, chapter seven.

There, we see that Israel finds itself in a difficult spot. God had given the land to Israel, but there is a repeating pattern. God delivers Israel. Eventually, Israel rejects the one true God and goes after some false god. This results in Israel being overwhelmed and the victim of injustice and hardship. In each case, Israel repents, is delivered, and the cycle repeats. In this cycle, Israel is being abused by the Midianites. Midian was one of Abraham's sons. Sadly, his descendants had long since abandoned Abraham's faith and were now enemies of Israel. God raises up Gideon to defeat the Midianites. In this, Gideon can follow one of two extremes. He can raise an army of sufficient size to guarantee victory over the Midianites, or he can simply pray and wait on God to get rid of the Midianites. God commands Gideon to follow a third path. In chapter seven, we read that the Midianites had an army of overwhelming numbers. Gideon gathers his own army of some 32,000 Israelites. This is how I tend to respond to things that worry me. I look for a way to use my own resources to resolve the problem. God tells Gideon that he has too many soldiers. He warns Gideon that Israel would not see God's hand in delivering them if he keeps that number. Through different tests, God reduces the number of soldiers in Gideon's army from 32,000 to three hundred. God doesn't tell Gideon to do nothing. He does tell Gideon to take action but also to allow sufficient room for God to deliver.

What can we learn from this story? First, we see that it's not uncommon that the things that worry us are due to our own poor choices. Israel would not have had to worry about the Midianites if Israel had not worshiped false gods. Second, we see that when we encounter difficulties that threaten us, we can't simply be idle and do nothing. We can't sit in our homes and be filled with worry and dread over our circumstances. Instead, our actions must be in partnership with our Creator. Our efforts must demonstrate our trust in Him. As in most things, there is a wise balance that we should seek. Third, if God delivers us from our worry-producing circumstances, we should consider if poor decisions created the issue. If they did, we should learn from our mistakes.

Elsewhere, we see Jesus going to be with his friends Mary and Martha. This would have been a special time. In the story, we see Mary sitting with Jesus and enjoying his company. Meanwhile, Martha is in the kitchen working to prepare a meal. Martha is upset that Mary isn't helping. Jesus tells Martha:

> *"The Lord answered her,"Martha, Martha, you are worried and upset about many things, but one thing is necessary. Mary has made the right choice, and it will not be taken away from her."* -- Luke 10:41-42 (CSB)

Here, the word translated worried is from the Greek *merimnate*, which is a form of the same word Jesus uses when telling us not to worry. I think I understand where Martha was coming from. I have many friends from that part of the world. In Middle Eastern culture, hospitality plays a much more significant role than we see in most of American culture. I have often visited Muslim friends. Regardless of the time of day, they will go into the kitchen and prepare a full meal for me, even if my visit was spontaneous. This seems to be a universal value for them and one that is likely profoundly ingrained. Martha was doing what she felt she had to do. She was worried that she would be a bad hostess. Martha was upset that Mary didn't share in that worry. Jesus isn't telling Martha that she should not care about making him feel welcome. He isn't suggesting that Mary should not help. He's recognizing it was more important that Mary needed to be with him. I have often asked my Muslim friends to just sit and talk instead of disappearing into the kitchen. Martha was worried about something that didn't matter to Jesus.

I find that I am guilty of this. I don't only worry about genuinely serious things. I can easily obsess over things with little to no consequence. I can magnify their importance. How often is God telling me that I'm worried about many things, but most are not needed? I think that's a point to consider when we are anxious. Is this thing essential? If the worst was to happen, would it truly be that bad?

Jesus promises us that he is the most trustworthy source of peace and freedom from worry.

"Peace I leave with you. My peace I give to you. I do not give to you as the world gives. Don't let your

heart be troubled or fearful." -- John 14:27 (CSB)

Paul reminds us that God promises us peace, and he gives us the steps for finding peace.

> *"Do not be anxious about anything, but in every situation, by prayer and petition, with thanksgiving, present your requests to God. And the peace of God, which transcends all understanding, will guard your hearts and your minds in Christ Jesus."* -- Philippians 4:6-7 (NIV)

Note that Paul doesn't say, "present your requests to God, and He will fulfill your shopping list." The promise here is that God will give you peace in the moment. Jesus continues. He points out that how we deal with money and worry demonstrates what our priorities are. We can think about what we need to eat, but that should always be secondary to our focus on the kingdom.

> *"But seek first the kingdom of God and his righteousness, and all these things will be provided for you."* -- Matthew 6:33 (CSB)

When we place other things ahead of seeking the kingdom of God, we virtually ensure that we will encounter worry. We can have complete confidence in an eventual future where God's kingdom will come to pass. We can have no such faith in anything else. When Jesus says, "*Is not life more than food,*" he is reminding us to not sacrifice the eternal as we struggle for the temporal.

In the 1986 movie *The Mission*, we find Rodrigo, played by actor Robert DeNiro. Rodrigo is a cruel soldier and slave trader. He has come to South America to capture indigenous natives to sell into slavery. When the power of the gospel calls Rodrigo, he feels compelled to perform an act of penance for the wrongs he has done. Tying together the weapons and armor he had used to enslave and harm others, he struggles to carry the burden up a steep, rocky, and treacherous cliff. In a moving scene, Rodrigo arrives at the summit, where he is met by the native tribe, which he had previously attempted to enslave. A tribesman pulls out a knife and wrestles with the choice of killing or freeing the man who had abused his people. He cuts the burden from Rodrigo and casts it away. The joy of that scene is infectious. It frees not only Rodrigo but also the tribesman. Enemies become friends.

Worry is much like guilt. It blinds, binds, and bends us into grim caricatures of the creations that God intends. Be prudent and wise, but Jesus wants to free us of what binds us.

Today's thought and challenge:

God doesn't want us to worry. Pull out a sheet of paper and make a list of things that worry you. Those worries can be monetary, relational, or any challenge or concern.

First, consider whether the concern is an actual need or simply a desire. God will never grant a desire if it threatens an essential need.

Second, ask God to reveal what concrete actions you can take to resolve the issue. Consider seeking counsel from others on this. Make a plan to accomplish those steps.

Third, write the worry on a piece of paper and hand it over to God. Ask Him, in faith, to take control over it. Trust Him to guide and direct you. Remember that you have placed it in God's hands if you find yourself worrying about that issue. If you have taken wise and concrete steps and placed your trust in God's provision, there is no reason to continue worrying.

At that point, worry will simply impede your ability to move forward. If you find that you are still worrying, give yourself a break. God knows that you are human. Don't condemn yourself. Take the issue back to God and ask for His help. Consider the times when God has previously shown you that He can be trusted and rest in that.

Additional points on this topic:

I think that it would be irresponsible and dishonest to not address an additional reality. While God does work miraculously to answer prayer, that isn't always His plan. Yes, Jesus tells us to not worry. He tells us that God is aware of our needs. Still, what do we do with the reality that millions today won't have their needs met? Every day, untold numbers of children, parents and those without families will starve. They will exist without shelter, medical care, education, freedom, or many other basic necessities. The vast majority do not suffer because of poor choices or laziness. The mere reality of where they were born, the color of their skin, nationality, or family practically ensures that they will struggle to meet even their most basic needs.

Jesus doesn't say that every need will be met. He says that God knows what our needs are. Consider also that Jesus was speaking this in a society that was commanded to care for the poor. Consider his birds of the air picture. Young birds are incapable of going to gather food. While they are incapable, the capable parents provide for them. Much of scripture addresses our responsibility to stand in the gap for those who need help. It is one of the most common topics in all of scripture. What does the bible say about poverty and our response to this common source of worry?

> *"When you are harvesting in your field and you overlook a sheaf, do not go back to get it. Leave it for the foreigner, the fatherless and the widow, so that the LORD your God may bless you in all the work of your hands."* -- Deuteronomy 24:19 (NIV)

God gives us an essential principle that His provision for us is not license to be selfish or obscenely wealthy, certainly not at the expense of others. While rich farmers could have squeezed every last penny out of their fields, God prohibits them from doing that. He commands them to give a portion to the poor.

> *"At the end of every seven years you must cancel debts."* -- Deuteronomy 15:1 (NIV)

In Deuteronomy chapter fifteen, we read about the

concept of the year of Jubilee. While there is some disagreement about what it means, this verse seems to make it clear that unending debt is not part of God's plan. Usury is the act of loaning at high interest. All too often, we have been utterly silent or even standing with those who promote usury, which is clearly prohibited in scripture -- Exodus 22:25; Leviticus 25:36,37.

I recently read about a couple who started with a combined student loan debt of $54,000. Over the past 24 years, they have paid $140,000 toward that debt. They still owe $130,000. This is because of ungodly and greedy laws, passed largely by conservative politicians (who often appeal to Christian values.) These laws allow financial institutions to take advantage of ill-equipped young people. They permit immorally high-interest loans and a prohibition against student bankruptcy. Combine that with the reality that schools are not required to disclose career realities to students and they have no route to escape poverty. This has resulted in $1.3 trillion dollars in student debt in America. I believe there are more verses condemning usury than homosexuality. Still, I can't remember a single criticism or protest with Christians carrying signs condemning unjust lending practices.

In nearly every case, systemic injustice plays a significant role in the lives of children living in poverty. God tells us that we are to respond to the poor with generosity.

"There will always be poor people in the land.
Therefore I command you to be openhanded toward

your fellow Israelites who are poor and needy in your land." -- Deuteronomy 15:11 (NIV)

The problem of widespread poverty, injustice, hunger, and lack is persistent. There has always been poverty, and scripture demonstrates God's heart on the issue. God knows our needs. He also sees our greed. Faithful followers of Jesus should not respond with silence and inaction. When we promote political policies that add to that injustice, I can not think that God is pleased.

> *"Do not pervert justice; do not show partiality to the poor or favoritism to the great, but judge your neighbor fairly."* -- Leviticus 19:15 (ESV)

> *"Away with the noise of your songs!*
> *I will not listen to the music of your harps.*
> *But let justice roll on like a river,*
> *righteousness like a never-failing stream!"* -- Amos 5:23,24 (ESV)

When we gather to worship God, it should be to give Him what gives Him joy. The purpose is not to make us feel ecstatic. I believe that God cares more that we love the poor and mistreated. Yes, God is aware of our needs, but He has devised a system to make sure that those needs are met. He expects us to be a part of the solution. In our nation, people of faith only have three options.

First, we can give sacrificially. However, to meet even the most basic of those needs, we would have to give exponentially more than we do currently. I don't see us doing this to the degree that makes a significant

271

difference.

The second option would be for us to promote political and social policies that meet those needs. That would require us to change how we interact with political power. Whether we like it or not, the Government is currently best equipped to address widespread poverty and injustice. At this point, this approach is anathema to much of the Church.

The final option is to ignore the issue, blame the poor, and embrace the powerful. All too often, I see us doing the third, which should be unthinkable for followers of Jesus.

> "I was a stranger and you did not invite me in, I needed clothes and you did not clothe me, I was sick and in prison and you did not look after me." -- Matthew 25:43 (NIV)

The way we treat the poor, in regards to meeting their most basic needs, is a direct reflection of our love of God. God does not call us to worry about meeting our own needs. I do think that we should be concerned if our response to the needs of others is heartless. Do you want to show the world the reality of your love for God? Putting a bumper sticker on your car, demanding public prayer, and promoting conservative or liberal causes may make us feel godly but it does nothing to show the world our love of God. If you truly want the world to see your love of God, take concrete steps to love your neighbor. Love the poor, the immigrant, the disenfranchised, and those treated unjustly. If we don't do that those bumper stickers mean nothing.

Day Thirty-five: Search My Heart

" Search me, God, and know my heart;
test me and know my concerns.
See if there is any offensive way in me;
lead me in the everlasting way." -- Psalms 139:23-24
(CSB)

As we come to the end of Matthew chapter six, I want to stop and give us a moment to reflect and ask God to speak directly to us. We all think that we are the *good guys*. There's a joke from a comedy team, where two Nazi soldiers are sitting around a fire, and one notices a skull on their uniforms. He asks the other, "Are we the baddies?" It's hilarious but also tragic because so few ever ask themselves that question. While repentance is foundational to our faith, many in the Church only see others' need for it.

So, if so few recognize their need for repentance, if very few question their personal priorities, values, and outlook on life, why is the world in such a mess? If our opinion of ourselves was accurate, shouldn't the world be a kinder, gentler place?

It doesn't take a prophetic gifting to see that things are terribly broken in our world and seem to be progressively deteriorating. We can't deny that there are two paradoxical views- that everyone thinks they are good, and the world is full of evil thinking and behavior. Both viewpoints can't be correct. I think we all need to acknowledge that there is a destructive force at work in each of us.

I am no exception to this. Before I point the finger of judgment at someone else, I am fully aware that four more are pointing back at me. I recognize my failings and the harm that I have done to myself and others over six decades of life. This is despite my sincere desire to live a just, kind, and Christlike life. Sometimes, I have done this intentionally. Typically, it was because I acted rashly and without maturity.

Still, I learned long ago a core tenet of my faith:

> *"If we confess our sins, he is faithful and righteous to forgive us our sins and to cleanse us from all unrighteousness."* -- I John 1:9 (CSB)

From the early days of my journey with God, I recognized the importance of asking God to search my heart and help me acknowledge and correct my flaws. Part of my desire to be transparent and honest with myself is recognizing that God already knows my shortcomings. I can hide nothing from Him. Still, before we can connect with God, we must own up to our failings.

"Go and learn what this means: I desire mercy and not sacrifice. For I didn't come to call the righteous, but sinners." -- Matthew 9:13 (CSB)

When we only see ourselves as righteous, what do we leave for Jesus to do in our lives? He comes to us only when we recognize our need for him and our frailty and propensity toward selfishness.

Over the decades of my faith, I have often gone to a brother and asked for forgiveness. The reverse has rarely occurred. I genuinely try to be kind and respectful, but there have been times when my tongue took off before my brain or spirit was in gear. In the times when I realize it, I try to make it right. It has been harder when someone else accuses me of saying something unkind and unloving, and I honestly disagree with their assessment. I try to make things right, but it's not always possible to avoid conflict or hurt feelings.

This may be one of those times. If I am honest and listen to God's call in my life, I feel compelled to offer criticism I believe to be truthful. I don't criticize those I disregard. I don't plead for change or repentance from those who I believe are beyond redemption. Criticism of one thing doesn't negate other positives that we should acknowledge. However, this study of Jesus' sermon addresses an audience quite similar to today. This includes the American Church. It's prudent to point it out and pray that it is received and considered openly and with grace.

Today, we see far too many who hold positions of religious influence, who rarely reflect the same values that Jesus embraced. Are they listening for God's still, small voice -- I Kings 19:12? Like the Pharisees, they seem more focused on retaining social stature, attaining political influence, defending their culture, increasing their economic holdings, and wielding power. They sprinkle in *Christian* vocabulary and use Jesus' name but I wonder if building the kingdom of heaven is their objective. I don't think so. While they proclaim a Creator of earthquake or whirlwind, Jesus spoke, as God did to Elijah, in a still small voice. They speak of honoring God by enforcing their personal religious rules on others. They pick and choose scripture in a way that supports their personal interests without actually knowing God. They quote:

" What should I bring before the Lord
when I come to bow before God on high?
Should I come before him with burnt offerings,
with year-old calves?" -- Micah 6:6 (CSB)

But they ignore that burnt offerings, or posting the Ten Commandments on Public Property, are not what God wants. Two verses later, God says what He wants:

"He has shown you, O mortal, what is good.
And what does the LORD require of you?
To act justly and to love mercy
and to walk humbly with your God." -- Micah 6:8 (NIV)

Like the Pharisees, far too many of today's religious

leaders not only fail to promote justice, display mercy, and embrace humility, they seemingly oppose those things. Like the Pharisees, they seem to despise justice. They embrace or fabricate half-truths and lies and promote political and social agendas which foster injustice. Instead of embracing mercy, they seemingly rejoice in the pain and hardship of those they see as sinners. Rather than loving the world that God "*so loved*," they portray the entirety of those outside as either a threat to be opposed or a resource to be tapped. They often portray humility as weakness. They promote and raise leaders who never question themselves, much less ask the complex and soul-searching questions that genuine faith requires.

Of course, not all Pharisees were stone dead in their faith. Still, Nicodemus and Joseph of Arimathea seemed to be the exception and not the most influential. Today, some religious leaders listen for God's still small voice. They authentically question whether they are embracing and promoting the values of Micah, chapter six, verse eight. We can't paint the entire Church community with that broad brush, but neither can we ignore the fact that the portraits of the Pharisees and many of today religious influencers and followers are strikingly similar.

Jesus's message to the Pharisees on that hillside rings true for the many who corrupt our faith today. His *you have heard it said, but I tell you* antitheses seem to be pointed at them- all those years ago and today. Just as the influential religious leaders, in Jesus' day, had

278

misinterpreted, misled, and harmed God's message and attacked those who questioned, they often do much the same today. Few of the Pharisees had hearts soft enough to receive Jesus' message. I pray that today's *wolves in sheep's clothing* will reject their traditions, take a step back, and listen to Jesus' words. Jesus' accusation of their being vipers and potential food for the devil was not addressed only to those on that hillside.

"Be on your guard against false prophets who come to you in sheep's clothing but inwardly are ravaging wolves." -- Matthew 7:15 (CSB)

Today, our world is troubled with many of the same vexations that those on that hillside experienced. Irrational, sometimes violent, and unrighteous political extremism is just as common. Like the Pharisees, they tell us to fear *those people*; those from other cultures, those with different beliefs, those with different political opinions, those outside our community, and those they don't understand. Instead of spreading the great news of the gospel, which demands we go outward, they call us to turn inward, be disconnected, and even adversarial.

Of greater significance is how few, in the wider Christian community, push back. It's concerning that so few ask questions or point to how far we have strayed from Jesus' commission to "*go, and make disciples*" -- Matthew 28:19,20. Consider the bracelet that many wore a few decades ago- *What Would Jesus Do?* How much of what characterizes the wider American Church today reflects Jesus? While none of us are perfect, where does the concept of genuine repentance fit into the life of the Church today?

A commonly repeated verse, often shared a few years back, was:

> *"and my people, who bear my name, humble themselves, pray and seek my face, and turn from their evil ways, then I will hear from heaven, forgive their sin, and heal their land."* -- II Chronicles 7:14 (CSB)

I've attended numerous prayer meetings and rallies where the preacher would reference this verse. He would say something to the effect that *America must return to God.* I could almost audibly hear God say, "You first!" This verse was not addressed to the citizens of a secular, non-sectarian nation. When King Solomon said this, he wasn't standing in Greece or Egypt. He wasn't in Babylon or Assyria. Solomon wasn't addressing a secular crowd or the non-believer. He was explicitly addressing believers at the dedication of the Temple.

This call to humility and repentance was addressed to the Church then, and it is today. Often, when calls within the Church point out her desperate need to change, it is met with claims that the person is critical, negative, hostile, or divisive. Perhaps, that is true, at times, but what was the response to Peter, when he wrote the following to a group of exiled believers:

> *"For the time has come for judgment to begin with*

God's household, and if it begins with us, what will the outcome be for those who disobey the gospel of God?" -- I Peter 4:17 (CSB)

Another verse is often used in calling non-believers to faith in Jesus. It says:

"See! I stand at the door and knock. If anyone hears my voice and opens the door, I will come in to him and eat with him, and he with me." -- Revelation 3:20 (CSB)

The problem with how this verse has been used in evangelism is that it is not addressing those outside the faith. It is addressing us. Jesus is knocking at the door of the Church. The question is whether we will let him in. In large parts of the American Church, he doesn't appear to be welcome. It's undeniable that in many churches and movements his teachings are no longer embraced.

Suppose we want the nation to recognize the extraordinary grace, love, and joy that God offers them. In that case, it's fair to ask whether we are communicating it the best way and whether it's truly at the core of our identity. It's critical that we, as a body of believers, look at ourselves first. I think that Jesus was pointing to this with his list of antitheses. Jesus challenged his audience to put aside what they had been taught and pointed them toward a radically different path. He did it then, and I believe he is doing it today.

Today's prayer:

Lord Jesus,

I have been told what it means to honor God and live in this world, but perhaps, some of that was incorrect. Others have offered examples of their belief of how a godly person should think and behave. I should indeed honor and respect those who have taught me, but only you have the words of life. Only you have authority in this. Help me put aside beliefs, thoughts, values, and loves that don't reflect your nature. Even if it puts me at odds with those I love, set my feet on a path that follows you, where you direct my faith. Lead me to genuine and honest repentance, and change.

Day Thirty-six: Judgment

"Do not judge, so that you won't be judged.

For you will be judged by the same standard with which you judge others, and you will be measured by the same measure you use. Why do you look at the splinter in your brother's eye but don't notice the beam of wood in your own eye? Or how can you say to your brother, 'Let me take the splinter out of your eye,' and look, there's a beam of wood in your own eye? Hypocrite! First take the beam of wood out of your eye, and then you will see clearly to take the splinter out of your brother's eye. Don't give what is holy to dogs or toss your pearls before pigs, or they will trample them under their feet, turn, and tear you to pieces." -- Matthew 7:1-6 (CSB)

"Be on your guard against false prophets who come to you in sheep's clothing but inwardly are ravaging wolves. You'll recognize them by their fruit. Are grapes gathered from thornbushes or figs from thistles? In the same way, every good tree produces good fruit, but a bad tree produces bad fruit. A good tree can't produce bad fruit; neither

can a bad tree produce good fruit. Every tree that doesn't produce good fruit is cut down and thrown into the fire. So you'll recognize them by their fruit."
-- Matthew 7:15-20 (CSB)

This first section of Matthew seven, regarding judgment, is complex. I believe that it is often misunderstood and poorly applied. Like much of what Jesus said, I think the key to understanding it is to have Christ's heart and the Spirit's wisdom. In application, it requires balance and humility.

I'd like to draw some analogies from J.R.R. Tolkien's epic, *The Lord of the Rings.* If you aren't familiar with the story, I encourage you to read the books or watch the movies. In the story, you find various characters. While they aren't meant to be intentional metaphors, we can see aspects of metaphor in them. We find the wizard and Christ figure Gandalf is speaking with Frodo. Gandalf has called Frodo to embark on a dangerous and challenging journey. This adventure will require tremendous courage and wisdom. Frodo quickly realizes that he will come face to face with evil. Added to this, Gandalf tells Frodo about Gollum. Frodo, a young, innocent hobbit, is upset that Gollum is even around since his uncle, Bilbo, had the opportunity to kill him. Gollum is a horrid creature. Gollum was once very much like Frodo. Now he is a mere shadow of his former self, more at home in the dark than in the light. Understandably, Frodo wants to be rid of him.

Frodo expresses his frustration that Bilbo didn't kill someone that he solely views as vile, dangerous, and without value. Gandalf reminds Frodo of the value of

284

pity, of our limited qualifications to enact judgment, and that we are unable to foresee the future.

Both Frodo and Gandalf recognized that Gollum had become deeply corrupted by the Ring. The Ring was an instrument of corrupting power. Their discernment of the depth of Gollum's brokenness was eventually proven to be accurate. This part of the story teaches us a few things. First, there is a significant difference between discernment and condemnation. Second, even those who are broken often serve an essential role in moving our story forward. Third, even beautiful, gentle hobbits can become corrupted by power and pervasive lies.

Frodo and Gandalf wisely took note of the evidence of Gollum's brokenness and treachery. They didn't ignore it. They didn't encourage it. They never portrayed him as someone worthy of following. They held him responsible and warned others about him. They were honest with Gollum about the danger he was in. What they didn't do was wish him into the fires of Mount Doom. They didn't kill him. Frodo genuinely seemed to hold out hope that Gollum would change.

Of all of the things that Jesus says in this sermon, this section is the one that most concerns me and causes me to pause and examine my own heart. Over the last forty years and during much of this study, I have spoken at length about my sadness and occasional disgust at what I see happening in some segments of today's Church. While much of the Church seems to take seriously Jesus' command to love God and neighbor, it seems to me that large segments don't. I've often responded with criticism.

This section is both confusing and terrifying. Did Jesus really mean that all judgment is wrong? Clearly, there are many times when Jesus, the Apostles, prophets, and other people of faith are highly critical. Most often, that criticism is directed to those who were once seen as believers. That judgment of the Church is both expected and required, and it is shown in scripture.

> *"For the time has come for judgment to begin with God's household, and if it begins with us, what will the outcome be for those who disobey the gospel of God?"* -- I Peter 4:17 (CSB)

Their criticism was almost always far more damning and hyperbolic than anything I've said. Still, Jesus makes it clear that the way I show, or don't show, grace to others will be the measure used in my own judgment. That is something I don't want to take lightly.

So, what did Jesus mean when he said that we should not judge? The Greek word that is translated as *judge* is *krinete*. It is the present active imperative form of the word *krinō*. This word means to judge, pass judgment on, or condemn. So, is Jesus saying that we should not make any discernment at all? Clearly not. One of the first things God tells Adam is about discernment.

> *"If you do what is right, won't you be accepted? But if you do not do what is right, sin is crouching at the door. Its desire is for you, but you must rule over it."* -- Genesis 4:7 (CSB)

Discernment of right and wrong is foundational to living life in the kingdom of heaven. Does Jesus mean that we can judge sin but not judge people? If that was true, then we wouldn't have the Mosaic Law. The Prophets, Peter, Paul, and Jesus would have never confronted and called out the religious leaders and believers of their day. Paul even tells us that believers will play some role in the implementation of eternal judgment.

> *"Or don't you know that the saints will judge the world? And if the world is judged by you, are you unworthy to judge the trivial cases? Don't you know that we will judge angels — how much more matters of this life?"* -- I Corinthians 6:2-3 (CSB)

Judgment of our own behavior and the behavior of others, especially believers, is clearly something that has been a part of God's plan. So, what is Jesus prohibiting? Let's take a look at a few other verses that use the word *krinete*.

> *"He also said to the crowds, "When you see a cloud rising in the west, right away you say, 'A storm is coming,' and so it does. And when the south wind is blowing, you say, 'It's going to be hot,' and it is. Hypocrites! You know how to interpret the appearance of the earth and the sky, but why don't you know how to interpret this present time?*
>
> *Why don't you judge for yourselves what is right?"* -- Luke 12:54-57 (CSB)

> *"You judge by human standards. I judge no one. And if I do judge, my judgment is true, because it is not I alone who judge, but I and the Father who sent me."* -- John 8:15-16 (CSB)

In these verses, the same word for judgment is used. We are permitted, even encouraged to judge the spiritual environment of our time. This form of judgment is discernment. Both discernment and warning are necessary. I believe the type of judgment that Jesus is prohibiting is condemnation. He is prohibiting any judgment that excludes grace. Jesus is warning us to not judge others from a place of self-righteousness. He is also prohibiting judgment that is not based on truth. Any judgment that is self-righteous, dishonest, or comes from bad intentions is what Jesus is warning us about.

An early Church father speaks to this difference:

> "But some explain this place after a sense, as though the Lord did not herein forbid Christians to reprove others out of goodwill, but only intended that Christians should not despise Christians by making a show of their own righteousness, hating others often on suspicion alone, condemning them, and pursuing private grudges under the show of piety." -- Pseudo-Chrysostom

There is a significant difference between a holy, kingdom-based judgment and an unholy, worldly-based, and sanctimonious condemnation. The former comes from a desire to protect, restore, and build up others. The latter often comes from a place of hurt and anger. It seeks to belittle and insult. The former has no desire to offend. A sense of insult may come, but that isn't the desired result. The desired outcome would be to shine a light on an issue of concern and reach a joyful resolution through either clarification or repentance.

Another issue of balance is between the tendency of some to find fault and outrage in everything and those who are utterly silent on truly harmful and horrendous behavior. Neither extreme is healthy. People tend to gravitate to one extreme or the other. At times, I have seen my own tendency for the former. That is no more wrong than those who are silent to injustice, cultural idolatry, and dishonesty.

As in the story from the Lord of the Rings, I don't believe that Jesus means we are not to discern the difference between evil and good or recognize how others approach evil. Jesus tells us to do just that. Soon after warning us to not judge, he says that we can discern false prophets by their fruit -- Matthew 7:15-20 above. Decades later, the Apostle Paul lays out which fruit demonstrates the work of the Spirit in someone's life and which fruit demonstrates its absence.

> *"But the fruit of the Spirit is love, joy, peace, patience, kindness, goodness, faithfulness, gentleness, and self-control."* -- Galatians 5:22-23 (CSB)

> *"Now the works of the flesh are obvious: sexual immorality, moral impurity, promiscuity, idolatry, sorcery, hatreds, strife, jealousy, outbursts of anger, selfish ambitions, dissensions, factions, envy, drunkenness, carousing, and anything similar."* -- Galatians 5:19-21 (CSB)

I see few in this world, either within or outside the Church, who consistently demonstrate the fruits of the Spirit and never exhibit the works of the flesh. We are all flawed. We all need to grow. Still, lives that exhibit these fruits and works tell us something about a person's spiritual health. Like physical health, a person's spiritual health is not static. It can change. Often, external intervention is critical to healing, but it can also harm.

More importantly, people who have a vital faith will grieve over their personal choices to disobey God. They will never feel comfortable devaluing their love for God or neighbor. Godly people will desire to daily be more like Jesus. None of us will arrive on this side of the grave, but all who genuinely love God and neighbor will strive to be more holy. We will mourn our spiritual failings. I fail to see how any faithful follower of Jesus would promote or defend evil. We will fail, but a believer's desire will be to promote kingdom values. Even when our worldly strength fails to follow through, a follower of Jesus has the desire to be like Jesus.

> *"The spirit is willing, but the flesh is weak."* --
> Matthew 26:41 (CSB)

We may disagree with other believers on some moral, ethical, theological, cultural, or political issue. When we do, we should be open to hearing another point of view. Our understanding of the world's reality might be incorrect. We may have been misled. We should prayerfully research and go to God for direction. The desire to *let us reason together* -- Isaiah 1:18 should include rational, humble, and respectful discussion on matters where we disagree. If we are not open to loving dialog on issues where we disagree can we truly say that we are open to the Spirit's prodding in our lives?

So, it's my opinion that Jesus is not prohibiting us from discerning right from wrong or wisely recognizing someone's spiritual health based on these outward signs. Those who quote the first verse of Matthew seven often do so when they sense a criticism of themselves or their own tribe. Often, these same people have no problem offering criticism of those outside their tribe. However, Jesus makes an important point of priority. We need to get our own house in order before we criticize someone else's home.

I will be candid. There are still rooms in my spiritual home that I need to tidy. Using this analogy, though, I don't present my personal mess with pride and pretend that it should be on the cover of some spiritual version of *Better Homes and Gardens*. What bothers me is when so many live in spiritual hovels and pretend that those places are godly mansions. As believers, we should welcome honest, accurate, and well-meaning observations about flaws in our spiritual houses. If there are cracks in our foundation, overflowing septic tanks, or house fires that threaten our neighbors' homes, we have a responsibility to lovingly and humbly point it out to them. When that house fire is seemingly intentional and threatens others, we should stand with those being threatened by such reckless behavior. The intent should always be to help and serve the wider community.

The issue here is honesty in our criticism and our motivation.

First, we must begin by recognizing that each of us are imperfect. Only God is perfect. He knows our failings and weaknesses, so we must approach judgment and discernment with humility and grace. Regardless of how corrupt, hypocritical, or even harmful a person's character and behavior may seem, we must be as gentle as possible. If we approach any correction with a hint of superiority, we are criticizing the wrong person. We must look in the mirror before criticizing. Not being perfect doesn't mean that we should respond to evil with silence. It just means we should respond with humility, love, and grace.

Second, while we can get a sense of a person's spiritual health by their behavior and apparent values, we can never fully know their motivation or thinking. Only God knows those things. Perhaps there is an inner struggle that we aren't aware of. Maybe the issue is not a matter of rebellion or selfishness but of incorrect understanding. These days misinformation, propaganda, and *group-think* have misled and harmed many. This is especially true in some segments of the Church. We may be able to discern the act but not fully see the person.

Third, we don't have a clue or the authority to judge the person's eternal state. Perhaps in eternity, but not today. Only God can judge our eternal destiny. Only He knows the future or how His grace and justice will be applied.

At times I have criticized or expressed disgust about a church or brother who promoted policies that harmed the poor, ignored injustice or practiced what I believed to be political idolatry. The response was often, "You shall not judge." In that case, I'm wasn't saying they were going to hell. I'm wasn't even saying that everything about that person was evil. I was simply saying that those views and actions were not biblical or ethically just. However, that person may be quick to say someone else will spend an eternity in constant torment because they have a somewhat different view of some theological concept. Which of those two responses is condemnation?

Unholy judgment is a widespread problem. We often are comfortable with offering unkind and possibly erroneous judgment of someone outside our tribe. We may entirely reject any judgment directed at our tribe or ourselves. This is true of conservatives and liberals. It is true of those inside and outside the Church. Our tribal mindset makes us blind to our own faults and exaggerates the flaws of the other tribe.

Another critical point is whether offering criticism might be an utter waste of energy. I think this is what Jesus means by not offering pearls to swine. There's nothing less productive than continually trying to persuade or convince someone whose mind is already made up. I fell into this black hole for many years. It's still a tempting challenge. While we can hold out hope that we can find agreement or that something will change, it's rarely wise to continue trying to open a door that's firmly shut. Sometimes, the best approach is to say nothing. At other times, you may feel led to address a concern. If your concern is rejected, leave it to God to judge. In many cases, God will prompt a person's heart. Sometimes, a person will refuse to reconsider. I think this is what Jesus meant when he told his disciples:

"Greet a household when you enter it, and if the household is worthy, let your peace be on it; but if it is unworthy, let your peace return to you. If anyone does not welcome you or listen to your words, shake the dust off your feet when you leave that house or town." -- Matthew 10:12-14 (CSB)

None of this is easy or to be taken lightly. There have been times when I was critical and truly judgmental. In those cases, I not only misrepresented God's grace, but I also lost any opportunity to lovingly get the other person to think. I may have lost the chance to discover that I was in the wrong. Conversely, there have been times when I probably should have spoken up more forcefully. I may have heard a brother share a lie, belittle another person, express an arrogant and hateful view, and I remained quiet.

For almost four decades, I felt that I had a prophetic calling to speak what I believed was biblical truth to my brothers and sisters and offer a call to repentance. Only God knows if I was misled in thinking that. I will leave it to Him to discern when I have been motivated by a desire to see the Church be salt and light and when I have simply had a critical and negative mindset. I do know I was never primarily motivated by a desire to diminish or harm. Building myself up was never my goal. The goal of judgment is always to call God's people back to living lives that bless, heal, and restore. The purpose of repentance is not to make us feel miserable or unworthy. The goal is to make us whole and be a blessing to our community.

"Even now — this is the Lord's declaration —

turn to me with all your heart,
with fasting, weeping, and mourning.
Tear your hearts, not just your clothes,
and return to the Lord your God.
For he is gracious and compassionate,
slow to anger, abounding in faithful love,
and he relents from sending disaster." -- Joel 2:12-13
(CSB)

Today's prayer:

Heavenly Father,

Help me to recognize my own dire need for repentance and growth. My own failings are all too persistent and damaging. I need to embrace Your desire to make me whole through fundamental change and recognize the depth of Your grace. As I am confronted with behavior by my Christian family that shocks, grieves, and saddens me, give me peace, courage, and wisdom to know how best to respond.

"God, give us grace to accept with serenity
the things that cannot be changed,
Courage to change the things
which should be changed,
and the wisdom to distinguish
the one from the other." -- Reinhold Niebuhr

Day Thirty-seven: Ask, Seek, Knock

"Ask, and it will be given to you. Seek, and you will find. Knock, and the door will be opened to you. For everyone who asks receives, and the one who seeks finds, and to the one who knocks, the door will be opened. Who among you, if his son asks him for bread, will give him a stone? Or if he asks for a fish, will give him a snake? If you then, who are evil, know how to give good gifts to your children, how much more will your Father in heaven give good things to those who ask him. Therefore, whatever you want others to do for you, do also the same for them, for this is the Law and the Prophets." -- Matthew 7:7-12 (CSB)

Ask. Seek. Knock. If you look up the word *faith* in the dictionary, it is defined as a noun. A thing. However, in practice, I believe that Jesus is telling us that faith is a verb. It is an action. Faith is less a thing that we possess than a lifestyle we practice. Throughout his sermon, Jesus has been talking about life in the kingdom of heaven. Here, he continues to describe how his followers should live within that kingdom.

Within much of today's Church, faith is often described as an inventory. It is seen as a list of opinions to be embraced as fact. We are told that salvation comes by believing certain concepts and rejecting other ideas. Faith is described in terms of some theological agreement. Never mind that many of those theological concepts are beyond human comprehension or limited scriptural support exists for many of those doctrines. We are told that to have saving faith, we must agree to believe certain things. I won't argue with that. Perhaps, some of those doctrines are essential to living a life of faith. Still, when Jesus talks about life in God's kingdom, he seems to put little emphasis on doctrine, a noun. Instead, he emphasizes actions. Instead of describing faith as an expression of doctrine, he defines it as a life of values to be pursued.

In these verses, the verbs ask, seek, and knock, are commands in the present imperative. This indicates that they are seen as continuous actions. In essence, Jesus is saying, "Keep asking. Keep seeking. Keep knocking." Back in the 1970s, I was involved in a mission outreach campaign with the odd title- *I Found It*. While there was much good in that program, I now think it was simplistic and somewhat misleading. Since those days, decades ago, I have continued to *find it*. In fact, when it comes to seeking God and living in His kingdom, I want to always be in the process of *finding it*. In this life, we will never arrive. Kingdom faith demands that we constantly question and challenge our limited understanding of an infinite and invisible God.

297

Kingdom faith should never be static. A faith that never changes is likely one that has stopped asking, seeking, and knocking. Jesus' faith never changed, but he was unique. He arrived with a fully formed faith. Still, even with that, he lived a life that was constantly seeking God's direction and guidance. His faith was not simply something he believed. It was something that he pursued.

What is Jesus asking us to seek? In context, I think that Jesus is continuing his statement from the previous chapter:

> *"But seek first the kingdom of God and his righteousness, and all these things will be provided for you."* -- Matthew 6:33 (CSB)

There, he was telling the crowd to not worry about their daily needs. He was reminding them of their priorities. Seek the kingdom first. He said then that God will take care of our needs if we have our priorities in order. Still, what are we to continually seek, ask, and knock on God's door for?

Many see this section as solely related to our prayer life. I agree that it does give us guidance in how we should *pray constantly* -- I Thessalonians 5:17. However, I suspect Jesus is touching on an issue that extends beyond our prayer life. Still, let's address these verses as they relate to prayer.

Jesus is making a confident *if-then* statement. If you ask, you will receive. If you seek, you will find. If you knock, the door will be opened. How many of us have experienced that? We pray with all our might for a
298

friend to be healed, and they still die. We cry out to God about a sense of despair and loneliness, and nothing seems to change. Whether it's a prayer for something miraculous or mundane, the asking, seeking, and knocking may often result in no apparent external change. Your friend dies. Your prayer seems to go unanswered. Was Jesus misleading us here? Was he "writing a check that couldn't be cashed?" I don't think so. I think the problem is that we don't understand what is best for us or what Jesus is promising.

"But the Lord is good, who often gives us not what we would, that He may give us what we should rather prefer." St. Augustine

I was a rare child because I preferred vegetables to candy. I wish that was still the case. If a child approaches their parents to have candy for dinner, we know what a loving parent's response would be. To the child, the denial of their request may seem that their parents aren't listening or don't care. In fact, a good parent will give a child what they need. A good parent will never withhold a child's need in order to give them what they want.

"You do not have because you do not ask. You ask and don't receive because you ask with wrong motives, so that you may spend it on your pleasures." -- James 4:2-3 (CSB)

Those who teach a prosperity gospel are misrepresenting the purpose of prayer. While God is concerned about our daily needs, He recognizes the harm that comes from a love of material wealth. No amount of faith is likely to move God's hand to grant material wealth to a spiritually poor person.

In promising these *good gifts*, Jesus may have been pointing back to his blessings in chapter five. If we continue asking, seeking, and knocking, we will develop lives that God will bless. If we seek first God's kingdom, what sorts of people does God promise will we be? We will:

- be humble
- mourn over the damage done by sin
- be gentle
- have a genuine desire to be righteous
- be merciful
- have a heart of purity
- promote peace
- respond to difficulties with joy

Our prayer requests for a miracle or some external blessing may not be answered as we wish. However, if we prioritize seeking God's kingdom, God will definitely give those things to us, which will eternally bless us.

Jesus concludes this section with, perhaps, his most well-known statement. Even those who wrongly think the Bible says "God helps those who help themselves" likely know this verse.

> *"Therefore, whatever you want others to do for you, do also the same for them, for this is the Law and the Prophets."* -- Matthew 7:12 (CSB)

This verse has become known as *The Golden Rule*. I suppose we call it golden because it is so important.

Jesus was a master at cutting through the tangle of theological confusion and summarizing God's intent. His summary here is a matching bookend to:

"He said to him, "Love the Lord your God with all your heart, with all your soul, and with all your mind. This is the greatest and most important command. The second is like it: Love your neighbor as yourself. All the Law and the Prophets depend on these two commands." -- Matthew 22:37-40 (CSB)

Suppose we were to commit the entire Old and New Testament to memory. If we fail to treat others the way we want to be treated or if we fail to love God and neighbor, then we have failed to live a kingdom life.

While I haven't found specific historical documentation for this, I've read that The Golden Rule is an update to a concept that predates the Sermon on the Mount. It is said that both Greek and Jewish scholars taught that we should "not do to others what we don't want to be done to us." This has been referred to as *The Silver Rule*. There's little doubt that the Silver Rule is the bare minimum for any ethical human. If we don't like being attacked, we shouldn't attack others. If we don't want to be robbed, we shouldn't rob others. If we don't want others to lie about us, we shouldn't lie about others. But Jesus took this minimal prohibition against doing harm to others and greatly expanded on it. It's not enough to simply not harm others. Jesus commands us to do good to others. Jesus even connects the act of doing good to others to showing love to him.

"Truly I tell you, whatever you did for one of the

*least of these brothers and sisters of mine, you did
for me."* -- Matthew 25:40 (CSB)

Jesus' Golden Rule demands that we don't simply avoid
harming others but that we actively put ourselves in
their shoes and promote justice for them.

Since verse twelve begins with *"therefore,"* Jesus is
giving a condition for receiving what we are asking,
seeking, and knocking. If we don't consider the needs of
others, we shouldn't expect God to answer our prayers
for other things. When we are genuinely seeking God's
kingdom, we will actively be pursuing the common
good of our neighbors. If we are blind to the suffering
and injustice a neighbor is experiencing, our vision is
on the worldly kingdom rather than the heavenly
kingdom.

Today's prayer:

Lord God,

Help me to never become complacent in my walk of
faith. Forgive me for the times I have felt that I had
arrived. Drive me to my knees in prayer. Give me a
heart and mind that challenges what I have been taught
and the courage to honestly question. As I connect with
the believing and unbelieving, help me to demonstrate
humility, gentleness, mercy, and peace. Help me
attempt to understand their view of the world and work
to promote truth and pursue justice.

Day Thirty-eight: The Narrow Gate

"Enter through the narrow gate. For the gate is wide and the road broad that leads to destruction, and there are many who go through it. How narrow is the gate and difficult the road that leads to life, and few find it.

Be on your guard against false prophets who come to you in sheep's clothing but inwardly are ravaging wolves. You'll recognize them by their fruit. Are grapes gathered from thornbushes or figs from thistles? In the same way, every good tree produces good fruit, but a bad tree produces bad fruit. A good tree can't produce bad fruit; neither can a bad tree produce good fruit. Every tree that doesn't produce good fruit is cut down and thrown into the fire. So you'll recognize them by their fruit.

Not everyone who says to me, 'Lord, Lord,' will enter the kingdom of heaven, but only the one who does the will of my Father in heaven. On that day many will say to me, 'Lord, Lord, didn't we prophesy in your name, drive out demons in your name, and do many miracles in your name?' Then I will announce to them, 'I never knew you. Depart from me, you lawbreakers!'" -- Matthew 7:13-23 (CSB)

See also- Luke 13:24-30

From chapter five to this point, Jesus has gone into detail about life in the kingdom of heaven. When Jesus talks about the kingdom of heaven, he isn't referring only to life beyond the grave. He is primarily talking about God's values in the present. Up to this point,

- Jesus has used the beatitudes to point to having kingdom **attitudes** (*Be-attitudes*).

- He used a series of *you have heard it said* statements to provide correct **doctrine**.

- In talking about prayer, fasting, judgment, and giving, Jesus informs us of godly **practices**.

The combination of these provides a map to the *narrow road* that Jesus is telling us about in this passage.

Now, Jesus moves past the blessings of following God's kingdom values and provides a warning. In this section, he addresses the consequences of not living according to those values. Soon after telling us not to improperly judge others, he reminds us of God's judgment.

I could write an entire book on various interpretations of the ideas this passage raises. It leaves me with so many questions. Who is Jesus addressing here? Is this a warning for this life or life beyond the grave? What are the conditions that might result in God saying, "*Depart from Me*?" Broadly, there seem to be three different views of this passage. Typically, the conservative/fundamentalist view is that Jesus is talking about hell. Many believe that most outside their particular belief system will be permanently banned from God's presence and eternally tortured. A more measured orthodox/mainline view may include some version of Purgatory, where sinners will be denied entry but can still be restored in eternity. A liberal view might see this as a description of the misery of a life lived without God.

I'd prefer to avoid discussing this, but this passage requires we consider it carefully. I could repeat the hard-line view of hell. As a young believer, I read cartoon *Chick Tracts* which portrayed a hideous and obscene depiction of hell and God's complicity. In my opinion, they also presented an overly simplistic view of how someone would end up there. I've seen this view presented by both Christian and Muslim fundamentalists. I'd read these tracts and hear those who embraced those views speak of God's love. I tried to embrace that interpretation. Still, as much as I tried, that never made sense to me. More importantly, it made me question if promoting that view was an insult to God's character. This interpretation didn't seem to match our view of God as our father unless our father was sadistic.

Alternately, I could posit that there is no judgment. I

could say that there is a heaven but no hell. But, if I did that, I'd have to ignore the sad reality of man's brokenness and the awful things we do. I'd have to deny the hate, dishonesty, and selfishness that has destroyed countless lives. An eternity with souls who are still unwilling to love God and others would not allow heaven to be heaven.

I can't embrace either view. On the issue of hell, I will only briefly say that there is so much that I don't know. I find verses that seem to provide opposing views on God's judgment in eternity. I firmly believe in the concept of judgment. I think that we will have to make an account of our actions and attitudes in this world. I am uncomfortable in stating, with certainty, what the result of that judgment will be. I am equally hesitant to provide a formula for how God will judge. I think those who do that, with apparent ease, are guilty of speaking without authority. I believe that is the sort of judgment Jesus warned us to not do.

I will use a word here that will likely cause some to misinterpret what I mean. I hope you will hear me out. I tend to consider myself a hopeful, Christian universalist. I know that, for many, that last word may label me a heretic, but I don't mean it in the way it is often interpreted. By this, I mean that scripture gives me some hope that Jesus' sacrifice on the cross may somehow provide redemptive and restorative grace for all of God's creation. I'm not suggesting and I don't believe the old maxim "all roads lead to heaven." My hope is that Jesus' death on the cross while providing the *only way* to God, may somehow be applied to all. In

306

studying the issue, I find more verses supporting the concept of some eventual restoration than I do for the horrific image that is often painted.

In short, I see two problems with the concept that judgment is once for all eternity, with no avenue for redemption following that judgment.

The first is the many scriptures that seem to indicate a different outcome.

"For just as in Adam all die, so also in Christ all will be made alive." -- I Corinthians 15:22 (CSB)

If we accept this verse is theologically accurate and believe in the concept of original sin, what are we to believe? The most obvious explanation seems to be the following. The righteousness imputed by Christ is applied universally in the same way that the rebellion of Adam was applied universally. See also -- Isaiah 57:16, Lamentations 3:31-33, Luke 3:16, John 1:29, John 3:17, John 6:33, John 3:35, John 6:39, John 12:32, Acts 3:21, Romans 5:18-19, Romans 6:23, Romans 11:32, II Corinthians 5:19, Colossians 1:19-20, I Timothy 2:6, I Timothy 4:10, I John 2:2, I John 4:14, Revelation 21:4.

I will leave it to you to read and pray over these scriptures. As with the verses used to promote the fundamentalist view, there are different interpretations for these verses. I freely admit that some verses support the fundamentalist view. Still, I think they conflict with everything else scripture teaches us about God's nature. I could be wrong, but anyone who embraces a more harsh view should at least consider what these verses mean.

The second issue is one of justice. Many say something to the effect, "God is love, but He is also just." They use this concept of justice to defend an eternal, inescapable hell. An appeal to justice is precisely where I find a problem with that view. God is indeed loving. Undoubtedly, God is just. However, I see neither love nor justice in imposing a sentence of eternal, unrelenting agony. A finite crime can never be given an infinite punishment and still be considered just. A just court will prescribe a punishment that fits the crime. For me, to accept an eternal, inescapable hell, I have to believe that God is neither loving nor just. I can't do that.

Perhaps judgment will be like an incident from my past. As a young Elementary School teacher, I was always looking for *teachable moments*. One Summer day, I was at the home of a family who were like adoptive parents to me. As I walked up their driveway, I saw a six-foot black snake winding its way over the driveway. I've never had much fear of snakes, so I got a stick, held down its head, and picked it up. The family's grandson was visiting, and I thought I'd take it to show him how to tell it wasn't poisonous. Without thinking, I went into the house to find him. When the mother came upon me with that snake, her response was emphatic. "Get that snake out of my house!" Of course, I hadn't thought through my bringing it into the house. She was one of the most loving, gentle, and kind people I knew, but she would not have that snake in her home. Perhaps, Jesus' *depart from me* is similar to that. I never questioned whether I would be forever barred from that home. I simply knew I couldn't go in with that snake. I had to make a choice. I got rid of the snake. I suspect that judgment may be similar to that.

So, on the issue of hell, I'll only say that God has the authority, right, and power to judge us as He chooses. The God I see, best illustrated by Jesus, is not a God who would do that. The fundamentalist view of hell doesn't seem to match any definition of love or justice in any dictionary. The liberal idea of a non-existent hell doesn't seem to address our need to change and be restored. I will never tell anyone that hell doesn't exist or assure them that they won't go there. God is the judge, and I am not. I trust His goodness enough to leave it in His hands. I believe that He knows how best to deal with the sins of Hitler, Mother Teresa, and myself.

Moving beyond the issue of hell, it is clear that Jesus is saying that there will be consequences for those who don't follow the narrow road. Perhaps those consequences will extend beyond the grave, or they may be experienced in this present life. He talks about consequences and the indicators of what not being on that narrow road looks like.

I think the narrow road can best be illustrated with a Venn Diagram. We see three circles that overlap in the middle.

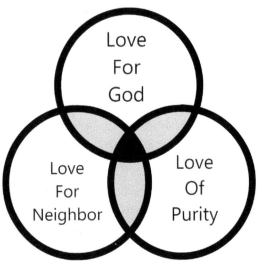

The Narrow Road

- One circle is labeled *Love for God.*
- A second circle is labeled *Love for neighbor.*
- A third circle is labeled *Morality and ethics (Love of Purity).*

Many may be able to point to existing in one of those circles, but very few of us are consistently in that small space where all three overlap.

These days, there seems to be an increasing number who don't land in any of these circles. Those who fail to love God, love their neighbors, or live by kingdom standards of ethics and morals are walking a broad road. They will leave a path of destruction in their wake. That destruction may not immediately fall on them. Destruction will more likely impact those they come into contact with.

310

While those three circles are independent, they do interact. A person who genuinely loves God must also love their neighbor.

> *"If anyone says, "I love God," and yet hates his brother or sister, he is a liar. For the person who does not love his brother or sister whom he has seen cannot love God whom he has not seen."* -- I John 4:20 (CSB)

If we don't show love for our neighbor, we can't truly love the One who created us both.

Likewise, many indeed care about their neighbors. They may not be believers, but they are involved in programs that show their genuine concern for the well-being of others. At times they are more giving than many inside the Church. That is admirable and should be commended. However, that love for our neighbor is diminished if they don't live a righteous life or if we show disdain for God or fail to appreciate God's goodness. Humans are both physical and spiritual beings, so true love will address the needs of both. By not allowing God to be a part of their lives, they are missing the joy and peace that can come from having a daily relationship with their Creator. Not having that peace may conflict with their attempt to love their neighbor.

You may be someone who loves God and cares about your neighbor but make little effort to live a righteous life. God wants to transform and heal us. He wants to make us new creatures.

> *"Therefore, if anyone is in Christ, he is a new*

311

creation; the old has passed away, and see, the new has come! Everything is from God, who has reconciled us to himself through Christ and has given us the ministry of reconciliation. That is, in Christ, God was reconciling the world to himself, not counting their trespasses against them, and he has committed the message of reconciliation to us."
-- II Corinthians 5:17-19 (CSB)

When Jesus talks about the narrow path, I believe he is talking about the convergence of these three loves- the love of God, the love of neighbor, and the love of purity. Very few of us live in that space consistently.

As I look at the Church today, I suspect we tend to focus on only one circle and ignore the others.

Fundamentalist and Conservative churches tend to focus on the circle related to purity. Sometimes it's genuine. Sometimes it's an external and fake holiness like the Pharisees were known for. They spend much of their time isolating themselves from the world and avoiding things they deem to be unholy. Too often, when it comes to loving their neighbor, at best, their actions are simply band-aids to problems their politics helped create.

Liberal churches tend to focus on the circle related to loving our neighbor. Sometimes, it's a genuine love that actively fights injustice and meets physical and spiritual needs. Sometimes, the love of neighbor is more talk than action. They sometimes overreact to the phony righteousness they see from Conservative churches and almost embrace external immorality in protest.

312

If we ignore either love of neighbor or a desire for purity, we call our love of God into question. The world is watching, and they see our actions. Our actions will always communicate more convincingly than our words.

We spoke in the last section about outward signs that indicate the condition of our heart. I won't go into depth on this but will reiterate that the things we say have little value if they are not made concrete by our actions. Only God knows the entirety of a person's heart. Only God knows a person's eternal destiny. Still, Jesus warns us that there will be those, apparently among the visible community of believers, who are not who they claim to be. False prophets may quote scripture, but if their lives and ministries don't display a love for God, a love of neighbor, and a desire for purity, then they are not ready to be trusted. As in our own lives, we need to distinguish between the fruits of the Spirit and indicators of worldly affections. Most of the failures that the Christian Church has seen over the last two millennia are because we failed to discern between good and bad fruit. When the Church follows false prophets and con-men, it suffers. Consequently, the world lacks the salt and light we are called to provide.

Today's verse and challenge:

"Therefore produce fruit consistent with repentance. And don't presume to say to yourselves, 'We have Abraham as our father.' For I tell you that God is able to raise up children for Abraham from these stones. The ax is already at the root of the

trees. Therefore, every tree that doesn't produce good fruit will be cut down and thrown into the fire." -- Matthew 3:8-10 (CSB)

Next, I hope to build on today's topic. At this point, I hope we more clearly see the narrow path that Jesus is calling us to. What it requires is for us to honestly inspect our hearts, priorities, words, and actions. In preparation, the challenge is to consider the three components of the narrow path- Love of God, Love of Neighbor, and Love of Purity. Prayerfully consider if there are ways that your approach to life conflicts with these loves. In what ways are we demonstrating growth in these areas?

Day Thirty-nine: Test Yourselves

"Test yourselves to see if you are in the faith. Examine yourselves. Or do you yourselves not recognize that Jesus Christ is in you? — unless you fail the test. And I hope you will recognize that we ourselves do not fail the test. But we pray to God that you do nothing wrong— not that we may appear to pass the test, but that you may do what is right, even though we may appear to fail. For we can't do anything against the truth, but only for the truth." -- II Corinthians 13:5-8 (CSB)

"Let's examine and probe our ways, and turn back to the Lord." -- Lamentations 3:40 (CSB)

From the day we are born until we die, assessment is a universal component of the human experience. Sometimes that assessment is affirming. Often, it is correcting. Too often, it is condemning. Ideally, our parents affirm and guide us as we grow and mature. Our teachers praise, encourage, and challenge us so that we will build our knowledge and skills. Upon entering the workforce, our employers and customers let us know what they expect and when they want more from us. Occasionally, they praise and promote us.

I always dreaded getting report cards and work assessments. Even when I had done my best, there was always a nagging voice in the back of my mind that criticized me. Sometimes, the criticism seemed unfair. More often, it was just and accurate. When I had a good boss or teacher, I walked away from the evaluation, sensing I was appreciated and valued. Still, I was aware of areas where I needed to grow.

Evaluation is even more critical in our spiritual lives. In the physical world, our progress is often easy to determine and unavoidable. We succeed in potty training, sell enough widgets, or pass the test. In this material world, it's easy to develop objective criteria, a rubric, to determine if we are progressing. When it comes to evaluating our walk with Jesus, that evaluation can become murky. We may put off self-evaluation and simply hope that we will *graduate*. We hope that we won't hear God say:

> *"Then I will announce to them, 'I never knew you. Depart from me, you lawbreakers!"* -- Matthew 7:23 (CSB)

Instead, those of us who love Jesus long to hear him say:

> *"Well done, good and faithful servant! You were faithful over a few things; I will put you in charge*

of many things. Share your master's joy." --
Matthew 25:23 (CSB)

I don't think that it's necessary or wise to wait for that eventual, ultimate evaluation. Instead, we should be daily allowing God to reveal our true nature to us. This is the point of a well-known verse:

"Search me, God, and know my heart;
test me and know my concerns.
See if there is any offensive way in me;
lead me in the everlasting way." -- Psalms 139:23-24 (CSB)

As is the case in most things, we tend to gravitate to extremes. This is especially true when it comes to how we evaluate ourselves. Many of us never see any wrong that we do. Perhaps we learned this from a privileged or permissive childhood. Regardless of how bad we did the job, how little we studied, or how unlike Jesus we look, we may deceive ourselves into thinking we can do no wrong. As a young and immature Christian musician, I remember playing for a group of people, and I forgot the words to my song. Instead of acknowledging that I hadn't adequately prepared, I made the patently absurd comment that "the devil is trying to confuse me." I wasn't honestly evaluating my failure.

Alternately, some never cease to condemn and criticize themselves. Regardless of how sincere they are or how diligently they try, all they see is failure. Neither extreme is healthy or helpful. Both this and failing to recognize spiritual sickness are examples of spiritual dysmorphia. In both extremes, we are failing to see ourselves as we actually are.

While earthly evaluation is often flawed and occasionally motivated wrongly, God's evaluation of us is always accurate. It seeks to build us up and give us peace. It seeks to make us whole and instruments in establishing His kingdom.

Since God's evaluation of us is always gracious, loving, and beneficial, why do we so often fail to seek it? It may be that our self-image is so fragile that we see any criticism as a threat. Perhaps it's because we fear discipline:

> *"My son, do not take the Lord's discipline lightly or lose heart when you are reproved by him, for the Lord disciplines the one he loves and punishes every son he receives."* -- Hebrews 12:5-6 (CSB)

While it's true that evaluation and discipline are related, regular self-evaluation is the best way to avoid reproof and discipline.

More importantly, today, I think that the need to evaluate our spiritual health is rarely taught or practiced in much of the Christian Church. One strength of Catholic tradition is the practice of regular witnessed confession. If all confession is private and internal, it is easy to become unpracticed. While we should confess our sins directly to God, there is also a need to confess to one another and for corporate confession.

"Therefore, confess your sins to one another and pray for one another, so that you may be healed. The prayer of a righteous person is very powerful in its effect." -- James 5:16 (CSB)

The privacy of this confession should be respected and practiced with discretion.

While we are only responsible for our own sin, corporate sin is also very real. It is, perhaps, more damaging to the reputation of the Church than individual failings. We see many instances of corporate confession of sin throughout scripture:

"they cried out to the Lord, saying, "We have sinned against you. We have abandoned our God and worshiped the Baals." -- Judges 10:10 (CSB)

"Woe to us, for we have sinned." -- Lamentations 5:16 (CSB)

"Why are we just sitting here?
Gather together; let's enter the fortified cities
and perish there,
for the Lord our God has destroyed us.
He has given us poisoned water to drink,
because we have sinned against the Lord." -- Jeremiah 8:14 (CSB)

We can't claim to be *one body* and then fail to recognize the need for corporate evaluation and repentance.

I believe this is a particular weakness in much of today's contemporary worship services. Before we can truly worship our Creator, we have to recognize and repent of our sin and seek God's forgiveness and cleansing. The book of Amos illustrates this. In chapter five, we see how God feels about worship when we are ignoring His teaching:

"I hate, I despise, your feasts!
I can't stand the stench
of your solemn assemblies.
Even if you offer me
your burnt offerings and grain offerings,
I will not accept them;
I will have no regard
for your fellowship offerings of fattened cattle.
Take away from me the noise of your songs!
I will not listen to the music of your harps.
But let justice flow like water,
and righteousness, like an unfailing stream." --
Amos 5:21-24 (CSB)

This meaning of this section seems apparent. A church that ignores injustice or right behavior is incapable of worship. The weekly service that fails to promote repentance and transformation is a *weakly* service. The apostle John reminds us how knowing God is evidenced:

"This is how we know that we know him: if we keep
his commands. The one who says, "I have come to
know him," and yet doesn't keep his commands, is a
liar, and the truth is not in him. But whoever keeps
his word, truly in him the love of God is made
complete. This is how we know we are in him: The
one who says he remains in him should walk just as

320

he walked." -- I John 2:3-6 (CSB)

Agreeing to a statement of faith is worthless if we don't reflect Jesus. Daily we should be challenged to ask ourselves whether we walk as Jesus did.

Before we go further, we need to remember that God's grace is far greater than our rebellion or failings. We are all flawed. What I say in this book is, I believe, a universal call. It applies to me first. Fortunately, we have a God and savior who forgives freely. All He asks is that we acknowledge and take steps to change.

"If we confess our sins, he is faithful and righteous to forgive us our sins and to cleanse us from all unrighteousness." -- I John 1:9 (CSB)

A call to repentance is not an act of condemnation. It is an act of concern, honesty, and love and is a spiritual necessity. Like a visit to a doctor's office, the only way to heal spiritually is to be tested and treated. A call to repentance is not an excuse to belittle or demean. The goal is always to encourage growth and build up the Church.

As we examine our hearts, we must recognize how easily we can be deceived. We come with decades of programming that may fight against the Spirit's revelation to us. If spiritual forces have deceived others in my church community, do I verify the things they tell me before I believe or repeat them? Do I recognize how easily the Church's enemy can lie and mislead?

"The heart is more deceitful than anything else, and incurable — who can understand it?

I, the Lord, examine the mind,
I test the heart to give to each according to his way,
according to what his actions deserve." -- Jeremiah
17:9-10 (CSB)

Repentance is not the act of being like our pastor, teacher, or mentor. It's not the attempt to mimic them or gain anyone's approval. It may be precisely the opposite. Only God's Spirit, honest prayer, and the scriptures can reveal our actual needs. The goal of repentance is to:

> *"For whoever wants to save his life will lose it, but*
> *whoever loses his life because of me will save it."* --
> Luke 9:24 (CSB)

Genuine repentance may mean abandoning some aspects of your identity that you have connected with your religion (or secular worldview.) In those places where your religious view of the world doesn't mesh with Jesus' character and teachings, true repentance requires us to follow Jesus. This may require us to lovingly part ways with one group in order to pursue Jesus more honestly. Of course, this should be approached with caution and wisdom.

Today's challenge, prayer, and verse:

With that as background, I believe today's exercise should be an ongoing process. In essence, it is where the rubber meets the road. Jesus has told us a lot about the narrow path. He has called us to live life within the kingdom of God. The challenge is in how we can evaluate our walk in that kingdom. Below, I will offer a suggestion that I will try myself. You may choose to evaluate your walk by some different method. This is definitely just my way of approaching this, and you should pray about the best way to go forward in your own life. What is essential is to develop a rubric, a plan of measurement, to determine where repentance is needed and go to God for cleansing and healing.

In yesterday's segment, I mentioned using a Venn diagram of overlapping circles. It may be easier to use three columns. Label the top of each column: Love of God, Love of Neighbor, Love of Purity. You may want to spend a few days praying and studying the indicators of these loves.

See the following scriptures: Deuteronomy 11:1, Joshua 22:5, Psalm 1:1-6, Jeremiah 7:1-11, Micah 6:8, Matthew 3:10, Matthew 7:15-20, Matthew 22:37-40, Matthew 23:23, John 14:15, Romans 13:10, I Corinthians 13:4-8, Galatians 5:19-21, Galatians 5:22,23, Ephesians 4:2, Ephesians 5:9, Colossians 3:12-15, I Thessalonians 4:4, Titus 3:2, Titus 3:5, James 2:18, James 3:17, I Peter 4:8, II Peter 1:5-9, I John 2:5, I John 3:17,18, I John 4:8, I John 4:20, I John 5:3.

What are some indicators that you love God, neighbor, and purity? You may find that you see growth in one area but not in another. This may reveal that you don't truly understand what the narrow path is. For instance, scripture is clear that we can't love God if we don't obey Jesus' commands -- I John 2:3 or if we don't love our neighbor -- I John 4:20. Also, our love of purity and neighbor should be the natural out-flowing of our love of God.

When I look at the decades-long course of my Christian walk, it's reasonable that I should question my faith.

How truly do I love God? Do I love to spend time in prayer? Is my desire to honor and please God motivated by love, social pressure, or fear? In the battle between my earthly attachments and love of God, where is my heart, and where do I spend my time? Do I sense God's presence in my life?

Is my love of my neighbor factual or just a concept that I claim to embrace? In thinking about the *Silver Rule*, do I practice business or promote views and politics that "do to others what I wouldn't want to be done to me?" If so, how can I possibly claim to love them? Do I actually follow Jesus' command to love them with the same protection and value as I do myself?

In God's call to live a life of purity, do I look to God to determine what is and isn't a kingdom value? My neighbor, pastor, family, social influencer, or favorite musician doesn't set the standard I should follow. Do I seek to live a life that looks like Jesus' life?

For me, I recognize both the need for repentance and growth in all three areas. When it comes to repentance, I've often found myself to be a serial offender. I have to recognize that repentance is not simply a sense of regret and remorse. It means enacting tangible steps to work toward following a different path.

I'd like to make one point on the issue of confronting personal and persistent sin. I've mentioned this illustration before. While we should attempt to avoid sinful behavior, finding victory over any sin is less about running away from evil than pursuing good. Walk into a dark room. As hard as you try, you can not remove darkness. The only way to remove darkness is to turn on the light. The best thing we can do when we seek to repent is not simply to turn from sin but to turn toward Jesus.

To walk Jesus' narrow path is not to repeat some statement of faith or cloister ourselves away with others who repeat that statement. To walk that path requires us to seek it for ourselves and with our whole heart. We must look at those three loves, which are evidence of true saving faith. You may want to keep a daily log of whether you lived out those loves. The world is keeping a record of our actions. They see large segments of the Church community which don't seem to look like Jesus. While some evaluation is unfair and painted with a broad brush, much is accurate and damning. They see our fruit, and their damning conclusion is often not complimentary. In many instances, they see the Church as a force for evil instead of good. If our religion is a reflection of our social or cultural values we may be reflecting a god that isn't biblical. Individually and corporately, the Church must take God's call seriously to search our hearts and repent. I hope you will join me in that today.

God,

Give me a heart that desires to grow, eyes that see clearly, a mind that thinks critically, a desire for justice, a commitment to honesty, a hunger for righteousness, a gracious spirit, and a willingness to change.

"Purify me with hyssop, and I will be clean;
wash me, and I will be whiter than snow.
Let me hear joy and gladness;
let the bones you have crushed rejoice.
Turn your face away from my sins
and blot out all my guilt.
God, create a clean heart for me
and renew a steadfast spirit within me." -- Psalms 51:7-10 (CSB)

Day Forty: A Firm Foundation

"Therefore, everyone who hears these words of mine and acts on them will be like a wise man who built his house on the rock. The rain fell, the rivers rose, and the winds blew and pounded that house. Yet it didn't collapse, because its foundation was on the rock. But everyone who hears these words of mine and doesn't act on them will be like a foolish man who built his house on the sand. The rain fell, the rivers rose, the winds blew and pounded that house, and it collapsed. It collapsed with a great crash." -- Matthew 7:24-27 (CSB)

"Why do you call me 'Lord, Lord,' and don't do the things I say? I will show you what someone is like who comes to me, hears my words, and acts on them: He is like a man building a house, who dug deep and laid the foundation on the rock. When the flood came, the river crashed against that house and couldn't shake it, because it was well built. But the one who hears and does not act is like a man who built a house on the ground without a

foundation. The river crashed against it, and immediately it collapsed. And the destruction of that house was great." -- Luke 6:46-49 (CSB)

Teachers are instructed to routinely summarize and repeat. We repeat because the concepts have become ingrained in us and because repetition, ideally, will instill those concepts in our students. We don't spend just one day explaining the multiplication tables and hope for the best. We progressively present, repeat and practice them with our students, so the skill is readily available. Jesus, the greatest rabbi, was a master teacher. He also used repetition and summary to get his point across. The things Christ taught were an integral part of his life. He could teach about God's blessings because he lived a life that demonstrated kingdom blessing. He could teach about prayer and fasting because he had mastered both. He made real the narrow path every day. He could teach about the true meaning of scripture because he was united with the God who inspired scripture.

Now, we arrive at the final summary of this great sermon. Jesus begins this section with "*therefore*." In essence, Jesus is saying:

"Everything I have told you, up till now, has been about the kingdom and the narrow path. Now, let me tell you what to do with what you've been told."

Jesus tells us of God's nature, God's expectations for us, and what true and false faith looks like. He presents this package to us, fully formed, and suggests what we might do with it.

Jesus was a carpenter by trade. I suspect he built and repaired chairs, but he may have had a hand in building or repairing Palestinian houses. Jesus never built mansions. If he did build houses, they would have been humble and simple, by today's western standards. His lengthier construction experience is taking place now:

> *"In my Father's house are many rooms. If it were not so, would I have told you that I am going to prepare a place for you?"* -- John 14:2 (CSB)

The mansions he is building for us now will certainly eclipse any he constructed when he was first occupied as a carpenter. Still, Jesus was probably aware of the steps to correctly build a house and the consequence of poor construction. He is preparing a room for us in his Father's house. He isn't building a mansion for us where we will live apart from our Creator. He wants us to join him in his Father's house.

To conclude his sermon, Jesus gives us a parable. Jesus never got bogged down in meaningless philosophy or tedious theological argument. His use of parables provided imagery that causes us to think and question their meaning. Once again, he takes this approach.

In this parable, Jesus offers the story of two ordinary people who set about building a house. The same parable, with minor differences, is given in the book of Luke. Jesus compares life in the kingdom of God to the construction of a house. He tells us of the blessing to a life constructed on the foundation he has just described.

Additionally, he warns us of the consequences of building on a faulty foundation.

Living in a country plagued with the curse of homelessness, I am grateful to have a home of my own. My wife and I built our house nearly thirty years ago. I can go back and look at videos I took of its construction. Today, when I come home, I appreciate the visible parts of the house. I see the floor, the walls, and the windows. I appreciate the plumbing and electrical fixtures. I rarely think about the foundation. That is until we have a storm. In the last twenty years, we've experienced several *once-in-a-century* storms. Global Climate change has brought tremendous downpours and violent winds that were rare a century ago. Through all of those, apart from some minor drainage issues, our house has endured. The walls still stand, the roof doesn't leak, and the elements remain outside. The reason for this is found in those videos of the early days of construction. The contractor dug down deep and built a foundation that was sturdy and dependable.

Jesus' parable compares two people. They both may have had pride in their houses. The world sees them both as homeowners. However, Jesus is saying that they are nothing alike. One builds his house on a rock (Matthew) which is dug deep (Luke). Rain, river, and winds pounded the house (Matthew) and was hit by flood (Luke). It didn't collapse (Matthew) and couldn't be shaken (Luke). The other builds his house on sand (Matthew) without foundation (Luke). Rain, river, and winds pounded that house, and it collapsed. In Luke, it adds:

> *"the destruction of that house was great." -- Luke 6:49 (CSB)*

Saint Augustine says of this last verse that it is "fear-inspiring."

In this parable, Jesus is comparing the consequences of how a house is built to how we approach religion and faith. In effect, he is saying, "even though both are houses, with walls and a roof, one will stand, and one will fall." You can own a house that is destined to collapse, and you can profess a religion that is equally doomed. If we want our home or our faith to last, Jesus tells us what we must do to accomplish that.

Jesus takes everything he has taught up to this point and tells us this should be our foundation. He tells us we must *"hear his words and act on them"* (Matthew) and *"comes to me, hears my words, and acts on them."* (Luke) Two words are critical to building that foundation: *hear* and *does them* (acts on them.)

The Greek word *Akouei*, which we translate as *hears*, means more than simply acknowledging background noise. It means to pay attention or to understand. Jesus may have used parables because he wants us to meditate on what he is saying and consider them deeply. Satan was likely there at Jesus' sermon and heard what was said, but he never comprehended what it meant. The Pharisees heard it, in addition to countless multitudes since then. While many have read it, how many have struggled to understand it? The

331

Greek word *Poiei* is translated here as *acts on them*, is perhaps the most important word in all of Jesus' sermon. It means *to do, make, practice, produce,* or *perform*. When Jesus talks about the narrow path, I believe this is what narrows it.

Jesus' brother, James, speaks of this:

> *"But be doers of the word and not hearers only, deceiving yourselves. Because if anyone is a hearer of the word and not a doer, he is like someone looking at his own face in a mirror. For he looks at himself, goes away, and immediately forgets what kind of person he was. But the one who looks intently into the perfect law of freedom and perseveres in it, and is not a forgetful hearer but a doer who works — this person will be blessed in what he does."* -- James 1:22-25 (CSB)

Jesus alluded to the foundation of the kingdom on another occasion:

> *"And I also say to you that you are Peter, and on this rock I will build my church, and the gates of Hades will not overpower it."* -- Matthew 16:18 (CSB)

In this recounting, Jesus isn't saying that the individual we know as Peter was the Church's foundation. Jesus responds to Peter's recognition that Jesus is the savior and the son of the Living God and that his words give life.

This is where the Church tends to divide into two

332

groups. This disagreement existed when James was writing and continues today. One group sees the foundation of the kingdom as based on faith. Martin Luther's assertion of *sola fida* (meaning *only faith*), has defined much of the history of the Protestant Church. Another group places emphasis on our actions as the foundation of life in the kingdom of God. Both views have fallen victim to extremism. The *faith-only* group may embrace such a devotion to creeds and theological affirmations that, for them, what we claim as our belief is all that matters- at least in terms of eternal destiny. The *works-only* group may embrace the false notion that God will weigh our charity on a scale to determine if our good deeds outweigh our bad ones. This view ignores God's grace and Jesus' sacrifice on the cross.

Neither view is biblical or healthy. Both extremes result in a Church that will fail to be salt and light. I recently heard a story from a friend who attended a seminary I was at briefly. He told me about two seminary students who actually got into a fistfight over some theological disagreement. This insanity was perfectly described by Jesus when he said:

> *"Blind guides! You strain out a gnat, but gulp down a camel!"* -- Matthew 23:24 (CSB)

Equally misinformed are those who believe they can earn favor with God through an ascetic lifestyle or acts of charity. That said, between the two, the latter is less of an embarrassment to the gospel. It also seems to be less of a problem. The Church has rarely been accused of being too charitable.

As to theological doctrine, when I read Jesus' words in this sermon, where does he continually place emphasis? Where in all of this does he promote a creed or the importance of doctrinal purity? I don't see it. He does say:

> *"Believe in God; believe also in me."* -- John 14:1 (CSB)

but this is in the context of offering solace to his frightened followers. It was not given as a theological command. Believing in Jesus was never divorced from being like Jesus.

Time and again, Jesus returns to our actions being what is most important in following him. Yes, we should know who Jesus was and what his death and resurrection have done for us. We should indeed be on guard against false teaching. Still, I suspect that much of today's false teaching is due to focusing on theological concepts at the expense of simply telling us that we need to look and act like Jesus.

Throughout scripture, most of God's prompting has been directed at our actions rather than our doctrine. We see God speaking to Ezekiel and commenting on this very thing:

> *"So my people come to you in crowds, sit in front of you, and hear your words, but they don't obey them. Their mouths go on passionately, but their hearts pursue dishonest profit."* -- Ezekiel 33:31 (CSB)

I think that a part of Jesus' comparison of a house built on a rock and one built on sand points to how the Church's focus must be on eternal values instead of temporal ones. This is especially true when it comes to how much of the Church seems to be led more by local culture than by eternal values.

Culture, whether conservative or liberal, rural or urban, contemporary or traditional, is fleeting. It has no eternal value. It is part of our earthly identity that may conflict with our eternal identity. So much of the world is rejecting the Church. This isn't because they reject Jesus, but because of the homogeneity of their local church. To be blunt, the only way the conservative church can survive is by appealing to conservative culture. To a lesser degree, I see the same form of cultural and political idolatry in liberal churches.

From my own experience, I struggled to remain in the conservative Church for decades but had to leave. Opposing views were never welcome, and each meeting was a struggle that prevented me from freely seeking God. Now, I am in a more liberal church. While there are a number of views there I disagree with, I am freer to honestly challenge and question those views. I never had that freedom when I was in the conservative Church. In my current church, I am free to *"work out my salvation with fear and trembling"* -- Philippians 2:12. In too many churches I've attended I simply feared working out my faith.

Jesus calls us to become new creations:

335

"Therefore, if anyone is in Christ, he is a new creation; the old has passed away, and see, the new has come!" -- II Corinthians 5:17 (CSB)

The easy path, the house built on sand, is to take Jesus and attach him to our existing view of the world. This is simply a form of syncretism. It is not following Jesus. It's not true Christianity. If we take conservatism, liberalism, or any other ism and simply place Jesus on top of it, we are no longer on the narrow path. Even worse, we become false prophets who mislead others.

We can erect a massive cross at our church buildings, prepare an exacting creed, and develop complex programs. We can construct immense buildings, create radio and television programs, and have multimedia worship services. While those things aren't automatically bad, none are essential. Jesus is telling us in this sermon what is essential. Come to him. Meditate on his words and put them into action.

Jesus' sermon directs the path we must follow. He shows us what evidence we will exhibit if we follow that path. He reminds us that the foundation of God's kingdom is not simply a matter of signing a statement of faith. The foundation is recognizing that Jesus is that foundation, and we must, daily, strive to live as he commands.

Today's verse and questions:

"For no one can lay any foundation other than what has been laid down. That foundation is Jesus

Christ." -- I Corinthians 3:11 (CSB)

Here are some questions to ask ourselves:

- How much of what I identify as part of my Christian faith is really a reflection of Jesus and how much is a product of my upbringing and those I hang out with?

- To what degree are my view of the world, values, and priorities shaped by sources that might have a hidden agenda? Do I study to make sure the things I promote are empirically true and align with kingdom values?

- Do my political, social, community convictions reflect God's heart? Am I willing to have God and other voices challenge my views?

- Do I value truth enough to study, question, and challenge what my friends, family, and tradition tell me?

- If someone outside of my faith looks at my values do they see Jesus or my culture with Jesus' name attached?

Day Forty-one: Who is in Charge?

"When Jesus had finished saying these things, the crowds were astonished at his teaching, because he was teaching them like one who had authority, and not like their scribes." -- Matthew 7:28-29 (CSB)

In March 1981, President Ronald Reagan was shot and rushed to emergency exploratory surgery. Vice-President George H.W. Bush was on a plane returning from Dallas. For some time, there was some question of who was in charge. The twenty-fifth amendment to the constitution included four sections related to relieving a President of their duties. In this instance, section four was applicable, but it had never been implemented before. For eight hours, the President's cabinet wrestled with whether to implement the temporary transfer of power. In, perhaps, the most embarrassing moment of his life, Secretary of State Al Haig went to the podium to address the press pool.

When he was asked the question:

"Who is in charge?"

Secretary Haig answered:

"Constitutionally, gentlemen, you have the President, the vice president, and the secretary of state, in that order, and should the President decide he wants to transfer the helm to the vice president, he will do so. As of now, I am in control here, in the White House."

Haig apparently forgot that the House speaker and the Senate's president pro tempore come before the secretary of state in the line of succession. Even if the vice president had been unavailable, Secretary Haig would not have been *in control*.

Secretary Haig claimed authority that he had not earned, did not deserve and did not have. Had he wanted to issue an executive order, sign a piece of legislation, or issue a command to the military, he would have likely failed. The claim to have authority is not the same as possessing it.

As we come to the end of Jesus' sermon, we note that the power of Jesus' words came directly from him and his unique authority. Paul tells us of Christ's authority:

*"For this reason God highly exalted him
and gave him the name
that is above every name,"* -- Philippians 2:9 (CSB)

Dr. Grant C. Richison refers to Jesus as *the Great Unlike*. If you place Jesus in a *Where's Waldo* drawing, you will note two things. He stands with and amid everyone, and yet he still stands alone. Dos Equis may claim in their ad that their guy is "the most interesting man in the world." He isn't. Undoubtedly, Jesus is the most unique and interesting.

The scribes and Pharisees of his day often defended their claim of authority by referencing the teachings of some ancient rabbi. Jesus' foundation, like the foundation we discussed yesterday, rested directly upon his connection with his Father and daily walk. He *walked the walk*, which gave him authority to t*alk the talk*.

The crowd's reaction to Jesus likely occurred often. This is seen in Mark 1:22:

> *"They were astonished at his teaching because he was teaching them as one who had authority, and not like the scribes."* -- Mark 1:22 (CSB)

The Greek word in verse twenty-eight that we translate as *astonished* is *exeplēssonto*. It means to be amazed, astonished, to strike out of one's wits, to astound, or be amazed. To be overwhelmed. It can also mean to have produced fear. Perhaps we could say that Jesus' words *knocked them out* or *terrified them*. When I was a teacher, there were many days I heard yawns in my class. I doubt that anyone was bored with Jesus' words. They undoubtedly caused a stir. Some were moved to follow him, and some conspired to oppose him.

The Greek word in verse twenty-nine that we translate as *authority* is *exousian*. It means authority, power, the right to control or govern; dominion, the area or sphere of jurisdiction. Coming from the lips of a Roman soldier, we see the same word used in the verse below:

"For I too am a man under authority, having soldiers under my command. I say to this one, 'Go,' and he goes; and to another,'Come,' and he comes; and to my servant, 'Do this!' and he does it." -- Matthew 8:9 (CSB)

Jesus was himself a *man under authority*. He took direction from his heavenly Father. His authority wasn't self-proclaimed, arrogant, or delusional. It was handed to him by our Creator, exercised in humility, and grounded in truth.

As I write this book, I acknowledge that I may come across as preachy or even pushy. That's not my intention. Perhaps some will read my thinking as arrogant. The truth is that I have no authority to tell anyone how to follow Jesus' narrow path. While I have spent decades studying, questioning, and trying to understand a relationship with a God who is invisible, ultimately, I see through the glass darkly -- I Corinthians 13:12. All that I have said in this study is my honest but limited understanding of the text. I have tried to apply it to my sincere but limited knowledge of the world I live in and the Church I love.

No pastor, teacher, radio or television pundit, politician, zealot, know-it-all, neighbor, elder, relative, or friend can speak authoritatively on the full nature of the kingdom of heaven. We can and should listen to others and intelligently and prayerfully consider their views. We should take our individual pursuit of a godly life seriously:

"Be diligent to present yourself to God as one approved, a worker who doesn't need to be ashamed, correctly teaching the word of truth." -- II Timothy 2:15 (CSB)

Ultimately, there is only one authority on the kingdom of heaven. Only one can speak authoritatively about what it looks like, how we should live it, and how to promote it. That authority is Jesus. The heart of that authority is contained in this sermon. The entirety of scripture can provide context, wisdom, and guidance. The advice of wise brothers and sisters may help us to see it more clearly. Prayer can clear misconceptions and change our affections. Still, all that we do as followers of Jesus should be filtered through this message and Jesus' life.

When the world considers the Church, it thinks of 2,000 years of her history. It considers the myriad of cultural expressions that the Church has reflected. It might picture stained glass and a thirteenth-century Pope or a country church that handles snakes. It may think of how William Wilberforce's faith led to the abolition of slavery in England or the molestation of children by predators in some churches. The Church has produced great good but also horrific evil. The world's view of the Church and the Church's view of itself is often biased, inaccurate, and incomplete. We should acknowledge and mirror the good, but we must recognize and confront the evil.

Secretary Haig's view of his authority was misplaced. Likewise, the Church must guard against placing trust in sources of information and teaching that don't reflect truth, compassion, or our struggle to live like Jesus. When Secretary Haig made that incorrect assessment, most knew that he was wrong.

While it's entirely fiction, imagine if many had believed him. What if he had gathered together supporters who backed his unconstitutional claim? It would have constituted a political coup. I think a similar spiritual coup has taken over significant portions of today's Church.

Had Secretary Haig actually instigated a coup, you would have seen various groups respond. Some may have actively supported him. Their support would demonstrate an act of treason and a violation of their oath. Some may have felt that doing nothing was the wisest course. Perhaps, out of fear or ignorance, they may have chosen to not *rock the boat*. Eventually, the lie behind this theoretical coup would likely have corrupted their reasoning so that they embraced it.

Some may have actively opposed him. Their opposition may have been seen as contrarian or argumentative. Still, they took a vow to protect the constitution, so the only honorable and honest thing to do would be to oppose the coup. This would produce disagreement and a negative response but would be necessary. The only correct course would have been to oppose the coup. Fortunately, Secretary Haig's misunderstanding was corrected. Reagan temporarily transferred power to Vice President H.W. Bush and no coup occurred.

I believe today, various forces are trying to remove Jesus from his position of authority in the Church. Political, social, cultural loves have stood at the podium. Instead of directly saying, like Haig's, "I am in charge here," they are more subtle and devious. They lie. They claim to be carrying out the will of the true authority. In fact, they are usurping that authority to enact their own agenda.

We all have a different history, culture, worldview, background, and political perspective. However, if our desire is to follow Jesus and promote the kingdom of God, we should recognize the real danger of a spiritual coup. The devil doesn't have to convince the Church to renounce Jesus. He simply has to confuse the Church into believing that doing the devil's will is doing God's will. That lie has done the majority of the damage that the Church has experienced in her lifetime.

Most of this boils down to choosing who we will serve. Typically, the choice is between serving God and neighbor or serving ourselves. These days it seems our social group and cultural identity are demanding our worship. I will be blunt. I don't believe that you can be an advocate for any ism and fully follow Jesus.

"No one can serve two masters, since either he will hate one and love the other, or he will be devoted to one and despise the other. You cannot serve both God and money." -- Matthew 6:24 (CSB)

While Jesus directly addressed the love of money in this verse, it applies to anything that will compete for our

344

affection. You can not follow Jesus and truly be a Republican or a Democrat. You can not promote the kingdom of God and see yourself as a liberal or a conservative. Those labels and identities reflect a worldview that exists apart from being a disciple of Jesus. They all contain agendas that oppose Jesus'.

We are primarily citizens of heaven and are here as ambassadors for God's kingdom. As temporal citizens of a transitory nation, we interact with the political, but we do so as ambassadors for Jesus. When we interact with the political or cultural, it should always submit to kingdom objectives. No party or worldview deserves our unconditional allegiance. Any partnership with those entities should always be limited, wise, studied, honest, and conditional.

In that temporary partnership, Jesus gives us direction. We should do to others what we would want them to do to us. We must consider how our vote and worldview will positively and negatively impact our neighbors and their freedom to freely choose their response to God's love for them. We must recognize the danger that comes from aligning ourselves with any worldly power. Throughout Church history, such marriages of Church and political power have consistently harmed the Church, the gospel, and the nation.

These choices are not easy or straightforward. No political or worldly ideal will ever entirely match Jesus' values. We may choose to vote differently. Still, we must consider why we support the policies we do. We must search and study. We must not simply be led by propaganda. We shouldn't merely follow the thinking of our church friends or blindly trust what we hear on "Christian" media (which often has little to do with Jesus.)

Most importantly, we must take responsibility for our social and political involvement. The party or candidate you support may defend a policy you believe to be godly. If they also support policies you know are evil, you must do three things. First, let them know they can't unconditionally depend on your vote. No party or candidate should ever feel they can depend on the unconditional support of followers of Jesus. Push them to promote policies that demonstrate the love of God and our neighbor in all areas. Second, your party or candidate's policies may harm or oppose Jesus' values. If so, you have a responsibility to stand in the gap for the harm your vote helps to create. If your vote ethically addresses one sin while defending another you must responsibly own your participation in that. Third, recognize that our involvement with worldly parties, cultures, and worldviews has a corrupting influence. Not just individuals but whole churches and church movements have been corrupted by political and cultural lies. We must guard against this and call for repentance when we see that corruption.

The good news is that even when we fail (and even a faithful Church fails), we know that God will restore a remnant. Read through Revelation chapters two and three. God will remove some churches and protect others. Even when many churches harm the gospel and actively oppose the kingdom, God has promised that:

"I am sure of this, that he who started a good work in you will carry it on to completion until the day of Christ Jesus." -- Philippians 1:6 (CSB)

Verse twenty-eight begins by telling us that Jesus had *"finished saying these things."* Jesus could have continued teaching for days and not exhausted his knowledge of the kingdom, but he stopped. Why? Being fully human, he knew that even a perfectly compelling sermon was heard by human ears. He knew that people had limitations. He stopped because he likely gauged the audience. Long sermons and long books produce exponentially dwindling results. Jesus was always compassionate in his dealings with the crowd. I hope this book wasn't unnecessarily long or needlessly repetitive.

As a younger man, I went hiking with a friend up a mountain outside Los Angeles. As we traversed switchbacks to the summit, we passed rocky ravines that seemed to offer a straight path to our destination. Being impatient and lacking understanding, we got off the trail and attempted to follow the gorge to the top. The ravine was filled with loose rock. No trees or foliage grew there to hold the rocks together. We soon noticed that the rock around us would come loose and slide toward the bottom with every step. We realized that a false step could trigger an avalanche that could kill us and harm those below us. For the next six hours, we were forced to crawl on our bellies up the ravine, till we reached the next switchback. We used our walking sticks to dig into the loose stone and pull ourselves up. What we thought was a sensible alternate path turned out to be a frightening and dumb decision.

Much of what I have written here has been my estimation of paths we take that we think are valid but aren't. For me, this study has forced me to embrace my need to follow Jesus more faithfully. It has revealed where I have lost my way and challenged me to correct my course. I suspect neither my liberal nor conservative friends will embrace everything that I've said. I don't expect them to. I only want to encourage honest self-evaluation. I suspect some will have stopped reading this early on. I wish there was a gentler way to address needed change. The danger in performing CPR is that ribs might be bruised or broken. Still, that is never the purpose. It's not my purpose either.

I hope that you will take what I've said in earnest but with a grain of salt. I believe most of what I've said is correct, but I'm equally confident that I could be wrong in parts of it. If honest and prayerful consideration leads you to a different understanding than mine, that is fine. I would like to continue making this sermon a primary focus in my walk of faith. I would like to see that from more who profess our Christian faith. My hope is that as you have read this it has challenged you to return to Jesus.

Today's verses:

"If you continue in my word, you really are my disciples. You will know the truth, and the truth will set you free." -- John 8:31-32 (CSB)

"You must follow the Lord your God and fear him. You must keep his commands and listen to him; you must worship him and remain faithful to him." -- Deuteronomy 13:4 (CSB)

"Therefore, be imitators of God, as dearly loved children, and walk in love, as Christ also loved us and gave himself for us, a sacrificial and fragrant offering to God." -- Ephesians 5:1-2 (CSB)

Day Forty-two: Closing Thoughts

"We used to hate and destroy one another and refused to associate with people of another race or country. Now, because of Christ, we live together with such people, and pray for our enemies." - Justin Martyr, around 150 AD

Justin, known commonly as Justin Martyr, lived less than a hundred years after Jesus. He was a Greek, born in Samaria. He identified as Samaritan, in a place and time where Samaritans were often disrespected. This speaks to his humility. Justin had studied the classic Greek philosophers but converted to Christianity. He lived at a time when Christians were being tortured and killed simply because they identified as followers of Jesus.

In his *First Apology*, Justin defends earnestly the character of the Christian life. He presents his *apology* (meaning argument) to Antoninus. Antoninus was the Roman emperor who was, at that time, persecuting the Church. Justin provides his reasoning for why

350

Antoninus should not persecute Christians. He points out that, while some individual Christians had behaved immorally, they should be judged individually, rather than the group as a whole. Instead, he points to the overwhelming evidence of the good things that were being done by Jesus' followers.

A tidal wave of compassion, selflessness, and charity was an indicator of the vitality of the faith of the early Church. When a massive and deadly plague struck the area of Caesarea in the early fourth century, the majority of the healthy fled the area. However, the Church stayed behind to care for the sick. Early Church historian, Eusebius, wrote:

"All day long, some of them [the Christians] tended to the dying and to their burial, countless numbers with no one to care for them. Others gathered together from all parts of the city a multitude of those withered from famine and distributed bread to them all....

[their] deeds were on everyone's lips, and they glorified the God of the Christians. Such actions convinced them that they alone were pious and truly reverent to God." - Eusebius, *The Church History* trans. Paul L. Meier (Grand Rapids: Kregel, 2007), 293

Compare those actions of the early Church to today. Today, we are experiencing a similar plague that is killing hundreds of thousands. Has today's Church responded similarly? Instead of volunteering to help the medical community and the sick, many have angrily demanded their "right" to not be vaccinated, wear a mask, or socially distance. By doing this, they have added to the stress on an already fragile medical system and likely caused needless physical harm and death. They have claimed, without factual support, that those who died did not die from this plague. Where the early Church stepped in to help and serve, many in the Church today have responded with anger, arrogance, ignorance, and selfishness. They have repeated disproven information that could endanger others and arrogantly claimed to know better than those who have demonstrated knowledge about the best medical and scientific practices. How has this affected the world's image of the Church? Does any of this look like Jesus?

Not long after Eusebius wrote about this, Roman Emperor Julian was lamenting how pagan worship of idols was declining and being replaced by followers of Jesus. He wrote, in a letter to a pagan priest of the Roman gods: (words in *italics* added for clarity.)

"When it came about that the poor were neglected and overlooked by the *pagan* priests, then I think the impious Galileans *the followers of Jesus* observed this fact and devoted themselves to philanthropy......

They support not only their poor, but ours as well, all men see that our people lack aid from us.......

It is their benevolence to strangers, their care for the graves of the dead, and the pretended holiness of their lives that have done most to increase atheism *disbelief in the pagan idols.*" - To Arsacius, 69-70; cf.

Fragment of a Letter to a Priest, 336-37

Soon after Pentecost, the infant Church gathered together. They didn't meet in some ornate building. Their teacher didn't have a six-figure salary. The members weren't the wealthy or the powerful. They didn't see their faith as an avenue to material prosperity or a tool to achieve political influence. They weren't seeking to alter the government or laws of the day. They avoided controversy. Rather than seeking to *Judaize* the world, they chose to simply tell the gentile world of a culturally neutral but transformative hope. They *"shared all things in common"* -- Acts 4:32.

At least up to when Emperor Julian feared the growth of Christianity, the Christian Church largely endeavored to reflect the values that Jesus taught in his sermon. For this reason, Justin was able to honestly point out that most of the derogatory stories about the Church were not based on fact. While there were bad actors within the group, they did not represent the values that the group tried to embrace. The vast majority presented a positive influence toward the common good.

I wonder how Justin might address the often poor image of Christianity today. There are still so many followers of Jesus who truly take seriously Jesus' call on their lives to love God and neighbor. These are people you won't see on the news. They care for their neighbor and don't defend politicians, policies, biases, bigotry, or share questionable or distorted information. They recognize that truth is a characteristic of the God they seek to serve and guard themselves against believing or

353

spreading lies and half-truths. They realize that the entirety of the Law, and the Prophets, boils down to the love of God and neighbor. They seek the common good of everyone. They don't fear the world but love it, just as God does. They recognize that we are simply visitors and guests in this world and that Jesus is preparing an eternal home for us. As guests, they honor God's creation. They seek to treat others with dignity. They promote God's kingdom desire for justice, and mercy on Earth, as in the heavenly kingdom.

Only God knows how many who call themselves Christian can provide support for Justin's claim with evidence. Justin had significant evidence to defend the greater Christian community of his day. Their existence was a net good for the world.

While there are many whose faith is genuine; while we all fail, and are flawed; while God puts His *"treasure in jars of clay"* -- II Corinthians 4:7, and God knows our shortcomings, a healthy Church should be asking itself if we have lost sight of who we've been called to be. If we were called to provide our *apology* for the work of God through today's Church, could we demonstrate an overwhelming good? I suspect not.

Only God can judge our faithfulness, but the world is watching, and shouldn't we challenge ourselves to do better? Yes, God has entrusted the gospel to us. He has placed that hope in human, jars of clay. The scripture goes on to say:

> *"We are afflicted in every way but not crushed; we*

are perplexed but not in despair; we are persecuted but not abandoned; we are struck down but not destroyed." -- II Corinthians 4:8-9 (CSB)

There is a true Church that will survive. No phony, religious politician, televangelist, or any amount of political idolatry by large segments that claim our religion will destroy the true Church. Still, these fruits do reveal our spiritual health. These distractions drive us farther and farther away from what Jesus was calling us to in his sermon.

Tragically, when the testimony of the Church fails, the spread of the gospel suffers. Anyone who has a heart for evangelism must first disciple the Church. If we seek to disciple, we can only do that by being honest with ourselves.

As we meditate on the Sermon on the Mount, I hope that we, as a corporate body of believers, will bring Jesus, and the values of God's kingdom, into our daily lives and loves. My prayer is that as we live in the twenty-first century we will live more by the priorities of the early Church. Only Jesus' words give life. If we have strayed from them, let us return to them. The world needs us to look more like Jesus.

The world doesn't need culture warriors or partisan loudmouths. It doesn't need prosperity preachers or fake miracles from ethicless conmen. It doesn't need a watered-down faith that fears to hold on to eternal truth. While statements of faith have their place, they aren't what the world needs. The world needs to see simple, humble, compassionate, honest, and thoughtful people who long to look like Jesus. I'm still on my journey to get to that place and am overjoyed when I meet others on the same path.

Justin was ordered to sacrifice to the Roman idols but refused. He was whipped and beheaded. As significant as the sacrifice and commitment to his faith was, more importantly, he pointed to the overwhelmingly positive character of the Church of his day.

I say it once more. None of us are perfect. Like everyone else, I fail. Still, I pray for two things. First, I pray that the name of Jesus, his message, and the reputation of his followers would be recognized as an unquestionable positive in a world that needs hope, grace, and love. For that to happen, it has to be true. Second, I pray that the Church would recognize that, as ambassadors for Christ, we represent Jesus to the world and that we would, individually and as a corporate body, commit to fleshing out his image.

Today's prayer:

Lord Jesus,

Help me set aside every false artifact of religion, utterly abandon my cultural, ideological, and political idols, and fully seek to look like you.

> "And the word of the LORD came again to Zechariah: "This is what the LORD Almighty said: 'Administer true justice; show mercy and compassion to one another. Do not oppress the

widow or the fatherless, the foreigner or the poor. Do not plot evil against each other.'

But they refused to pay attention; stubbornly they turned their backs and covered their ears. They made their hearts as hard as flint and would not listen to the law or to the words that the LORD Almighty had sent by his Spirit through the earlier prophets. So the LORD Almighty was very angry.

'When I called, they did not listen; so when they called, I would not listen,' says the LORD Almighty. 'I scattered them with a whirlwind among all the nations, where they were strangers. The land they left behind them was so desolate that no one traveled through it. This is how they made the pleasant land desolate.'" -- Zechariah 7:8-17 (NIV)

Day Forty-three: Love and Truth

*"Now these three remain: faith, hope, and love —
but the greatest of these is love." -- 1 Corinthians
13:13 (CSB)*

It's critically important to value and defend truth. We should seek justice. Knowledge is critical in the struggle for both. Sadly, our nation is divided into different universes of truth, justice, and knowledge. It's essential that we objectively seek out each of these treasures, but sometimes in the process, voices are raised, unkind words are spoken, and relationships are broken. Which is worse? Losing truth, justice, knowledge, or losing relationships?

Is it possible to love someone, if, in one area that you believe to be essential, you don't respect their view? I think so, but it means that we can neither jettison our values/intelligence nor our civility. It's all too easy to walk away. We can walk away from civility, and allow passion to overtake us. Others walk away from concern and feel like there is nothing they can do. Others walk away from struggling to find the truth. Some walk away from relationships. I don't think that I've ever been guilty of the latter, but I have, at times, allowed righteous passion to become unrighteous impatience. At times I've let my desire for biblical justice become an excuse for an unkind or ill-spoken word.

In scripture, Paul tells us of the importance of faith, hope, and love. Like truth and justice, faith and hope are essentially important. Still, when set next to love, they defer to the supremacy of love. Making love preeminent doesn't diminish faith or hope. True and abiding love only serves to empower faith and hope.

In our struggle for our universes, in our divided world, let's do our best to give the wheel to love and let it drive us forward. For myself, I daily question my use of words, and want to do better, but not at the expense of disobeying what I believe to be true or abandoning my calling. If, after reviewing fact, logic, and reason, we fail to find common ground on some issue, let's look for other ways in which we are like-minded.

About the Author

James Jennings is a graduate of Emory and Henry College; took classes at Dallas Theological Seminary, Talbot Theological Seminary, and California State University. He is retired from a career in education and Information Technology. He is married and lives in the Virginia countryside, where he does battle with Stink Bugs, cat barf, and an expanding waistline. As a boy, he was taken with Socrates' mission as a "gadfly" and has since been an inveterate questioner and pest. He is uncomfortable speaking of himself in the third person. He is a work in progress.

If you have questions or comments about this book, feel free to contact me personally at:

approvedpress@gmail.com

Thanks for reading. If you enjoyed this book, please consider leaving an honest review on your favorite store.

9 798985 931204